PRE-INTERMEDIATE

Language
LEADER
COURSEBOOK
and CD-ROM

CENTRE	Lincoln
CHECKED	Jacl &
ZONE	Black
CLASS MARK / SUFFIX	428 LEB
LOAN PERIOD	one month

...beau   Gareth Rees

...d Extra Practice by Diane Hall

CONTENTS

Unit	Grammar	Vocabulary	Reading
1 Weather (p6–13)	Present simple and present continuous: state and action verbs Present simple and present continuous: questions	The weather Modifiers: *quite, very, really, extremely* Adventure holiday activities	Internet news reports about extreme weather Magazine interview with a documentary film-maker Guidebook entry
2 People (p14–21)	Past simple: time expressions Past continuous	Personality adjectives	Newspaper article about a marathon winner Biography of Frida Kahlo
3 The Media (p22–29)	Articles Relative pronouns	The media Nouns: *photography / photographer* TV programmes	Webpage interview with a media worker Article about news organisations around the world
REVIEW UNITS 1–3 (p30–31)			
4 Health (p32–33)	Present perfect (1): time expressions Present perfect (2): *for* and *since*	Medical words	Podcast directory for a healthcare charity Magazine article about food for a healthy mind
5 Natural world (p40–47)	Comparison: comparatives and superlatives, *less, the least* Expressions of quantity	Landscapes Adjectives to describe places Animals Nouns and verbs: *damage n / v*	Text from a travel book about Bora Bora Magazine article about animal invaders
6 Society and family (p48–55)	*will, might* and *may*: predictions First conditional	Ages Negative adjectives: *un-* and *-less*	An advert for an institute of future analysis Newspaper article about low birth rate in Germany
REVIEW UNITS 1–3 (p56–57)			

LANGUAGE LEADER   PRE-INTERMEDIATE

2005081
£20.90

UNITS 1-6

Listening	Speaking/Pronunciation	Scenario	Study & Writing skills
News report about a hurricane	Discussing extreme weather Talking about different types of weather and season preferences **Pronunciation:** intonation for agreeing/disagreeing	**Latin American adventure** **Key language:** Agreeing and disagreeing **Task:** Designing a holiday	Using your dictionary: Understanding meaning A guidebook entry Linkers: *and, but, also, when*
Interview with a marathon winner	Talking about Mother Teresa Discussing creativity and creative people **Pronunciation:** *was/were*, word stress	**Sharing a flat** **Key language:** Describing people **Task:** Choosing a new flatmate	Learning styles and strategies Keeping a learning diary Linkers: *until, at first, then, at the moment, afterwards*
Interview with a media worker A lecture to students on a language course	Discussing types of media Talking about news companies **Pronunciation:** sentence stress	**That's entertainment!** **Key language:** Making suggestions **Task:** Planning a TV programme	Working with others A TV programme review
Podcast extracts: healthcare charity workers	Talking about life experiences Discussing food and diets **Pronunciation:** intonation in *yes/no* questions	**Health at work** **Key language:** Giving advice and reasons **Task:** Giving health advice	Guessing the meaning of unknown words A thank you email
TV programme about islands Tutorial discussing problems with time management	Discussing islands Describing places Talking about animals **Pronunciation:** weak forms	**Animals online** **Key language:** Describing photographs **Task:** Choosing photos for a website	Time management A comparative essay Linkers: *in contrast, but* and *whereas*
Meeting between a futurologist and a business investor	Talking about the changes technology has brought in life Discussing family life and different types of families **Pronunciation:** *what'll*, word linking	**Family matters** **Key language:** Expressing opinions **Task:** Speaking on a talk show	Correcting your writing An article Linkers: *so, as, however, because of*

CONTENTS

Unit	Grammar	Vocabulary	Reading
7 Science (p58–65)	*must* and *have to* *had to* and *could*	Science and crime Nouns, adjectives and verbs with prepositions	TV programme reviews Webpage biography of Stephen Hawking Newspaper article about problems for women in science in the UK
8 The night (p66–73)	Verb patterns Future intentions: *going to, hoping to, would like to*	Sleep *-ing/-ed* adjectives	Email exchange Magazine article about people who work at night A Maori legend
9 Work and industry (p74–81)	*used to* Present simple passive	Work Compound nouns Business	Company email Webpage about the uses of gold in industry Process of the early stages of chocolate making
REVIEW UNITS 7–9 (p82–83)			
10 Global affairs (p84–91)	Present continuous for future arrangements Past simple passive	People and organisations Adjectives	Encyclopaedia entry about the United Nations History of Microsoft
11 The environment (p92–99)	Present perfect continuous Phrasal verbs	Global warming Containers and materials	Essay about global warming Email correspondence about packaging Action group newsletter
12 Sport (p100–107)	Second conditional *too* and *enough*	Sports Personality types	Open letter to the Prime Minister Magazine article about female football fans An advert for a sports psychologist
REVIEW UNITS 10–12 (p108–109)			

Communication Activities (p110–125) • **Language Reference and Extra Practice** (p126–149)

UNITS 7–12

Listening	Speaking/ Pronunciation	Scenario	Study & Writing skills
Interview with a forensic scientist	Discussing rules and regulations in everyday life Talking about attitudes to science Pronunciation: Voiced/ unvoiced consonant pairs	**Ideas and innovations** **Key language:** Developing an argument **Task:** Choosing the best invention	Making notes Describing charts
A talk about sleep	Talking about sleep Problem solving Pronunciation: Intonation in *Wh-* questions	**A night out** **Key language:** Expressing preferences **Task:** Planning a night out	Improving your memory A story Time expressions
Consultant interviewing employees	Ranking criteria for a job Asking people if they used to … Talking about industry Pronunciation: *used to*, sentence stress in proposals	**Import-export** **Key language:** Negotiating **Task:** Making a deal	Giving a short talk Describing a process Linkers
Conversation about a schedule A talk about Interpol	General discussion about the United Nations Talking about big businesses and globalisation Pronunciation: Pausing and emphatic stress	**An Olympic bid** **Key language:** Adding emphasis **Task:** Making a presentation	Improving your listening Predicting content, Predicting vocabulary, Importance markers A for and against essay Linkers: *although, on the other hand, therefore*
Documentary about global warming	Talking about the causes and effects of global warming Discussing ways to reduce waste Pronunciation: Intonation in question tags	**Local regeneration** **Key language:** Question tags **Task:** Allocating funds	Exploring reading texts A report
Current affairs programme on TV Lecture: Giving students advice about an English exam	Talking about sports What would you do if … Discussion about the FIFA Football World Cup Pronunciation: Intonation in lists	**Sports psychology** **Key language:** Conversation fillers **Task:** Doing a survey	Doing exams A formal email Register, Punctuation

Audioscripts (p150–165) • **Irregular Verb List (p166)** • **Phonetic Charts (p167)**

Weather

In this unit

Grammar
present simple and
present continuous

Vocabulary
the weather
modifiers
adventure holiday
activities

Scenario
Latin American
adventure

Study skills
dictionary skills
(understanding
meaning)

Writing skills
a guidebook entry

1.1 EXTREMES

A

Climate is what we expect, weather is what we get.
Mark Twain, 1835–1910, US writer and humorist

| **VOCABULARY: the weather** |

1a Match the photos A–D with the types of weather in the box. Do you have any of this weather in your country?

| blizzard   drought   hurricane   storm |

1b Read these Internet news reports. Which situation is the most serious. Why?

2 Choose the correct word 1–8 in the news reports.

| **LISTENING** |

3a 1.2 Listen to this British news report about Florida, in the USA, before a hurricane hits. Number the sections of the report in order (1–4).

a) latest information about this hurricane ☐

b) interviews with members of the public ☐

c) the connection with global warming ☐

d) news about the police ☐

3b Listen again. Are these sentences true or false?

1 The man in the house does not have much food.

2 The weather at the coast is currently bad.

3 Hurricanes are unusual in this area.

4 The police officers are in the police station.

5 Every year there are more strong hurricanes.

○○○

◄ ► C +

Apple (114) ▼   Yahoo!   Amazon UK   News (1177) ▼

Online**News** | WEATHER

It's three days after Hurricane Katrina hit the US coast, but New Orleans is still suffering from strong [1]*wind / fog* and heavy [2]*rainy / rain*. Thousands of people are waiting for help. Half of the city is underwater and the army is still repairing the river walls.

The green and pleasant land of England is turning brown. After two cold, [3]*humid / dry* winters and [4]*hot / rain* summers, the south-east of England is experiencing a serious drought. Many lakes and rivers are now [5]*wet / dry*.

Following yesterday's blizzards and the heavy fall of [6]*snow / cloudy*, the police in New Zealand are using helicopters to reach hundreds of people in the countryside. It is still very [7]*warm / windy* and the [8]*ice / sun* is causing problems for the rescue teams.

GRAMMAR: present simple and present continuous

4a Which of these sentences are in the present simple (PS)? Which are in the present continuous (PC)?

1 At the moment, I'm covering the windows with wood.

2 We always help everyone.

3 The number of strong hurricanes is increasing.

4 Warm seas cause hurricanes.

How do we make negative sentences with these tenses?

4b Match the sentences 1–4 above with these grammar notes.

a) This is a regular action or habit.

b) This is an action happening now, or around now.

c) This is a fact or general truth.

d) This is a trend (i.e. a changing situation).

➡ Language reference and extra practice, pages 126–127

4c Complete these sentences. Use the present simple or present continuous of the verbs.

1 'Be quiet! I _____ to the news on the radio.' (listen)

2 In India, most rain usually _____ in the summer months, June to August. (fall)

3 Lightning _____ the Empire State Building in New York 500 times every year. (hit)

4 These days, more rain _____ in Australia because of global warming. (fall)

5 It _____ in tropical countries like Brazil. (not snow)

6 'It _____ now. Let's go to the park.' (not rain)

There are two types of verbs: **state verbs** and **action verbs**. State verbs usually describe feelings and situations, e.g. *be, have*. Action verbs describe activities and movements, e.g. *hit, play*.

5 Underline the main verb in these sentences. Are they state or action verbs in these examples?

1 It is still very cold today.

2 It's coming towards Florida.

3 I have a lot of food in my house.

4 Hurricanes are getting stronger.

5 I know about the danger.

What tense do we usually use for state verbs?

6 Complete this Internet news report. Use the present simple or present continuous of the verbs.

Storms hit the UK

There are heavy storms in the UK. Winds of 60 kilometres per hour [1]_____ (hit) the west coast, with more storms later this weekend. Experts say that these storms are unusual. 'Today, these storms [2]_____ (be) very strong. We usually [3]_____ (get) this kind of weather in the winter, not now.'

The heavy rain [4]_____ (cause) major transport problems – currently, the trains and ferries [5]_____ (not work).

The emergency services are helping local residents. 'Right now, we [6]_____ (move) people to safe areas and we [7]_____ (give) them hot food.' A group of fishermen are lost at sea and a rescue team [8]_____ (look) for them. 'We [9]_____ (not usually fly) in this kind of weather, but today [10]_____ (not be) a normal day.

SPEAKING

7 Discuss these questions with a partner.

1 What extreme weather does your country have?

2 What problems does the extreme weather cause?

3 Do you think your country's weather is changing?

4 Which types of weather do/don't you like? Why / Why not?

hot, sunny days	rainy days
clear, cold days	warm, cloudy days
hot, humid days	cool, cloudy days
windy days	foggy days
stormy days	snowy days

WINTER

Liam O'Connor is a familiar face in homes all over the country. Millions of us watch his documentaries. Now he's making a new programme about life in Russia. Here he tells Gaby Redmond about winter in Siberia.

Surviving Siberia – Wednesday 14 May 8 p.m. on Channel 7

The Big Chill

A _____
Yes, it does. Generally speaking, winter starts in September and lasts until May – so for about nine months. In the north, the sun never rises in December and January and it's dark nearly all day.

B _____
Well, minus 30 or 40 degrees Celsius is normal, but in northern Siberia the temperature sometimes drops to minus 60 or 70 degrees.

C _____
One reason is that, in the far north, the sun is always low in the sky and produces very little heat, so the ground stays cold all year. Another reason is that freezing winds come down from the Arctic because there are no mountains or trees to stop them.

D _____
It often snows, but it's rarely heavy. In the far north, snow cover lasts between 260 and 280 days.

E _____
Yes, they are. Definitely. Western Siberia is getting warmer faster than anywhere in the world. In fact, it's actually melting. And in some places in eastern Siberia, dangerous gases are rising from the ground. They're stopping the surface from freezing, even in the middle of winter. But it's still very cold!

READING AND SPEAKING

1 **Discuss these questions with a partner.**

1 Are there seasons in your country? If so, what's your favourite season? Why?

2 Do you like winter? Why / Why not?

3 What do you know about winter in Russia? What do you know about Siberia?

2a **Read the introduction to the text quickly. Where is the text from?**

1 a guidebook to Siberia

2 a book about climate change

3 a magazine about TV programmes

2b **Read the rest of the text. Complete it with these interview questions.**

1 Really? Why do they do that?

2 How do people keep warm?

3 Is the climate changing? Are winters getting warmer?

4 Is it really cold?

5 Does winter last a long time?

6 What do Russians think about their cold winters?

7 I see. What about snow? How much snow is there in Siberia?

8 What about you? What do you think about winter in Siberia?

9 And what's life like? Is it very difficult for people?

10 That's incredible! Why is it so cold?

2c **Complete these sentences with one or two words. (The words you need are in the text.)**

1 Winter lasts for about _____ in Siberia.

2 Temperatures of minus 70 degrees are not _____ .

3 The ground stays cold because _____ produces very little heat.

4 In some places in eastern Siberia _____ are melting the frozen ground.

5 A lot of things _____ in the very cold conditions.

6 People wear _____ to keep warm in Siberia.

F _____

They wear fur. In the West, we consider fur a luxury, but it's the only thing that keeps you warm when it's extremely cold.

G _____

Yes, it is. Without gloves, your fingers freeze. The little hairs in your nose freeze too. It's quite scary! The tyres of cars and lorries burst. Sometimes children can't go to school because it's so cold. They have lessons on TV!

H _____

Actually, they don't mind them. They enjoy a lot of outdoor sports. Ice-skating is the number one sport – it's really popular. They also like cross-country skiing and ice-hockey. Reindeer racing is quite popular too. Some people swim in rivers and lakes in the sub-zero temperatures.

I _____

They say there are health benefits to swimming in icy water. It's a way to avoid colds. Also, it's a real community event. Everyone takes part – men, women and children.

J _____

Well, to tell you the truth, I love it! In my home city, Liverpool, the winters are usually cloudy and mild and I don't like them much. You don't get many days when the weather's fine, you know, sunny and not raining. In Siberia, it's different. On bright sunny days, it's very beautiful.

VOCABULARY: modifiers

3a Match these comments about cold weather in London with the temperatures.

1 It's very cold. / It's really cold.
2 It's extremely cold.
3 It's quite cold.

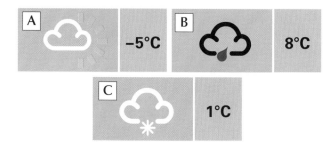

A −5°C   B 8°C

C 1°C

3b Use the phrases above to talk about the winter months in your country, or other places you know.

It's usually very foggy in my city in November, and it's extremely cold in January.

GRAMMAR: present simple and present continuous questions

4a Look at Exercise 2b. Which questions are in the present simple? Which are in the present continuous?

4b Match 1–3 with a–c to complete these grammar notes.

1 When _be_ is the main verb, we make present simple questions
2 When the main verb isn't _be_, we make present simple questions
3 We make present continuous questions

a) with the auxiliary verb _do/does_ + subject + infinitive of the main verb.
b) with the auxiliary verb _am/is/are_ + subject + _-ing_ form of the main verb.
c) with _am/is/are_ before the subject.

5a Underline the question words in Exercise 2b. What other question words do you know?

➡ Language reference and extra practice, pages 126–127

5b Put the words in order to make questions. Then ask and answer the questions with a partner.

1 sad   you   days   do   on   feel   cloudy   ?
2 wearing   your   teacher   what's   today   ?
3 English   are   fun   learning   you   for   ?
4 time   your   how   spend   free   you   do   ?
5 friends   doing   what   now   are   your   ?

5c Look at these answers to questions about the text in Exercise 2b. Write the questions.

1 In September. _When does winter start?_
2 In northern Siberia.
3 Because it's always low in the sky.
4 Dangerous gases.
5 Yes, it is. Faster than anywhere in the world.
6 Yes, they do. The hairs in your nose freeze too!

SPEAKING

6 Work in groups of three. Do the quiz about winter on page 110.

WRITING

7 Write four or five sentences describing winter in your country.

SITUATION

1a Look at the advert below for Double Action Adventures. Why does the company have this name? Would you like to go on one of their trips?

1b Match the different activities in the advert to the photos A–J.

2a Read this email from the boss of Double Action Adventures. What does he want his staff to do?

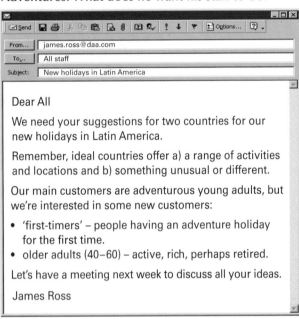

From... | james.ross@daa.com
To,... | All staff
Subject: | New holidays in Latin America

Dear All

We need your suggestions for two countries for our new holidays in Latin America.

Remember, ideal countries offer a) a range of activities and locations and b) something unusual or different.

Our main customers are adventurous young adults, but we're interested in some new customers:

- 'first-timers' – people having an adventure holiday for the first time.
- older adults (40–60) – active, rich, perhaps retired.

Let's have a meeting next week to discuss all your ideas.

James Ross

2b Look at these notes about two possible countries. Which do you think is best for Double Action Adventures? Why?

SOUTHERN ARGENTINA

	In the mountains	On the southern coast
Activities:	mountain trekking	three-day Antarctic wildlife cruise
	horse riding	sea kayaking with whales
Weather:		
Winter	cold and windy	very cold – no trips/visits possible
(March to October)		
Summer	windy and changeable	cold – trips/visits possible
(November to February)		

BELIZE

Activities:	On the coast:	diving, sea kayaking
	In the jungle:	jungle trekking, white-water rafting
Weather:	Rainy season:	June to October – heavy rain
		August to November – hurricane season
		average temperature 34 °C
	Dry season:	November to May
		average temperature 30 °C

3a 📻 **1.3** Listen to Diana and Simon (two DAA employees) discuss the two countries above. Which country do they think is the most interesting? Why?

A **B** **C** **D**

DOUBLE ACTION ADVENTURES

ONE HOLIDAY
TWO ADVENTURES!

F

E

Choose an adventure holiday with us and get double the action.
Spend your first week white-water rafting in the mountains.
Spend your second week diving and snorkelling at the coast.

3b Listen again. Who has these opinions: Diana, Simon or both of them? Write *D, S* or *B.*

1 The Antarctic trip is a good thing.   *B*

2 The summer season in the Antarctic is not very long.

3 The weather in the mountains is a problem.

4 Normal or simple activities are good for first-timers.

5 The activities in Belize are very good.

6 The dry season is the best time to go to Belize.

7 A seven-month holiday season is not very good.

KEY LANGUAGE:
agreeing and disagreeing

4a  Listen and complete these sentences from the conversation with *do, don't, so* or *neither.*

1 D: I think the Antarctic wildlife cruise is a great idea.

  S: Mmm. _____ do I.

2 S: I don't like the weather in the mountains.

  D: No, _____ do I.

3 S: I don't like the activities – they're very ordinary.

  D: _____ you? I do.

4 D: Seven months. I think that's good.

  S: _____ you? I'm not sure.

4b In which sentences do they agree? In which do they disagree?

Other activities available: mountain biking and trekking, sea kayaking, skiing and snowboarding, horse riding, wildlife watching and island cruises.

Trips to North America, Australia and Europe. All equipment, training and guides included.

5a  Intonation for agreeing/disagreeing Listen to these phrases 1–4 and match them with the intonation patterns a–b.

1 So do I.   3 Neither do I.

2 Don't you?   4 Do you?

a)   b)

5b Listen again and repeat.

6a Do you agree or disagree with these statements? Write your answers.

1 I think horse riding is interesting.

  Do you? I don't. / So do I.

2 I don't like walking in strong wind.

3 I don't think an Antarctic cruise is a good idea.

4 I think white-water rafting is dangerous.

5 I want to go sea kayaking.

6 I want to go diving.

6b Tell your partner your opinions. Does he/she agree with you?

I don't think horse riding is interesting.

– Don't you? I do. / Neither do I.

TASK: designing a holiday

7 You work for Double Action Adventures. Work with a partner to find out about two more countries.

Student A: Look at the notes on page 113.
Student B: Look at the notes on page 111.

8a Read the email from the boss in Exercise 2a again. What do you think of the four holidays? What do you think of the activities? How long is the best season for the holidays? Is the weather OK? Make notes.

8b Compare your ideas with your partner and choose the best two countries for Double Action Adventures.

OTHER USEFUL PHRASES
What do you think about …?
I think this is a good one because …
What about …?   I'm not sure.

STUDY SKILLS: using your dictionary: understanding meaning

1 Many words in English have more than one meaning. Look at this dictionary entry for *cold*. Match the example sentences a–c with the definitions 1–3.

> **cold** /kəʊld/ *adjective*
> 1 something that is cold has a low temperature and is not warm or hot
> 2 cold food is cooked, but is not eaten while it is hot
> 3 a cold person is not very friendly or kind

From *Longman Wordwise Dictionary*

a) We eat a lot of cold chicken and salad in the summer.

b) Some people think that the British are cold.

c) The weather's really cold today.

2 The words in bold below are used to describe the weather. Turn to page 121 and look at their other meanings. Write the number of the correct definition.

a) That's a really **cool** film.

b) Some Thai fish soups are really **hot**.

c) Gabriella's got very **dark** hair.

d) They always give visitors a **warm** welcome.

e) 'How are you?' 'I'm **fine**, thanks.'

f) His writing isn't **clear**.

g) This shampoo is for **dry** hair.

h) She's a **bright** child.

i) I don't like **mild** cheese.

3 Definitions often give you more information than just the meaning of a word. Work with a partner and answer these questions.

1 What colour is a **cloud**?

2 Where do we usually see **fog**?

3 What happens in **autumn**?

4 What kind of a storm is a **hurricane**?

5 Write down three facts about a **blizzard**.

6 What does the **sun** give us?

Check your answers in a dictionary or turn to page 111.

4a Dictionaries often tell us the opposites of words. Look at this entry for *loud*. We can see that the opposite of *loud* is *quiet*.

> **loud** /laʊd/ *adjective*
> something that is loud makes a lot of noise
> ⇨ opposite QUIET: *Turn that music down! It's too loud! | I could hear loud voices, arguing.*
> – **loudly** *adverb*: *'Stop!' she shouted loudly.*

From *Longman Wordwise Dictionary*

Think of the opposites of these adjectives from this unit. Check your answers in a dictionary.

1 long	_____	3 heavy	_____
2 strong	_____	4 major	_____

4b Complete these sentences with the opposites.

1 There are only _____ mistakes in your work.

2 It's only a _____ distance to the coast.

3 I don't like _____ coffee.

4 My bag's very _____ and easy to carry.

WRITING SKILLS: a guidebook entry

5 How important are these things for you in a guidebook? Give each a mark out of 5 (5 = very important; 1 = not important).

a) how to get there / travel around

b) information about the weather / when to go

c) information about the history of a place

d) places to visit / things to do

e) places to stay

f) what to eat and drink

g) prices (e.g. accommodation, food)

h) dangerous places / places to avoid

i) information about health services

j) local festivals and events

6 Read the text from a guidebook to Mallorca and answer these questions.

1 Why is spring the best time to visit Mallorca?

2 What happens to the countryside in the summer?

3 How long does the good weather last?

4 What's the weather like in winter?

5 The text tells us a lot about the weather. What other information is in the text?

6 Underline the different areas of the island that the text mentions, e.g. *beach*.

MALLORCA

WHEN TO GO
Mallorca has an average of 300 days of sunshine a year, but don't think you can have a beach holiday in November or December!

SEASONS

SPRING
The best time to visit Mallorca is in the spring when the sun is not very strong. At this time, prices (except during Easter week) are still quite low, but the weather is often warm and it is possible to enjoy the beaches. However, it can still be damp and cold, especially in the mountains, so come prepared.

SUMMER & AUTUMN
From mid-June, prices and temperatures rise. By July and August the island is extremely hot and, inland, the countryside becomes very dry. During these months, the coast becomes very crowded. From mid-September, prices and temperatures begin to fall. This is also a good time to visit as the fine mild weather often lasts into late October.

WINTER
November to February is winter, when many hotels and restaurants close. It can snow during this period, especially in the high mountains, and it gets extremely cold in some towns (Valldemossa, for example). This is also the rainy season.

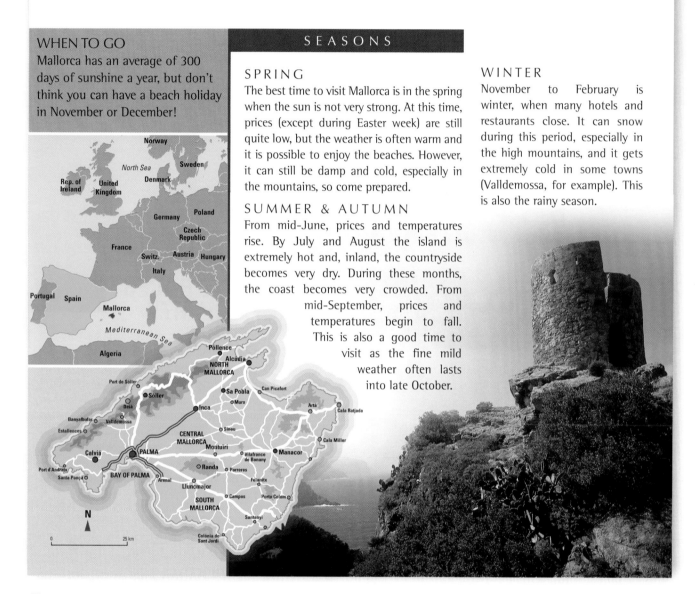

7a Linkers Words like *and, but, also* and *when* are linking words. We use them to join ideas. Underline the examples in the text above.

7b Complete these definitions with the words in the box.

| different   fact   time   words |

We use …

1 *and* to join two _____ or parts of a sentence.
2 *when* to talk about the _____ that something happens.
3 *but* to add something _____ or surprising.
4 *also* to add a new _____ .

7c Choose the correct words.

1 The waiters are friendly *and / but* they speak good English.
2 The weather's good in spring. It's *when / also* good in autumn.
3 You can go white-water rafting *but / and* you can't go kayaking.
4 A good time to visit Venice is in winter *also / when* it isn't crowded.
5 You can buy souvenirs in the hotel *but / also* the prices are often very high.
6 The beach is beautiful *when / and* it's *and / also* a good place to go snorkelling.

8 Write a 'When to go' section for a guidebook about your country, area or city. Write about the weather, but also about some other useful facts (e.g. prices, crowds).

2 People

In this unit

Grammar
- past simple
- past continuous

Vocabulary
- personality adjectives

Scenario
- Sharing a flat

Study skills
- learning styles and strategies

Writing skills
- keeping a learning diary

2.1 INSPIRATION

Well done is better than well said.
Benjamin Franklin, 1706–1790,
American politician and scientist

HOUSEWIFE RACES OUT OF POVERTY

Yesterday, Chimokel Chilapong, a Kenyan housewife and mother of four, beat hundreds of professional athletes and won the Nairobi marathon and $12,000. This was her first marathon race and she ran it in 2 hours, 39 minutes and 9 seconds. The other runners included professionals such as Joyce Chepchumba, the three times winner of the London marathon. Chimokel only started running a year ago, in April, to pay for her children's education. Now, in Kenya, she is a hero and an inspirational person. People think she is a determined woman, a dedicated mother and a talented person. Next week, there is a party in her honour.

READING

1a Look at the photo above and the newspaper headline. What do you think the story is about?

1b Read the article and check your ideas.

2 Read the text again and answer these questions.

1 What does Chimokel normally do in her life?

2 What is Joyce Chepchumba's job?

3 Why does Chimokel run in these races?

4 What do the Kenyans think of her?

LISTENING

3a `1.6` Listen to an interview with Chimokel after the race (you hear an interpreter). Tick (✓) the topics she talks about.

1 her reasons for running   4 her sports equipment
2 her brothers and sisters   5 her future plans
3 her husband and children   6 money

3b Put these events in order of time (1–8). Then listen again and check.

a) marry Benjamin ☐   e) train every morning ☐
b) sell a sheep ☐   f) win the marathon ☐
c) have children ☐   g) leave school ☐
d) start running ☐   h) travel to Nairobi ☐

VOCABULARY: personality adjectives

4a Find these adjectives in the text and Track 1.6 on page 150. Who do they describe?

dedicated	determined	friendly
hard-working	helpful	inspirational
kind	lovely	patient	talented

4b Choose the best adjectives. Use your dictionary.

1 She is very *dedicated / lovely / friendly*. She always does her training.

2 Her husband is *helpful / talented / determined*. He makes breakfast every morning.

3 She is very *kind / patient / determined*. She never stops and she wants to succeed.

4 She is *hard-working / inspirational / kind*. Many people now want to succeed like her.

14   UNIT 2 People

GRAMMAR: past simple

5a Match the beginnings and endings of these sentences about Chimokel.

1 Her mother died	one year later.
2 She left school	one year ago.
3 She married Benjamin	when she was sixteen.
4 She started training	in the same year.

We use the past simple to talk about finished actions and situations in the past. We know, and often say, the time of the action or situation.

5b Complete these grammar notes with the verbs in Exercise 5a.

You add -ed to the infinitive to make the past simple of most verbs. These are regular verbs, e.g. ¹_____ .

Sometimes you only add -d, e.g. ²_____ . We also sometimes make a spelling change, e.g. ³_____ .

Many common verbs in the past simple are irregular. We don't add -ed. We use a different word, e.g. ⁴ _____ .

5c How do we make negatives, questions and short answers? What is different when the verb is *be*? Look at Track 1.6 on page 150 and check.

➡ Language reference and extra practice, pages 128–129

6 Complete the rest of the interview between Chimokel and the journalist. Use the correct form of the verbs in the box.

be not come eat (x2) not have ~~prepare~~		
run speak stay train watch get up		

J: Tell us more about your training. How ¹*did* you *prepare* for the race?

C: Well, I ²_____ every day. I ³_____ about ten kilometres each time.

J: How did you feel before the race?

C: I ⁴_____ a bit nervous. I ⁵_____ at five o'clock because I couldn't sleep.

J: ⁶_____ you _____ special food? Did you have a special diet?

C: No, I didn't. I ⁷_____ my normal food, with my family every day.

J: ⁸_____ your family _____ the race?

C: No, they didn't. They ⁹_____ _____ to Nairobi. We ¹⁰_____ _____ the money for that. They ¹¹_____ in the village. I ¹²_____ to them on the phone after the race.

J: I'm sure they're very proud of you. Congratulations, Chimokel.

GRAMMAR TIP

We use **in** when we talk about years and months: *in 2006, in July*

We use **on** when we talk about days: *on Monday, on Sunday*

We use **at** when we talk about times: *at seven o'clock, at 8.15*

7a **Time expressions** Use these time expressions to make true sentences about you. Then compare your sentences with a partner.

ten years ago when I was sixteen last year		
last week in 2005 last night on Sunday		

7b Ask your partner about these things starting *When did you last …?*

cook a meal	enter a race or competition
watch a film	buy some clothes
lose something	go to a museum

SPEAKING

8a Look at the photo. Do you know this person? What did she do in her life? Discuss what you know about her with your partner.

8b Work with your partner to complete her life story.

Student A: Turn to page 112.

Student B: Turn to page 114.

8c Is there someone you think is inspirational? Tell your partner.

Frida Kahlo (1907 – 1954)

Frida Kahlo was a Mexican painter. Her colourful paintings show her powerful feelings about herself and the world around her. Some of her recent fans include Madonna
5 and Robert de Niro.

Life

Her life began and ended in Mexico City. When Kahlo was six years old, she had a serious disease (polio) that damaged her right leg forever. However, she was a clever and determined young woman
10 and went to one of the top schools in Mexico. When she was fifteen, she met the famous painter Diego Rivera. He was doing a painting on a wall at her school at that time. Then, at the age of eighteen, Kahlo was in a terrible accident. She was travelling on a bus when a tram crashed into it. She began to paint while she was recovering from the accident because she
15 was bored in bed. During the rest of her life she had over 30 operations to try to correct her physical problems.

In 1929, she married Diego Rivera but their relationship was often stormy. Soon after she got married, Kahlo started to wear traditional Mexican clothes and jewellery, and she also started to wear her hair high on her
20 head. She visited the United States and France, and met many important people. While she was staying in Paris, she appeared on the front cover of *Vogue* magazine. When she wasn't working, she liked singing and telling jokes at parties.

Work

Kahlo produced about 200 works in her life. Many of them were self-
25 portraits – a mixture of dreams and reality. In them, we can see that she was very proud of Mexico. Her paintings also tell us about politics, power relationships between rich and poor countries, Eastern and Western philosophy and the position of women in society. Many people admired her work, including Pablo Picasso.

READING AND SPEAKING

1 Discuss these questions with a partner.

1 Are you creative, e.g. can you sing, draw, paint, dance, etc.?
2 Which famous creative people do you know or like?

2a Read the text quickly. Write down two interesting things you remember. Compare with other students.

2b Are these sentences true or false, or does the text not say?

1 Frida Kahlo had a good education.
2 She had two very bad experiences when she was young.
3 She was on a tram when a bus crashed into it.
4 She started painting when she met Diego Rivera.
5 She travelled a lot in Mexico.
6 People didn't think that she was a talented painter.

2c Find words in the text that mean:

1 physically harmed something
2 becoming healthy again (e.g. after an illness or accident)
3 feeling pleased about your actions, your family or your country because they are good or successful
4 the study of ideas about life and how people should live
5 looked at something and thought that it was very good

3a What do you think about Frida Kahlo? Would you like to know more about her? Would you like to see more of her paintings? Why / Why not?

3b Think about some important events in your life. What happened? Did they change your life in any way? Tell your partner.

GRAMMAR: past continuous

We use the past continuous to talk about a longer background action in the past, when a shorter action interrupts it or happens during it. We use the past simple for the shorter action.

a) She **was travelling** on a bus when a tram crashed into it.

b) She began to paint while she **was recovering** from the accident.

4a Match these time lines with the sentences above.

4b Find two more examples in the text.

4c How do we make sentences in the past continuous (affirmative, negative and questions)?

We also use the past continuous on its own to talk about actions in progress in the past. We often use a time expression when we do this.

He was doing a painting on a wall at her school **at that time**.

'What were you doing **at eleven o'clock last night**?'
'I was watching TV.'

➡ Language reference and extra practice, pages 128–129

5 [1.7] Complete the texts. Use the past continuous or past simple of the verbs and write in the missing names. Then listen and check.

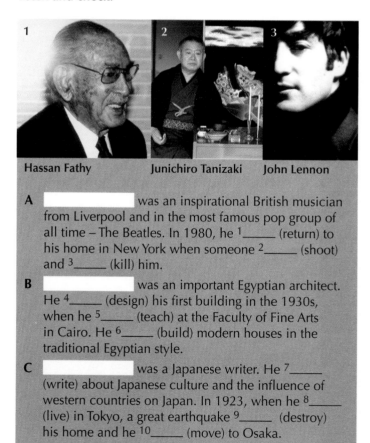

Hassan Fathy   Junichiro Tanizaki   John Lennon

A _____ was an inspirational British musician from Liverpool and in the most famous pop group of all time – The Beatles. In 1980, he ¹_____ (return) to his home in New York when someone ²_____ (shoot) and ³_____ (kill) him.

B _____ was an important Egyptian architect. He ⁴_____ (design) his first building in the 1930s, when he ⁵_____ (teach) at the Faculty of Fine Arts in Cairo. He ⁶_____ (build) modern houses in the traditional Egyptian style.

C _____ was a Japanese writer. He ⁷_____ (write) about Japanese culture and the influence of western countries on Japan. In 1923, when he ⁸_____ (live) in Tokyo, a great earthquake ⁹_____ (destroy) his home and he ¹⁰_____ (move) to Osaka.

pronunciation

6a [1.8] *was/were* Listen to *was* and *were* in these sentences. How do we pronounce them?
1 I was singing.
2 'Was she eating?' 'Yes, she was.'
3 We were studying.
4 'Were they running?' 'Yes, they were.'

6b [1.9] Listen and repeat these sentences.

7 Choose a time (e.g. ten o'clock last night) and ask your classmates what they were doing at that time. Make a note of their answers. Then report to the class.

At ten o'clock last night Kristina and Marina were doing their homework. Roman was watching TV.

SPEAKING

8a [1.10] You are going to invite a famous person from the past or present to dinner. Listen to the example and complete these sentences.

LOUIS ARMSTRONG

1 I think he was the greatest _____ ever.
2 He had amazing _____.
3 He could _____.
4 He had a big influence on _____.
5 He was also a _____ man. Later in his life, he gave _____.
6 How did you feel when you were eight years old, and _____ of New Orleans for money?

8b Work with a partner. Who would you invite? Make some notes under these headings:

his/her life (early, later)   personality
him/his abilities, skills   influence
two questions you would like to ask him/her

8c Work in groups without your partner. Tell your group about your guest. Listen to the other students. Then choose two guests to invite.

PREPARATION

1a Work with a partner. Talk about where you live. Do you live with your family? Do you share a flat with friends?

1b Imagine you are looking for a flatmate. Choose five of the following things that are important to you. What other things are important in a flatmate? Compare your ideas with your partner.

A flatmate should …

have similar interests to me	not smoke
be friendly and sociable	have a job
be good-looking	be rich
do his/her washing up	be a good cook
be quiet and polite	be tidy
be honest	be clever

2 **1.11** Match these opposite adjectives. Then listen and check.

1 polite	a) shy
2 friendly	b) horrible
3 confident	c) rude
4 nice	d) miserable
5 cheerful	e) unfriendly
6 hard-working	f) stupid
7 clever	g) quiet
8 chatty	h) lazy

pronunciation

3a **Word stress** The word *confident* has three syllables: con-fi-dent. How many syllables are there in the adjectives in Exercise 2?

3b **1.12** How do we pronounce *confident*? Listen and check.

• • •
1 confident   2 confident   3 confident

3c **1.13** Mark the stress on the adjectives in Exercise 2. Then listen and check.

3d Test your partner. Say one of the adjectives. Your partner tells you the opposite.

SITUATION

Stephanie (a PhD student from Germany) and Xu Ming (from Hong Kong and works for an advertising company) share a three-bedroom flat in London. They are looking for a new flatmate. Stephanie is in Germany at the moment and she missed the people who came to see the flat. Xu Ming telephones Stephanie and tells her about the different people.

4a **1.14** Listen to part of their conversation. Do you think Stephanie wants this person to be the new flatmate?

4b Listen again and complete Stephanie's notes. Write one word in each gap.

Name/Nationality/Job:
Martin, Canadian, 1_____.

Personality:
At first, not very 2_____. Not 3_____.
Hard-working. Seems honest and 4_____.

Likes/Dislikes:
Watching 5_____ on TV, cooking. Hates 6_____.

Appearance:
Looks 7_____. Wearing 8_____ clothes. Short 9_____ hair. Like actor Tom Cruise.

Xu Ming's opinion:
Happy to live with a 10_____ person. Would like to share with a Canadian.

KEY LANGUAGE: describing people

5a `1.15` Complete these questions from the conversation. Then listen and check.
1 What's he _____ ?
2 What does he _____ like?
3 What _____ he like?
4 _____ you like to live with him?

5b Match the questions above with the sections of the notes in Exercise 4b.

5c Complete these sentences from the conversation. Then look at Track 1.14 on page 151 and check. Which questions in Exercise 5a do they answer?
1 He's _____ short brown hair.
2 He _____ like that Hollywood actor.
3 He _____ honest and tidy.
4 He certainly _____ chatty.
5 He works long hours, _____ he's hard-working.
6 He _____ watching sport on TV.
7 He _____ nice clothes.

5d Choose someone you know, e.g. a friend or a member of your family. Prepare answers for the questions in Exercise 5a. Ask your partner about his/her person.

TASK: choosing a new flatmate

6a Work with a partner. You are going to find out about the other people who want to share the flat. Write notes about each person under these headings.

Name/Nationality/Job   Appearance
Personality   Other information
Likes/Dislikes

Student A: Ask about Toshi. Then turn to page 113 and answer B's questions.

Student B: Turn to page 114 and answer A's questions. Then ask about Isabelle.

6b You and your partner share a flat in London. You are looking for a new flatmate. Discuss each of the three people, Martin, Isabelle and Toshi. Who would you like to live with?

OTHER USEFUL PHRASES
What do you think of ...?
What about ...?
I like / don't like ... because ...
I agree/disagree.
So do I. / Do you?
Neither do I. / Don't you?

1a 🔊 **1.16** **Listen to two people talking about their experiences of learning a new skill and answer these questions.**

1 What did they learn?

2 Did they enjoy learning it?

1b Listen again and answer these questions.

1 Who helped them?

2 Was it easy or difficult to learn?

3 How did they feel when they could do it?

2a Work in a small group. Tell your partners about something that you have learned successfully in your life (e.g. a school subject, to ride a bike, to drive). Use the questions in Exercise 1a and b to help you.

2b Write down one or two things that you learned from the experience.

Everyone learns in different ways and very often we can't say that one way is better than another. However, there are things we can all do to improve our learning. One thing is to understand better how we learn, and to know our strengths and weaknesses.

3 Do this questionnaire to find out your learning style. Give each statement a mark out of 5 (5 = Yes, a lot / easily, etc. 1 = No / Not at all, etc.). Then turn to page 112 to read the analysis of your answers and tips to improve your learning.

What's your learning style

A

1 Can you remember any of the photos in Unit 1 of this course book?

2 Do you find it easy to understand charts and diagrams?

3 To remember the spelling of a word, do you write it down several times?

4 Can you find mistakes in your own writing?

5 Are you good at using maps?

6 Have you got a good memory for people's faces?

7 When you get a new piece of equipment (e.g. a DVD player), do you read the instruction book carefully?

8 When you were a child, did you enjoy reading books in your free time?

B

9 Do you enjoy discussions about the subjects you are studying?

10 Do you enjoy listening to lectures and talks?

11 To remember the spelling of a word, do you say the letters aloud?

12 Is it difficult for you to study in a noisy place?

13 Do you enjoy listening to books on CD?

14 When you think of a phone number, do you hear the numbers in your head?

15 When people tell you their names, do you remember them easily?

16 When you were a child, did you like listening to stories?

C

17 Do you learn best by doing things rather than reading about them?

18 Do you like doing experiments (e.g. in a laboratory)?

19 Do you enjoy role-plays?

20 Is it difficult for you to study when there are many things happening around you?

21 Do you move your hands a lot when you're talking?

22 When you get a new piece of equipment (e.g. a DVD player), do you ignore the instruction book?

23 In your free time, do you like doing things with your hands (e.g. painting)?

24 When you were a child, did you do a lot of physical activity in your free time?

WRITING SKILLS: keeping a learning diary

It is a good idea when you are studying English to keep a learning diary. Writing makes our thoughts and feelings clearer. It gives us thinking time and helps us to organise our ideas. It also helps us to make plans and to see our progress and development. Writing about our learning can help us become better learners.

Thursday 20th October

This morning we learned how to use phrases like *So do I* and *Neither do I*. Jane's a good teacher. She explained everything well and in the class I understood perfectly. Now, I'm not so sure! I need to look at the lesson again tomorrow – perhaps with my classmate Gozem – she's really clever and helpful! I'm glad I decided to come to this school (the teachers and students are great) and at the moment I'm very happy here.

Friday 21st October

Today I had lunch with some of my classmates and we spoke a lot of English! Afterwards, Gozem and I studied together and she helped me with the homework. I now realise that I enjoy working with other people like this – it's fun and I learn better than on my own.

Sunday 23rd October

I think my listening is getting better. I had a lot of trouble with it until I came here. This evening I watched a film in English on TV. At first, I didn't understand much, but then I started to understand what the people were saying. I wrote down some of the expressions they used in my vocabulary book.

4 Michal is a student at a language school in Cambridge. Read the entries from his learning diary and answer these questions.

1 What did Michal study on Thursday morning?
2 Did he understand the explanations in class?
3 Why is he glad that he came to this school?
4 Does he learn more on his own or in a group?
5 Why does he think that his listening is improving?

5 In a learning diary you can write about:

1 your feelings about the course/coursebook.
2 things you find difficult.
3 things you can do to help you learn.
4 things you learn about yourself.

Find examples of 1–4 above in Michal's diary.

6 Linkers Study the examples of the linking words *until, at first, then, at the moment* and *afterwards* in the text. Then choose the best word to complete these sentences.

1 *At first / At the moment* I couldn't do the homework but *until / then* a friend explained how to do it.
2 *At first / Until* I was shy and didn't ask any questions. *At the moment / Then* I became more confident.
3 I'm enjoying my new course in this country *at first / at the moment*.
4 I didn't use an English–English dictionary *at first / then* but *then / at the moment* I realised that it was better than translating words.
5 I was working hard *until / afterwards* my new flatmate arrived!
6 We had a very long and difficult exam this afternoon. I felt really tired *afterwards / at first* and went to bed early.

7 Start your own learning diary. Write about 100 words and show it to your teacher. After that, keep the diary for yourself. Try to write something every day or two. After about a month, read the diary from the beginning. Do you notice any changes in your English, yourself, or in the way you learn?

Vocabulary

Grammar

LONGMAN
WordWise

3 The media

In this unit

Grammar
- articles
- relative pronouns

Vocabulary
- the media
- nouns (*photography/ photographer*)
- TV programmes

Scenario
- That's entertainment!

Study skills
- working with others

Writing skills
- a TV programme review

3.1 MY MEDIA

I find television very educational. Every time someone switches it on, I go into another room and read a good book.
Groucho Marx, 1890–1977, US comedian

VOCABULARY AND SPEAKING: the media

1a Put these words into three groups: A for newspapers and magazines, B for television and radio, and C for computers and the Internet. (Some words can go in more than one group.)

> advert article celebrity comedy
> computer game reality TV show
> drama email journalist presenter
> producer programme documentary
> search engine series soap opera
> station webcast

1b Are these statements true for your country? Discuss them with a partner.
1 Newspapers are boring.
2 There are a lot of magazines about celebrities.
3 Soap operas are all the same.
4 Computer games are violent and expensive.
5 Journalists usually tell the truth.

READING

2a Callum Robertson works for BBC Learning English. Read the webpage about him on page 23 quickly. Do you think he has an interesting job/life? Why / Why not?

2b Complete the gaps in the text with these phrases.
a) I also watch a lot of TV
b) I sometimes travel abroad (e.g. China, Brazil)
c) learn the phonemic symbols
d) I started working for the BBC in 1998

LISTENING

Helen Francis is a journalist with a national newspaper. Every week, she writes an article for the newspaper. The article is about how media workers use the media themselves.

3a [1.17] Listen to her telephone interview with Callum. Which of these different types of media does he use a lot?

newspapers magazines television radio the Internet

3b Listen again. Are these sentences true or false?
1 Callum doesn't buy a newspaper every day.
2 When he cycles to work, he gets one of the free newspapers.
3 The magazines that he reads are mainly computer magazines.
4 He likes a variety of different TV programmes.
5 He listens to the radio when he's doing other things.
6 He only uses the Internet for business.
7 The physical feeling of holding a newspaper is important for him.

GRAMMAR: articles

4 Complete these grammar notes with the words in the box. Then find examples in the webpage text.

| a/an   the   no article |

1 Use _____ with plural nouns, to talk about people or things in general.

2 Use _____ with a singular noun, and to talk about a person's job.

3 Use _____ with singular or plural nouns, to talk about a particular person, place or thing, or to talk about people, places or things your listener knows about.

We use *a* when we talk about someone or something for the first time. We use *the* when we talk about that person or thing again.

*Helen Francis is a journalist with **a** national newspaper. Every week, she writes an article for **the** newspaper.*

5a Find examples of this use of *a* and *the* in the text.
➡ Language reference and extra practice, pages 130–131

5b Complete this description of a TV advert with *a/an* or *the*.

There's ¹_____ funny advert on ²_____ TV at the moment. This is what happens. ³_____ honest-looking man and ⁴_____ beautiful woman are getting married. ⁵_____ woman is wearing ⁶_____ expensive wedding dress. ⁷_____ man looks very happy. At the last minute, however, ⁸_____ woman runs away and ⁹_____ man is very surprised. Then we see why. Outside, ¹⁰_____ car is waiting for ¹¹_____ woman. We realise that ¹²_____ woman loves ¹³_____ car more than she loves ¹⁴_____ man!

5c Write four or five sentences about a TV advert you know.

SPEAKING

6 Interview your partner about how he/she uses the media. Use the questions in Track 1.17 on page 151 to help you. Ask about the things below and make notes of the answers.

newspapers   magazines   television   radio the Internet

Do you use the media in a similar way to your partner?

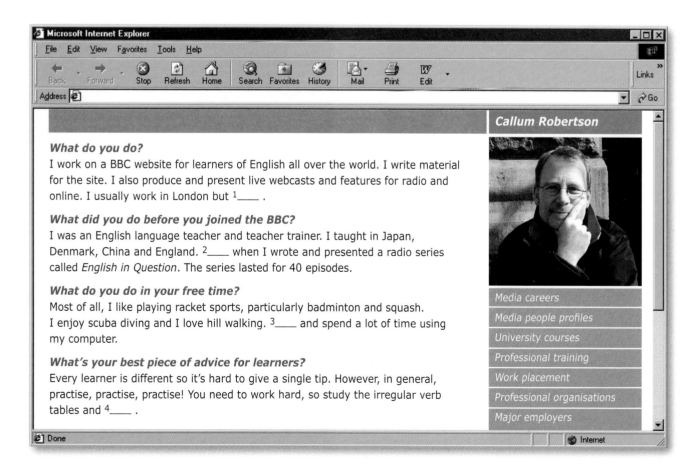

Callum Robertson

What do you do?
I work on a BBC website for learners of English all over the world. I write material for the site. I also produce and present live webcasts and features for radio and online. I usually work in London but ¹____ .

What did you do before you joined the BBC?
I was an English language teacher and teacher trainer. I taught in Japan, Denmark, China and England. ²____ when I wrote and presented a radio series called *English in Question*. The series lasted for 40 episodes.

What do you do in your free time?
Most of all, I like playing racket sports, particularly badminton and squash. I enjoy scuba diving and I love hill walking. ³____ and spend a lot of time using my computer.

What's your best piece of advice for learners?
Every learner is different so it's hard to give a single tip. However, in general, practise, practise, practise! You need to work hard, so study the irregular verb tables and ⁴____ .

Media careers
Media people profiles
University courses
Professional training
Work placement
Professional organisations
Major employers

1 Discuss these questions in small groups.

1 How often do you watch the news on television? Which channels do you watch?

2 What are the big news stories at the moment?

2a What do you know about these news companies?

BBC World   Al Jazeera International
OneWorldTV   AllAfrica.com   CNN
World News Network (WNN.com)

2b Read this article from a British in-flight magazine and find out more about the news companies. Choose the best title for the text 1–4.

1 The end of TV news   3 World news, global lies

2 Choose the news   4 Local news, real life

3a Complete these sentences with the names of the news companies in the text.

1 _____ and _____ are traditional, western news broadcasters.

2 _____ , _____ and _____ are not television companies.

3 _____ and _____ report some different stories from the main broadcasters.

4 _____ , _____ and _____ employ well-trained, professional reporters.

5 _____ does not usually pay its reporters.

6 _____ has a special interest in poor countries and their problems.

7 _____ and _____ are Internet sites that provide links to many news producers.

3b What do these words in the text refer to?

1 these (line 8)   4 it (line 28)

2 it (line 19)   5 these (line 34)

3 this company (line 26)

4 Discuss these questions with a partner. Give examples and explain your opinions.

1 Do you ever watch any of the international news channels or get your news from the Internet?

2 Which news channels do you trust?

3 Is the increase in non-professional journalism a good thing?

4 What are the advantages and disadvantages of newspapers, TV and Internet news?

5a Choose the correct word to complete these definitions.

1 A *journalist / journalism* is someone who writes reports for television, magazines, television or radio.

2 *Journalist / Journalism* is the job of writing reports for television, magazines, newspapers or radio, or the subject that people study.

After a long flight, you finally arrive in your hotel room and throw your bag on the bed. You turn on the TV and watch an international news channel that probably
5 *comes from the UK or the USA.*

5b Put these nouns into two groups: A for the person and B for the job or subject.

photographer   art   photography
scientist   politician   artist   science
psychology   politics   psychologist

A: *photographer*

B: *photography*

The main international broadcasters are BBC World and CNN. With an audience of over 1.5 billion people, these are popular channels that offer good quality news programmes. In both
10 companies, the journalists are experienced writers that produce journalism of a high standard.

However, there are alternative news channels which people watch because they want a less traditional or non-western view on world events.
15 Al Jazeera International is an Arabic television news company that started an English language international channel in 2006. With more than 15 offices and professional journalists all over the world, it says it gives a fresh view on the
20 big stories and it shows the news that we don't normally see.

The Internet offers even more variety. OneWorld is an Internet site which has stories about the developing world and human rights, rather
25 than the usual stories about US politics and business. The writers for this company are often local people who write the stories for free. This non-professional journalism is increasing and it certainly offers more choice.

30 AllAfrica.com and WNN.com are also Internet news sites, but they don't produce the news stories. Instead, they have links to more than 4,000 news organisations across the world. On sites like these, with a click of the mouse, you
35 select the news that you want to see.

So, next time you are in a hotel room, before you turn on the TV, perhaps you should turn on your laptop and discover the world's news yourself.

GRAMMAR: relative pronouns

6a Look at this sentence from the text.

The journalists are experienced writers that produce journalism of a high standard.

It has two pieces of information.

1 The journalists are experienced writers.

2 The journalists produce journalism of a high standard.

What are the two pieces of information in each of these sentences?

1 BBC World and CNN are popular channels that make good quality news programmes.

2 OneWorld is an Internet site which has stories about the developing world and human rights.

3 The writers for this company are often local people who write the stories for free.

6b Look at the sentences above and complete these grammar notes.

1 We use _____ and _____ to link information about people.

2 We use _____ and _____ to link information about things.

➡ Language reference and extra practice, pages 130–131

7 Join these pairs of sentences.

1 Politicians are very important people.
Politicians make the laws in a country.

2 The United Nations is a global organisation.
The United Nations tries to solve world problems.

3 Nelson Mandela was a great leader.
He made his country a fairer place.

8 We often use relative pronouns to make definitions. Match 1–3 with a–c and write *who/that* or *which/that*.

1 A journalist is someone _____

2 OneWorld is a company _____

3 Global is an adjective _____

a) means 'international' or 'all over the world'.

b) writes stories for television and newspapers.

c) provides news about the developing world.

SPEAKING

9 Work with a partner to complete a crossword.

Student A: Turn to page 114.

Student B: Turn to page 117.

SITUATION

1 Can you name any factual TV programmes about these topics? Do you like these programmes?

> politics   pop music   films   business   cars
> comedy   fashion   celebrities and fame
> design   nature and the environment

2a [1.18] Listen to the introduction to a new TV programme, *Fame and Fortune*. Which of the topics in Exercise 1 does today's programme include?

2b Listen again and answer these questions.

1 What is the interview with the Deputy Prime Minister about?
2 Where do the film directors come from?
3 What are 'The Hoodies'?
4 Who does Tony Cotton visit?
5 What does Lynne Miller do?
6 Who do you think is the main audience for this programme?
  a) children and teenagers
  b) young working adults
  c) families
  d) elderly people

pronunciation

3a [1.19] Sentence stress We stress some words more than others in sentences. Listen to the first sentence of the introduction to *Fame and Fortune*.

<u>Hello</u> and <u>welcome</u> to <u>Fame</u> *and* <u>Fortune</u>, the <u>programme</u> that <u>brings</u> you the <u>freshest</u> <u>news</u> and <u>views</u> from the worlds of <u>politics</u>, <u>business</u> and <u>entertainment</u>.

3b Listen again and repeat.

3c [1.18] Look at the rest of the introduction in Track 1.18 on page 152. Which words do you think are stressed? Underline them. Then listen again and check.

3d Practise reading the introduction aloud. Be careful with the stress.

4a [1.20] Listen to the programme development team brainstorm ideas for *Fame and Fortune*. What ideas do they decide to include in the programme? What ideas do they decide not to include?

4b Listen again. What is the fresh angle for each idea?

KEY LANGUAGE:
making suggestions

5a [1.21] Complete these sentences from the conversation in Exercise 4a. Then listen and check.

let's	any	about	don't	shall	anything
what	should	not			

1 _____ ideas?
2 Why _____ we get some politicians on the programme?
3 Let's _____ interview them about politics.
4 _____ ask them about their lives.
5 _____ else?
6 We _____ have a live band on the programme.
7 What _____ interviewing rich people?
8 What else _____ we put in the programme?
9 _____ about something with animals?

5b Which of the sentences in Exercise 5a:
a) give ideas or suggestions?
b) ask for ideas?

5c Look at Track 1.20 on page 152 and find more examples of this language. Notice the different grammar that follows each key phrase.

5d You are making plans for a friend who is visiting you next week. Complete the suggestions below. Then read your partner's suggestions.
1 Why don't we _____ ?
2 Let's _____ .
3 Let's not _____ .
4 We should _____ .
5 What about _____ ?

TASK: planning a TV programme

6a Work with a partner or in a small group. You work in the programme development department of a TV channel. You are going to design a weekly television programme for the channel. Read the instructions below and prepare some ideas and suggestions.

1 Decide on the target audience for the programme, e.g. teenagers, young adults, elderly people, professional people, housewives and house husbands, male or female …

2 Decide on the day and time for the programme, e.g. a weekday lunchtime programme, a Saturday evening programme …

3 Decide on the content of the programme, e.g. What topics should the programme cover? How can you make it interesting for your target audience? Can you think of any fresh angles for the topics? How many presenters should the programme have?

4 Decide on the name of the programme.

6b After you agree the format, imagine the first programme. Who are the guests? What are the topics? Write the presenter's introduction to the first programme.

6c Read your introduction to the other groups. Be careful with your sentence stress.

6d What do you think of the other programmes? Can you guess the target audience and broadcast time for these programmes? Would you like to watch any of them?

OTHER USEFUL PHRASES

Fine, but …	That's true.
I agree, but …	Perhaps that's not a good idea.
Exactly.	Great idea.
Really?	No, I don't think we should do that.

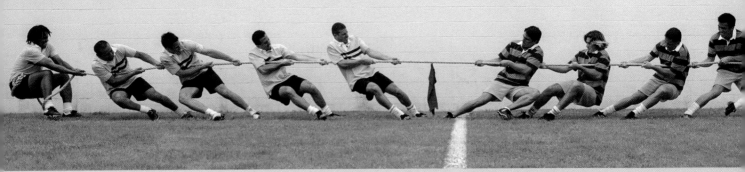

STUDY SKILLS:
working with others

1 Many tasks in this coursebook ask you to 'Discuss with a partner' or 'Work in small groups'. Make a list of things you like about working in class with others, and things you don't like. Compare your ideas in small groups!

I like exchanging ideas with other students.

It's sometimes quite difficult to understand my partner's accent.

2a **1.22** Listen to a talk to new students on an English language course in York. Does the speaker mention any of your ideas from Exercise 1?

2b Choose the words the speaker used. Then listen again and check.

1 It *increases / influences* the amount of time each student can talk.

2 It helps students become more *chatty / confident*.

3 It encourages students to become more *dedicated / independent* learners.

4 It provides *variety / energy* in the lesson.

5 You can learn *important / interesting* things from other students.

6 It gives the teacher the chance to see how everybody is working and *communicating / commenting*.

2c Can you think of any other advantages or disadvantages of working in pairs or groups? Are there more advantages than disadvantages?

3a **1.23** Two language students are discussing this question: *Do you always believe the news?* Listen to their conversation. Do you think they are working well together? Why / Why not?

3b Listen again. Who agrees with these statements; Ilwoo, Roberta or both of them? Write *I*, *R* or *B*.

1 You can trust the news on TV more than the newspapers.

2 It's sometimes interesting to read about celebrities.

3 The British don't feel part of Europe.

4 There isn't any news about South Korea in the British media.

3c Look at this list of things we find when students work well together. Match them with phrases a–j from the conversation.

1 Asking your partner what he/she thinks about a topic

2 Checking that you understand something

3 Asking your partner to explain something you don't understand

4 Agreeing with your partner

5 Disagreeing (politely!) with your partner

6 Showing interest in what your partner says

a) What do you think about …?

b) I think I agree with you, basically.

c) That's an interesting point.

d) Anyway, what do you think?

e) Sorry, I don't really understand. What do you mean, exactly?

f) I'm not sure I agree with you.

g) Are you saying that …?

h) You're right, actually.

i) Absolutely. / Exactly.

j) Yes, but …

4 Work with a partner. Discuss one or two of these questions. Use the language in Exercise 3c.

1 Which is better in your country, TV or newspapers?

2 Which are you more interested in, international or national news?

3 Is there too much news about celebrities in the media?

4 What do you think about TV news presenters in your country?

5 Is the Internet a good thing?

6 How important is radio these days?

WRITING SKILLS 3.4

WRITING SKILLS: a TV programme review

5a Do you know these words for TV programmes? Check any unfamiliar words in your dictionary.

> chat show   children's programme   soap opera
> current affairs programme   drama   sitcom
> documentary   game show   nature programme
> news   variety show   series

5b Discuss these questions in small groups.

1 Tell your group about a TV programme/series you watched recently. What was it about? Was it good? Why / Why not?

2 Are there any types of programme that you often or never watch?

6a Read this review of a TV series. Is it positive or negative? Would you like to watch this series?

LIFE ON MARS   BBC1

The fashion and culture of the 1970s are very popular today, but *Life on Mars*, a new police series, reminds us what life was really like then.

The story is simple. In Manchester, 2006, a car knocks down Detective Chief Inspector Sam Tyler (John Simm) while he is looking for a killer. He wakes up in 1973. He is still a police officer in Manchester and he is still looking for the same killer. However, the collar of his shirt is a lot bigger and there aren't any computers in the police station.

Life on Mars is an exciting police drama that is part thriller, part comedy. Simm gives a convincing performance as a man who is in shock, and writer Matthew Graham makes sure that there is also plenty of enjoyable comedy.

6b Read the text again and answer these questions.

1 Why is the collar of his shirt a lot bigger?

2 Why aren't there any computers in the police station?

3 Why do you think the name of this series is *Life on Mars*?

7 Look at paragraphs 2 and 3 in the text. Which is a description? Which gives us the writer's opinions?

8a We usually find these things in a TV or film review. Find them in the text.

1 a summary of the story

2 details of the main character(s)

3 a description of the place(s) where (and the time when) the action happens

4 a strong ending where the writer recommends (or does not recommend!) the programme/series/film

5 comments on the actors' performances (and/or other opinions)

6 an interesting beginning

8b What do you think is the best order for these things in a review? Discuss with a partner.

8c Remember: a common mistake when writing a review is to write a lot about the story, but very little about your opinions of the programme. How many sentences in this review tell us the story of *Life on Mars*?

9 A review needs a good beginning and ending. Look at these endings to TV reviews. Which do you like best? Which don't you like? Why? Compare your ideas in small groups.

1 Most TV is rubbish, but there are some programmes you have to watch. This is one of them.

2 I really liked this programme.

3 This comedy isn't funny. Don't watch any more. Go out with your friends instead – you can laugh more.

4 My conclusion: boring!

5 It was fascinating, magical and different – this was great TV.

6 For the next six weeks, millions of us have a date on Monday nights.

7 This programme had one good idea. But £4 million is a lot of money to spend on one idea.

10 Write a review for a student newspaper of a TV programme or series you saw recently.

REVIEW

GRAMMAR

1 Read the article and choose the correct form 1–12.

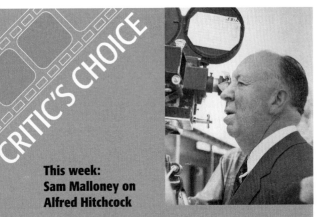

**This week:
Sam Malloney on
Alfred Hitchcock**

I ¹ *always enjoy / am always enjoying* a good thriller, and as I'm ² *the / a* film critic, I see a lot of them. One of my favourite movie directors is Hitchcock, or 'Hitch', the name he ³ *was preferring / preferred*. Born in London in 1899, Alfred Joseph Hitchcock was one of the most creative and inspirational directors of the 20th century. Many of his films are classics ⁴ *who / which* are still popular and important films today.

Hitchcock came from a poor family, and he ⁵ *left / was leaving* school early to start work. His first job in cinema was designing the text on the screen in silent films. He soon moved into directing, however, and his first major film was *The Lodger* (1926), a dark thriller. In ⁶ *a / the* film, he used new and interesting camera techniques.

Of the 53 feature films that Hitchcock made, perhaps his best came while he ⁷ *worked / was working* in the United States. He made some amazing films in the period of the 1950s and early 1960s. These ⁸ *include / are including*

the psychological thrillers *Rear Window* (1954) and *Vertigo* (1958) and, possibly his most famous, the terrifying horror film *Psycho* in 1960. Hitchcock ⁹ *was continuing / continued* to make films into his 70s; he made his last film, *Family Plot*, in 1976, four years before he died.

Hitchcock was a hard-working and talented film-maker, and he helped make the careers of many young actors. One of the interesting facts about him was that ¹⁰ *an / the* actor ¹¹ *who / which* appeared most often in his films was Hitchcock himself! He became famous for short appearances, and audiences still ¹² *watch / watched* for the scene where the director appears.

2 Correct the grammatical mistakes in these sentences.
1 Hitchcock was ~~the~~ film director in the 20th century. *a*
2 He made the thrillers and horror films.
3 My local cinema shows *Rear Window* at the moment.
4 Thrillers are films who shock audiences.
5 People in the UK go to the cinema more often these days.
6 Hitchcock was designing screen titles as his first job.
7 The DVD player stopped while we watched the film.
8 Wes Craven is a director which makes horror films.
9 Let's meet at a cinema in the high street.
10 I'm not often watching horror films – they scare me.

3 Discuss these questions with a partner.
1 Do you know any films by Alfred Hitchcock? Do you like them?
2 Do you have a favourite film director? Who?
3 Who is the most famous film director from your country?
4 What is your opinion of thrillers?

VOCABULARY

4a Complete the personality adjectives 1–9 using these clues. Three of the answers are adjectives from the text in Exercise 1.

1 caring about other people
2 someone who wants to help
3 an adjective from the text
4 calm, can wait for a long time and not get angry
5 likes talking, talkative
6 an adjective from the text
7 an adjective from the text
8 someone who tells the truth
9 opposite of *polite*

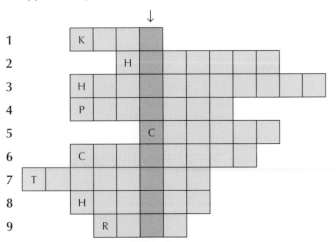

4b Check your answers by following the down arrow (↓). Which adjective is it?

5 Complete these newspaper extracts with the words in the box.

blizzards	celebrities	cloudy	fog
documentary	presenter	programme	
series	snow	storms	wet	windy

Tonight's weather

Weather warning for Scotland – expect 15 cm of
¹_____ and possibly ²_____ in the north. The north of
England will be very ³_____ with some ⁴_____ later
on in the evening. Wales will be cold and ⁵_____ , and
the south of England will be wet and ⁶_____ , with the
possibility of ⁷_____ during the night.

Scotland	England (North) (fog)
Wales	England (South)

TV previews – our recommendation

Don't miss Channel 7's new reality TV show, *Changing
Lives*, where ordinary people and ⁸_____ swap lives
for a week. In tonight's ⁹_____ , housewife and
mother-of-five, Maria Lester from Cardiff, learns how
to present the latest ¹⁰_____ about animals in the
popular ¹¹_____ , *Natural World*. The programme's
regular ¹²_____ , Alison Roberts, moves into Maria's
house and life. Expect a lot of problems but quite a
few laughs. Great for Friday-night viewing.

KEY LANGUAGE

6a Two TV producers want to choose a
presenter for a new reality TV show for young
people. Work with a partner. Discuss what kind
of person would be good in the role.

6b **1.24** Listen to their conversation. Did you
have the same ideas as the producers?

7 Listen to the conversation again and choose
the correct answer.

1 The two producers want a presenter who is:
   a) polite and smart.
   b) friendly and casual.
   c) confident and scruffy.

2 They decide to:
   a) invite Steve for a camera test.
   b) give Steve the job.
   c) invite Steve to meet the other people on
      the show.

8 Match the questions and suggestions 1–5 with the
responses a–e. Then look at Track 1.24 on page 153 and
check your answers.

1 What's he like?

2 I don't think we want a nice, polite person ...

3 What does he look like?

4 I think we need someone young and relaxed.

5 What about getting him to the studio for a camera test?

a) He's good-looking.

b) Yes, so do I.

c) Nice. He's very polite ...

d) Good idea.

e) Don't you?

9 Work with a partner to practise making suggestions.
Student A: Turn to page 113.
Student B: Turn to page 111.

LANGUAGE CHECK

10 Delete the extra word in these sentences. Then look
back at the pages and check your answers.

1 The weather is really good now at the moment. (page 7)

2 It's not quite very cold in London in winter. (page 9)

3 Do you are stay in the city in summer? (page 9)

4 We can go skiing but and we can't go trekking. (page 13)

5 I did trained every day for the marathon. (page 15)

6 We are were watching TV at 10.00 last night. (page 17)

7 'What's Julie like?' 'She's like very friendly.' (page 19)

8 I really don't like the chat shows. (page 23)

9 A newsreader is someone who it presents the news. (page 25)

10 What anything else shall we include? (page 27)

LOOK BACK

11 Find the exercise in Units 1–3 where you:

• learn about state and action verbs. (Unit 1)

• read a text about winter in Siberia. (Unit 1)

• write a guidebook entry for your country. (Unit 1)

• listen to an interview with a marathon runner. (Unit 2)

• talk about who to invite for dinner. (Unit 2)

• learn how to describe a person. (Unit 2)

• read an article about different news companies. (Unit 3)

• plan a new weekly TV programme. (Unit 3)

• write a review of a TV programme. (Unit 3)

4 Health

In this unit

Grammar
- present perfect 1
- present perfect 2 (*for* and *since*)

Vocabulary
- medical words

Scenario
- Health at work

Study skills
- guessing the meaning of unknown words

Writing skills
- a thank you email

4.1 DOCTORS WITHOUT BORDERS

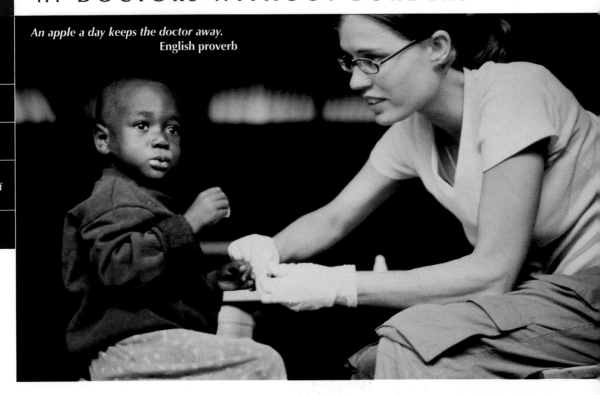

An apple a day keeps the doctor away.
English proverb

SPEAKING AND VOCABULARY: medical words (1)

1a Work with a partner. Which word is the odd one out in each group? Why? Use your dictionary.

1 doctor   surgeon   clinic   nurse

2 medicine   treatment   injury   surgery

3 disease   operation   malnutrition   illness

1b Describe the healthcare system in your country. Use the words in the box.

> private/state hospitals   health insurance
> taxes   local doctor   dentist

READING

International Medi-Aid (IMA) is a healthcare charity that works in poor and disaster-hit areas of the world. On its website, there are regular audio reports from the places they are working in.

2 Look at the list of podcasts for IMA and answer these questions.

1 Which podcasts are by and about people who provide care, e.g. doctors?

2 Which podcasts are about medical facilities?

3 Which podcast is about a financial problem?

International Medi-Aid  IMA

Podcast results 1–6 ▶

1 Field diary: New life begins
   A day in the life of one of our nurses, Beverly Timpleton, in Sri Lanka. She has worked in many different countries, but this is her most difficult position so far.

2 Healthy teeth for the young
   During their first week of action in rural areas, two new mobile clinics have treated more than 600 children.

3 Working in the Congo
   Miles Gallant, a surgeon from London, talks about his current work with us in the Congo. He hasn't worked in a foreign country before.

4 Hospital building continues
   To date, our team in Sri Lanka has built four hospitals, providing treatment to almost half a million people.

5 Treating malnutrition in Kenya
   During this year, we have trained 500 local people to treat malnutrition in their villages.

6 Forced closure of mobile clinics in Ethiopia
   We have closed our healthcare programme in Ethiopia because of a lack of funding.

LISTENING

3a `1.25` Listen to four extracts and match them to the podcasts in Exercise 2.

3b Listen again and answer these questions. Look at Track 1.25 on page 153 and check your answers.

1 How many IMA clinics were there in Africa last year?
2 How many African clinics will there be next year?
3 How did Miles feel in the UK?
4 Why is the jungle clinic 'the only hope' for the villagers?
5 When did IMA decide to train local people?
6 When did the training course begin?
7 When does Vera's course end?
8 What caused the damage in Sri Lanka?
9 In how many clinics does Beverly work?

GRAMMAR: present perfect (1)

4a These sentences all describe completed actions. Underline the actions in each sentence.

1 I've worked in Kenya, Nepal and Peru.
2 On January 1st 2004, we decided to solve this problem.
3 So far, in my time here, I've probably saved about a hundred lives.
4 Last year, we ran ten health centres in Africa.

4b Answer these questions about the sentences.

1 Which tense is each sentence in, past simple or present perfect?
2 Look at the past simple sentences.
   a) Which one is about a period of time in the past?
   b) Which one gives the exact time of the action?
3 Look at the present perfect sentences.
   a) Are they about finished or unfinished periods of time? What is the period of time in sentence 1?
   b) Do they give the exact time of the actions?
4 Match these time lines to the sentences.

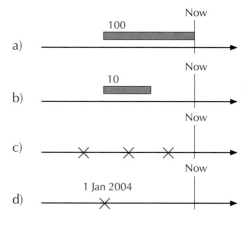

We often use the present perfect to talk about actions that are completed before now. These actions are completed in a period of time that is unfinished. We do not say the exact time in the past of the action.

4c **Time expressions** Which of these time expressions do we not use with the present perfect?

five months ago	last year	yesterday
this year	at five o'clock	today
in the last few days	never	this week
on December 20th 2007	so far	to date

4d How do we make the present perfect (affirmative and negative sentences, questions and short answers)?

→ Language reference and extra practice, pages 132–133

5 Complete these podcast summaries with the present perfect or past simple of the verbs.

International Medi-Aid IMA

Podcast results `1-6` ▶

1 A survivor's story One week ago, Asif _____ outside to collect some water. Seconds later, a bomb exploded. (go)

2 Training nurses So far this year, 110 local nurses _____ IMA training courses in Aceh province. (complete)

3 Images of survival Last week, IMA _____ a special exhibition of photographs by survivors. (organise)

4 Healthier futures We _____ two child nutrition clinics in Gaza and we hope to build two more next year. (build)

5 No deliveries Refugees in Darfur _____ any food supplies this month as the fighting continues. (not receive)

6 Soccer Aid Nearly 12,000 people _____ to raise vital funds for IMA at a charity football match on Christmas Day. (help)

SPEAKING

6 You are going to find out about students' life experiences (i.e. what have they done in their lives). Turn to page 115.

SPEAKING AND VOCABULARY: medical words (2)

1 **Discuss these questions in small groups.**

1 Describe your usual diet. What do you eat that's good / not good for you?

2 When you were at school, what food did you eat for lunch? Were school meals healthy?

3 Put these words into three groups: A for physical health and the body, B for mental health and the mind, and C for food and nutrition. Can you add any more words to each group?

carbohydrates	depression	heart disease
high blood pressure	insomnia	junk food
lack of motivation	nuts and seeds	salmon
poor concentration	poor memory	vitamins

READING

2a **Read the magazine article and answer these questions.**

1 How many of each thing a–d does the article mention?
 a) Types of food and drink
 b) Physical health problems
 c) Mental health problems
 d) Research studies

2 Complete the summary of the article with the words in the box.

| everyday | healthy | illnesses | mental | research |

Recent ¹_____ has shown that a ²_____ diet is good for your ³_____ health, from ⁴_____ problems (e.g. concentration levels) to serious ⁵_____ (e.g. Alzheimer's disease).

2b **Read the text again and answer these questions.**

1 Which did we know first: healthy food = healthy body, or healthy food = healthy mind?

2 What simple thing shows the link between food and the mind?

3 How many years ago did the school start serving healthy food?

4 What effect did the new diet have on the pupils?

5 How do you think 'our diets have changed a lot' (line 17)?

6 What is the result of these changes?

7 What two things does the Mediterranean diet do?

8 Do you eat any of the food recommended by the research in the last paragraph?

FEED YOUR

2c **Which of these definitions for words in the text are wrong? Can you correct them? Use your dictionary.**

1 mood (line 6): feelings and emotions at a particular time

2 link (line 7): the connection between two things

3 banned (line 10): officially allowed to do something

4 publicise (line 15): to tell people about something especially in the newspapers and on television

5 psychologist (line 16): a doctor who specialises in mental illnesses

6 prevents (line 25): stops something from happening

7 elderly (line 28): young people

Eat healthy food and have a healthy body. We have known this for a long time. Eat fruit and vegetables and stay physically healthy. However, we now know that there is also healthy food for your brain. Eat healthy food and have a healthy mind. This
5 is not perhaps a surprise. After all, we all know how chocolate can change our mood. However, new research clearly shows the link between diet and mental health.

For a few years, there has been a campaign to improve school meals in the UK. Daniel Brown is the head teacher of a school
10 that banned junk food and started serving healthy food in 2006. 'Our research shows that, since 2006, the children's behaviour in class has been a lot better. They are now calmer and they concentrate more. As a result, they are learning more.'

The UK Mental Health Foundation has started a campaign
15 *Feeding Minds* to publicise its own research. John Powell has been a psychologist for thirty years. 'This research shows that our diets have changed a lot, and the level of mental illness has increased. Now, I always consider my patients' diets, especially when they complain of depression and insomnia.'

20 The final piece of research concerns the Mediterranean diet. Since 1950, scientists have known that this diet (fruit, vegetables, fish, olive oil and red wine) helps you live longer. Since 2006, they have
25 known that it also prevents Alzheimer's disease, a serious mental illness that affects the elderly, and they are now telling the world about this important
30 discovery.

MIND

So, what does all this research suggest you eat? To improve your memory, eat salmon. To improve your concentration, eat vegetables. To fight insomnia, eat nuts. If depression is a problem, eat brown rice. If you worry about your later years,
35 cook with olive oil. Whatever you do, use your brain and shop for your mental health.

GRAMMAR: present perfect (2): *for* and *since*

3a Look at these sentences from the text and answer the questions below.

John Powell has been a psychologist for thirty years.

Since 1950, scientists have known that this diet helps you live longer.

1 When did John Powell become a psychologist?

2 Is he a psychologist now?

3 When did scientists discover the link between the Mediterranean diet and physical health?

4 Do they still know about this link?

3b We can use the present perfect to talk about states that began in the past and continue up to now. Find four more examples of this grammar in the text.

3c **Time expressions** We use *for* and *since* with the present perfect. Look at the sentences in Exercise 3a, then decide which of these time expressions go with *for* and which go with *since*.

2004	ten years	yesterday	a year	an hour
two o'clock	three days ago	a long time		

➡ Language reference and extra practice, pages 132–133

4 Complete these sentences with the present perfect of the verbs in the box. Then choose the correct word, *for* or *since*.

be (x2)   not be   have   know (x2)

1 Maxine _____ ill *for / since* a week. She should go to the doctor's.

2 We _____ about the link between smoking and cancer *for / since* 1950.

3 I _____ a cold *for / since* Monday.

4 He _____ a nurse *for / since* twelve years. He enjoys his job.

5 There _____ a hospital in my town *for / since* many years. In fact, it closed in 1994.

6 _____ you _____ about the advantages of this diet *for / since* a long time?

SPEAKING

5a You are going to interview your partner. Look at the questions below and choose one of the options in italics. Write similar questions for 7–9.

1 Do you have *a computer / a video camera*?

2 Do you have *a mobile phone / a watch*?

3 Are you a member of *a sports or health club / any Internet groups*?

4 Do you have *a job / a hobby*?

5 Do you have *a pet / a car*?

6 Do you know any *British / American / Australian* people?

7 Do you have …?

8 Are you …?

9 Do you know …?

5b Ask your partner the questions and find out how long he/she has had/been/known these things. Then find out more information and make notes.

WRITING

6a On a separate piece of paper, write a summary about your partner. Don't write his/her name.

6b Read some other summaries. Can you guess which student each is about?

SITUATION

1 What can you see in the photos on these pages? Have you ever been in or seen situations like these?

2a `1.26` Many companies have an occupational health officer who helps employees with health problems. Listen to a company's health officer, Mary, interview a new employee, Lucy. Complete the questions in the questionnaire below. Is Lucy in good health?

MORGAN&JONES

New Employee Health Questionnaire

Lucy Townsend

1 Have you seen a _____ recently?
2 Have you had any days off _____ in the last two years?
3 Do you have a _____ problem?
4 Do you suffer from _____ pain?
5 Do you have _____ eyesight?
6 Do you often get _____ ?
7 Do you often get _____ or 'flu?
8 Do you sometimes _____ stressed by work?

2b Listen again and note Lucy's answers. What extra information does she give with some answers?

pronunciation

3a `1.27` **Intonation in *yes/no* questions** Look at the intonation patterns. Which one is correct? Listen and check.

Have you seen a doctor recently?

1 ⟶   2 ⟶   3 ⤵

3b `1.28` Listen and repeat the health questionnaire questions in Exercise 2a.

3c Work with a partner. Ask each other the questions.

4a `1.29` Mary has consultation hours when she gives health advice to employees. Listen to a consultation with David. What are his problems?

4b What advice does Mary give David? Complete each gap with one word. Then listen again and check.

1 You should stretch your _____ .
2 You should take some _____ .
3 You should also eat _____ .
4 You should do some _____ .
5 You should go swimming _____ times a week.

4c Can you think of any more advice for David?

KEY LANGUAGE: giving advice and reasons

5a `1.30` Sometimes Mary explains the reasons for her advice. Listen and complete these sentences with the words and phrases in the box.

| because (x2)   to   so that   in order to |

1 You should stretch your arms _____ reduce the tension in your neck.
2 _____ you don't eat a lot of fruit, I think you should take some vitamins.
3 You should also eat garlic _____ it helps fight colds too.
4 _____ improve your general health, you should do some exercise.
5 You should go swimming three times a week _____ it really helps your health.

5b Match these pieces of advice 1–6 with the reasons a–f. Then choose the correct word or phrase.

1 You should try changing your chair *in order to / so that*
2 You should go to the optician's *because / to*
3 You shouldn't drink coffee at night *to / because*
4 You should take a lunch break *in order to / so that*
5 You shouldn't work late *because / so that*
6 You should bend your knees when you lift something, *because / in order to*

a) you can relax.
b) check your eyesight.
c) protect your back.
d) it makes you stressed.
e) it keeps you awake.
f) make your back better.

6 Work with a partner. What advice can you give for these health problems? Give the reasons behind your advice when you can.

1 I get headaches all the time.

2 My lower back aches a lot.

3 I've got the 'flu.

4 I'm tired all the time but I can't sleep at night.

5 I'm really stressed at work; I can't concentrate and I'm rude to people.

6 I only feel OK after my morning cigarette; before that I cough a lot.

TASK: giving health advice

7a Work in groups of four (A and B, and C and D).

Students A and B: You are occupational health officers. You are going to give advice to two employees for their problems. Look at Track 1.29 on page 153 and the Other useful phrases. Prepare to interview and advise the employees. You interview each employee in turn.

Students C and D: You are employees of Morgan and Jones. Look at your role cards on page 115 and prepare to tell the health officers about your problems. You visit each health officer in turn.

7b Employees: Which health officer gave you the best advice? Health officers: Which employee had the worst problems?

8 Swap roles and repeat the role-play.

Students A and B: Turn to page 123.

Students C and D: Prepare to be the health officers.

> ## OTHER USEFUL PHRASES
> What's the matter?
> How can I help?
> How often do you feel like this?
> How long have you had this problem?
> Does this happen every day?
> What kind of work do you do?

1 Discuss these questions with a partner.

1 What do you do when you read a word that you do not know? Do you look it up in your dictionary? Do you guess the meaning of the word? Do you ignore it completely?

2 What can you do to help you guess the meaning of words that you do not know?

2 Turn to page 116 and read the excerpt from a short story. Then answer these questions.

1 What are his problems?

2 What does the doctor say about them?

3 What do you think happens after the story?

3 Look back at the text and underline the words that you do not know or are not sure about. Compare with a partner. Can he/she explain any words you don't know?

There are a number of things you can do when you do not know a word. Read these strategies.

Using the context to understand the word

Does the rest of the sentence or text help you to:

a) understand the meaning of the word?

b) know the grammar of the word? (e.g. Is it a noun, a verb or an adjective?)

4a Look at the nonsense words in these sentences. What do you think they mean? Use the context to help you.

1 He survived the accident with only minor *gloobers*.

2 She's very healthy. She has never spent a day in *tong* in her life.

3 I can't remember the exact details of his case. I need to check his medical *donks*.

Dividing the word into different words

It's possible that you know one or more of the separate parts.

e.g. backbone = back + bone

4b Divide these words into two words. Then choose the correct meaning.

1 toothache
  a) a pain in a tooth
  b) a substance that you use for cleaning your teeth

2 sunburn
  a) light from the sun
  b) when your skin has become red and painful because you have stayed a long time in the sun

3 airtight
  a) flying through the air
  b) completely closed so that air cannot get in or out

Using your own language

Is the English word the same in your own language? If not, is part of the English word similar in your language?

e.g. French = <u>danger</u>eux   English = <u>danger</u>ous

Be careful! Sometimes you can find words in English that look the same as (or similar to) words in your own language, but they have a different meaning. For example, in Norwegian the word *sky* exists, but it means *cloud* in English. We call these words 'false friends'.

4c Work in groups. How many words can you think of in one minute which are similar in English to your own language?

4d Look at this list of false friends. Which English words are they similar to?

English word	Word in other language	What it means in other language
1 _____	fasto (Portuguese)	happy, fortunate
2 _____	caldo (Italian)	hot, warm
3 _____	bekommen (German)	to obtain
4 _____	librería (Spanish)	bookshop
5 _____	journée (French)	day
6 _____	komunikace (Czech)	road
7 _____	paini (Finnish)	weight
8 _____	rumah (Indonesian)	house

5 Look back at the text on page 116. Can you work out the meaning of any of the words you underlined?

6 Which of the strategies do you think is the most useful?

WRITING SKILLS:
a thank you email

7 Discuss these questions with a partner.

1 Do you send emails to your friends? How often?

2 What do you write about? How much do you usually write?

8 Read the email below and answer these questions. Use the ideas in the Study skills lesson to help you understand any difficult words.

1 What is the relationship between Harry and Abi?

2 What happened last week?

3 What is the connection between the email and the part of the story you read in Exercise 2?

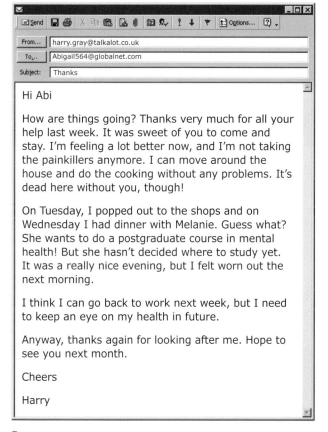

From...	harry.gray@talkalot.co.uk
To...	Abigail564@globalnet.com
Subject:	Thanks

Hi Abi

How are things going? Thanks very much for all your help last week. It was sweet of you to come and stay. I'm feeling a lot better now, and I'm not taking the painkillers anymore. I can move around the house and do the cooking without any problems. It's dead here without you, though!

On Tuesday, I popped out to the shops and on Wednesday I had dinner with Melanie. Guess what? She wants to do a postgraduate course in mental health! But she hasn't decided where to study yet. It was a really nice evening, but I felt worn out the next morning.

I think I can go back to work next week, but I need to keep an eye on my health in future.

Anyway, thanks again for looking after me. Hope to see you next month.

Cheers

Harry

9 Find one phrase in each section of the box that we do not use in informal emails or letters.

Greetings
Hello   Hi   Dear Jane   Hiya   Dear Sir

Opening phrases
How's life?   How are things?   How are you?
How are things going?   Hope you're OK/well.
Thank you for your message of 28 February.
Hope everything's OK.   Hope all's well.

Endings
Take care   Yours faithfully   Bye for now   Love
See you soon   Cheers   With love   Love from

10a Find the two examples of *thanks* in the email. Then decide if these statements are true or false.

1 We use *thanks* with *for* + a noun (phrase) or a verb ending in *-ing*.

2 We can put other words after *thanks*, e.g. *very much, again*.

10b After saying thanks, we often add another sentence for support. Match the sentences a–d with 1–4.

1 Thanks for your advice.

2 Thanks for doing the shopping.

3 Thanks for dinner.

4 Thanks for the chocolates.

a) I'll do it next time!   c) They were delicious!

b) It was lovely.   d) It's been really useful.

11 Look at these sentences. What does *'s* mean: *is, has* or *the possessive* (e.g. *Simon's health*)?

1 He's had an operation.

2 There's no problem with David's eyesight.

3 Jane's here!

4 It's been a difficult week.

5 The doctor's skills are very useful there.

6 John's broken his leg.

12 Write an email to a friend. Thank him/her for a present or for helping you to do something.

Natural world

In this unit

Grammar
- comparatives and superlatives
- expressions of quantity

Vocabulary
- landscapes
- adjectives
- animals
- nouns and verbs (*damage n/vb*)

Scenario
- Animals online

Study skills
- time management

Writing skills
- a comparative essay

5.1 ISLANDS

Let nature be your teacher.
William Wordsworth, 1770–1850, English poet

SPEAKING AND VOCABULARY: landscapes

1a How many of these things can you see in the photos A–C?

beach	cliff	coast	forest	hill	lagoon	lake
mountain	rock	sand	wave	sea	river	

1b Discuss these questions with a partner.

1 The places in the photos are all islands. Where in the world do you think they are?

2 Which islands have you visited? Describe them.

3 What do you think of when you think of an island?

I think of a tropical island with sandy beaches and a warm blue sea …

READING

2a Read the text. Are these sentences true or false?

1 There is a single mountain.

2 The water in the lagoon isn't very deep.

3 The colour of the water is the same everywhere.

4 You can drive round Bora Bora very quickly because it's a small island.

2b Read the text again. Use the information to draw a map of Bora Bora.

TROPICAL ISLANDS

Bora Bora

Many people have called it the most beautiful island in the world – a paradise of clear blue water and white sandy beaches in the Pacific Ocean.

The main island is surrounded by a lagoon and a large ring of smaller islands. There are green hills and two impressive peaks. At 727m, Mount Otemanu is the highest point.

The lagoon is the most important feature of Bora Bora and is three times bigger than the main island. The water is calm, shallow and transparent, with an amazing range of different shades of blue. You can go on trips to feed the sharks and friendly rays.

You can drive round Bora Bora in about an hour (it's only 6kms long and 3.5kms wide) but it's better to travel by bike. When you're thirsty, stop for a coconut drink. A man cuts off the top of your coconut with a huge knife!

B

C

LISTENING

3a **1.31** Listen to a TV programme about islands. Which islands do we learn about?

Great Britain   Greenland   Honshu   Iceland
Madagascar   Sumatra

Which island has a big problem? What is it?

3b Look at the statements 1–6. Can you remember which island they refer to? Listen again and check.

1 It's popular with tourists.
2 The nights are very short in summer.
3 The animals and plants are different from other places.
4 There's a tunnel connecting it to a continent.
5 There are big differences in climate between different parts of the island.
6 Its name doesn't describe it well.

3c Which island(s) would you like to visit? Why?

GRAMMAR: comparatives and superlatives

4 Complete these sentences with the comparative or superlative form of the adjectives. Then look at Track 1.31 on page 154 and check.

1 In the south, it's hot and dry, but the climate is _____ in the mountains that run down the middle of the island. (cool)
2 The island's _____ animals are the lemurs. (famous)
3 Great Britain is _____ many of its European neighbours. (crowded)
4 Wales and the north of England are hilly, while the south and east of England are _____ . (flat)
5 Greenland is _____ island in the world. (big)
6 Madagascar is _____ fourth _____ island in the world. (large)

5a Look at these sentences about the islands and answer the questions below.

*About 50,000 people live around the coast where the climate is **less cold** than in the centre.*

*Greenland is **the least green** of all the islands.*

*Some parts of the island are **less tropical** than others.*

*The area around London is probably **the least impressive** part of Great Britain.*

1 What are the opposites of the words in bold (e.g. *less cold – colder*)?
2 Do we use *less* and *least* with both short and long adjectives?
➡ Language reference and extra practice, pages 134–135

5b Complete these pairs of sentences using *less* and *least*.

1 a) The centre is colder than the coast.
   b) The coast is *less cold than* the centre.
2 a) Great Britain is greener than Greenland.
   b) Greenland is _____ Great Britain.
3 a) Scotland is the hilliest and the south of England is the flattest part of Great Britain.
   b) The south of England is _____ part of Great Britain.
4 a) In Bora Bora, the lagoon is more important than the main island.
   b) The main island is _____ the lagoon.

6 **Adjectives** Talk about the four islands using some of the adjectives in the box.

| beautiful calm cheap exciting impressive interesting mysterious peaceful pleasant popular romantic strange wild |

Greenland is probably the least popular with tourists.

SPEAKING

7 Think of two places and prepare to talk about them for one minute. Work in small groups. Take turns to describe your places.

I'd like to tell you about two different coasts in Spain …

VOCABULARY: animals

1a Which of these animals can you see in the photos A–G?

crab	red deer
elephant	giraffe
gorilla	hedgehog
human	leopard
monkey	panda
rabbit	snail
squirrel	tiger

A

1b Which of the animals above do you have in your country? Which do you think are cute? Are any of them dangerous? Are any of them nearly extinct?

READING

2a Read the article on page 43 and choose the best summary.

1 It is about the problems that new animals face in new environments.

2 It is about how foreign animals affect local animals and environments.

3 It is about the similarities between the natural environment and the business world.

2b Read the text again and find out where these animals came from, where they invaded and who or what they caused problems for.

1 grey squirrels   4 apple snails

2 red deer   5 mitten crabs

3 rabbits

3 Read the text again and answer these questions.

1 What do you think happens to the small food shop when a supermarket starts business?

2 Is the red squirrel like the small shop or the supermarket?

3 Why did the grey squirrel come to Britain?

4 Do all invasive animals cause the extinction of native animals?

5 Are there more large animal invaders than small ones?

6 Why do you think the apple snail doesn't cause many problems in Europe?

7 Is it common to find good things about animal invasions?

8 Who is Britain selling mitten crabs to, and why?

4 Are there any problems with invasive species in your country?

VOCABULARY: nouns and verbs

5a Many words are both nouns and verbs, without any change in form. Is *damage* a noun or a verb in these examples?

1 Grey squirrels don't damage the economy.

2 Apple snails cause a lot of damage in south-east Asia.

5b Find these words in the text. Are they nouns or verbs?

1 shop		3 cause		5 hope
2 harm		4 plants		6 ships

GRAMMAR: expressions of quantity

6 We can use *a lot of* with both countable and uncountable nouns. It means a large number or quantity. How do we use the other words in the box? Find and underline examples in the text.

a lot of   few   little   many   much

C

D

INVASION

7 Are these statements true or false? Use the examples you underlined in the text to help you.

1 We never use *much* in questions.

2 We often use *many* in positive sentences.

3 We don't usually use *much* in positive sentences. Instead, we use *a lot of*.

4 We never use *much* in negative sentences.

5 We can use *many* in questions and negative sentences.

➡ Language reference and extra practice, pages 134–135

Animal invaders

How much danger are we in? How many invaders are there?

Imagine you run a small food shop in your local neighbourhood. Suddenly, a giant supermarket opens for business opposite your shop. What happens to you and your business?

In the natural world, things are often the same. The red squirrel was living happily in England when, in the 1880s, many people brought grey squirrels from North America as pets. Since then, these pets have escaped into the wild. They now eat the same food as the red squirrels, and they eat it more quickly. Consequently, now there aren't many native squirrels in England and they are in danger of extinction.

There are many invaders that don't cause extinctions, but they do destroy plants and harm the economy. For example, European red deer are destroying the forests in South America because they eat the young trees. Rabbits have spread from Europe and now eat farmers' crops all over the world. These kinds of invaders are causing problems for humans, unlike the grey squirrels, which cause little damage to plants and don't damage the economy.

Few invaders are large land animals; most of them are fish or small animals like insects. There are thousands of these invaders and these smaller animals often mean farmers lose a lot of money. The apple snail from South America doesn't cause much damage in Europe, but it causes a lot of damage in south-east Asia because it loves to eat rice plants.

There are very few positive sides to these animal invasions. However, in Britain today, one invasion story offers some hope. Chinese mitten crabs first came on ships from China. These crabs destroy local environments and attack fish in fish farms. However, in China these crabs are an expensive food, so, now, Britain is selling them back to China. The crabs are travelling on ships again, but this time they are food, not invaders; and this time they are helping the British economy, not harming it.

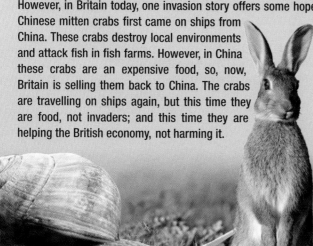

8 Complete this paragraph with *much, many, a lot of, little* or *few*.

There are [1]*many or a lot of* animals that are invaders, but perhaps there are [2]_____, if any, invaders that are worse than humans. 200,000 years ago there were very [3]_____ humans. Now there are nearly six billion of them. Unfortunately, there isn't [4]_____ information about the early history of this species, but it seems certain that the first humans came from Ethiopia in east Africa. After [5]_____ thousands of years (150–180) humans were living on every continent on Earth. How [6]_____ damage have these invaders caused? They have destroyed [7]_____ native plants and animals. Before humans, there was [8]_____ pollution. Now, there is [9]_____ pollution and it is causing [10]_____ harm to the global environment. It seems that humans need to change [11]_____ things about their lifestyle if they want to survive.

GRAMMAR TIP

In spoken and informal written English, we often use *not a lot of, not many* and *not much* instead of *few* and *little*, e.g. *There aren't a lot of students in my class. There aren't many cinemas in my city. There isn't much time left.*

SPEAKING

9a Use the sentence beginnings (or similar ones) to make true sentences about you.

In my country, there *are many / is a lot of* …

In my country, there *are few / is little* …

In my house, there are *many / a lot of* …

In my house, there *aren't many / isn't much* …

I've got *many / a lot of* …

I haven't got *many / much* …

I spend *a lot of* time …

I spend *little* …

9b Now ask your partner questions to find out if his/her life is similar to yours.

Is there much unemployment in your country?

Have you got many pictures in your house?

SITUATION

1a Look at the website on page 45. What kind of organisation is it for?

1 a business   3 an academic institution

2 a charity   4 a government department

1b Which link A–E do you click on for the following information?

1 people who kill animals illegally

2 special accommodation for animals

3 caring for ill animals

4 animals that are not free

5 saving animals from danger

The AAI Website Manager, Neil, is choosing some photos for the new AAI website. He needs to discuss them with the Communications Director, Katie. However, she is in the Congo and she does not have access to the Internet to view the photos. Neil telephones her to describe them and make his recommendations.

2 `1.32–33` Listen to the two parts of the conversation and answer these questions.

1 In what order does Neil describe the photos A–D?

2 Which photo does he recommend for the website?

3a `1.32` Listen to the first part of the conversation again and complete Katie's notes.

Whale pics
1) There are ¹_____ whales close to a beach. Two men are ²_____ whale off the beach. Loads of ³_____ watching.
2) On the left, we can see the large ⁴_____ of a whale. Two people throwing ⁵_____ on the whale. Pic is ⁶_____ .
1st pic is best – a ⁷_____ of people working together, they look very ⁸_____ – more dramatic.

3b `1.33` Listen to the second part of the conversation again and complete Katie's notes.

Bird pics
1) Man in the ¹_____ passing a ²_____ to someone on beach.
2) People ³_____ a bird. Woman in ⁴_____ shirt holding bird, woman on the ⁵_____ cleaning bird.
1st pic more ⁶_____ , makes you ⁷_____ the situation.
2nd pic shows what experts ⁸_____ , but not very ⁹_____ .

KEY LANGUAGE: describing photographs

4a `1.32–33` Complete these sentences from the conversation. Then listen again and check.

1 In the first one, _____ are four whales that are close to the beach.

2 There are loads of people _____ the background.

3 On the left of the picture, we can _____ the large head of a whale.

4 On the right, there are two people _____ are throwing water on the whale.

5 They _____ very professional.

6 He's _____ a bird to someone.

7 The second one _____ some people who are cleaning a bird.

8 The bird's _____ the middle of the picture.

9 There's another woman _____ the left.

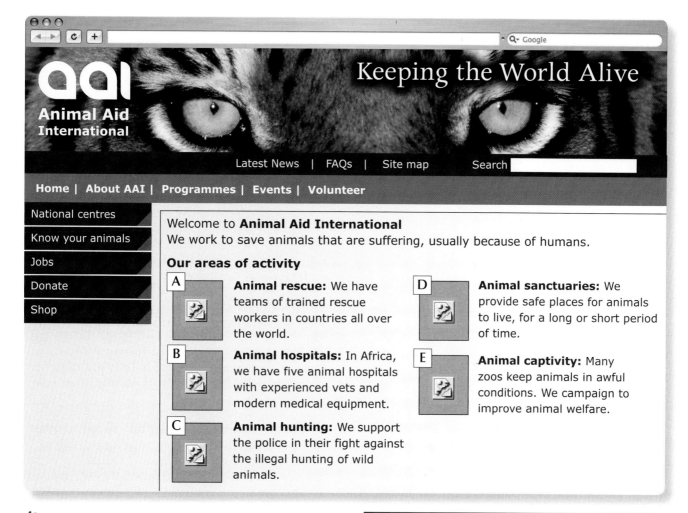

Keeping the World Alive

aai
Animal Aid International

Latest News | FAQs | Site map | Search

Home | About AAI | Programmes | Events | Volunteer

National centres
Know your animals
Jobs
Donate
Shop

Welcome to **Animal Aid International**
We work to save animals that are suffering, usually because of humans.

Our areas of activity

A **Animal rescue:** We have teams of trained rescue workers in countries all over the world.

B **Animal hospitals:** In Africa, we have five animal hospitals with experienced vets and modern medical equipment.

C **Animal hunting:** We support the police in their fight against the illegal hunting of wild animals.

D **Animal sanctuaries:** We provide safe places for animals to live, for a long or short period of time.

E **Animal captivity:** Many zoos keep animals in awful conditions. We campaign to improve animal welfare.

4b Answer these questions about the sentences in Exercise 4a.

1 Which tense do we use to describe someone's actions in a picture?
2 What type of word do we use after *look*?
3 Underline the phrases for describing the position of something in a picture.

pronunciation

5a 1.34 Weak forms Some words have both a strong and a weak pronunciation. We often use the weak form when the word is not stressed in a sentence. Listen and notice the weak pronunciation of *that, are* and *to*. Listen again and repeat.

In the first one, there are four whales that are close to the beach.

5b 1.35 Listen and repeat the strong and weak forms of *a, that, of, to, some, are* and *can*.

5c 1.36 Listen and repeat sentences 2–9 in Exercise 4a.

6 Work with a partner. Practise describing the four photos in Exercise 2. Can you hear the weak forms?

TASK: choosing photos for a website

7a Work with a partner. You are going to role-play a similar situation to the conversation in Exercise 2.

Student A: You are the Website Manager. Turn to page 116 and prepare to describe your photos.

Student B: You are the Communications Director. Find out which links the photos are for and take notes.

7b Swap roles and repeat the role-play.

Student B: You are now the Website Manager. Turn to page 125.

8 You are now back in the office. Look at the four photos that your partner described. Was the description good? Do you agree with his/her choice?

> **OTHER USEFUL PHRASES**
> This one is   nicer/clearer/stronger/weaker
>   more unusual/dramatic/powerful
> I like the way this one …
> I think this one is better because …
> It makes you feel sad/angry/…
> I think we should use this one because …

STUDY SKILLS:
time management

1 Look at these expressions with *time*. Which suggest the person has a problem with time?

1 I've got all the time in the world.

2 There aren't enough hours in the day.

3 Time's running out.

4 I've got time on my hands.

5 Time's on my side.

6 It's a race against time.

Which expressions best describe how you feel about time?

2 How do you use your time? Look at the list of activities in the time chart below. Guess how many hours a day you spend on each. Then keep a record for a few days. Which of the activities can you change to give yourself more time to learn English?

3a Work in groups of three or four. Look at these problems some students are having with time management. What advice would you give them?

1 I'm often late for appointments, or sometimes I miss appointments completely.

2 I spend a lot of time looking for my notes. I can never find anything.

3 I sometimes study for a long time, but I don't feel I'm learning anything. I read the material, but nothing's happening – it's not going in.

4 I can't finish all the things I need to do in the day.

3b **1.37** Listen to some students and their tutor discuss the problems above. Do they mention any of your ideas?

3c Match this advice with the problems 1–4 in Exercise 3a. Then listen again and check.

a) Find out when you study best.

b) Decide what's important.

c) Keep a diary – and check it!

d) Take regular breaks.

e) Make lists of things you need to do.

f) Organise your files.

g) Make sure you can concentrate.

h) Be nice to yourself!

3d Look at Track 1.37 on page 155 and underline the parts of the script that tell us about the advice a–h above. Which two tips do you think are most useful for you?

4a Think of ten things you need to do in the next week (e.g. write an essay, go to the doctor).

4b Which things in your list are urgent? Which can wait? Put them in order of priority (i.e. most important first). Then show your partner. Does he/she agree with your order?

5 It's also important to decide how to spend time on a particular task. Imagine that you are going to write an essay in class. You have 45 minutes to write 150 words. Put these stages in the correct order and decide how long you should spend on each.

1 checking your work

2 thinking and noting ideas; planning and organising notes

3 writing

Compare your ideas with three or four other students.

Keeping time?

- sleeping
- personal care (e.g. washing, dressing)
- eating and drinking (including preparation of meals, snacks, coffee breaks)
- travelling
- time at college

- time at work
- time with family
- housework
- socialising with friends
- sport/leisure activities
- (non-work) time on the Internet
- other

WRITING SKILLS: a comparative essay

6 Discuss these questions with a partner.

1 Are there any volcanoes in your country? Are they famous?

2 Have you ever been up a volcano? If not, would you like to go up a volcano?

3 We use special terms to talk about volcanoes. Do you know what these words mean?

> active   dormant   erupt   an eruption   cone

7 Read this essay and choose the best title.

1 Discuss the good and bad features of volcanoes.

2 Compare and contrast two volcanoes.

3 Consider the problem of volcanoes, and what people can do about this problem.

Volcanoes are one of the most impressive features of the natural world. Everybody can recognise a volcano, but are they all the same? This essay looks at two famous volcanoes in different countries.

The largest active volcano in the world is Mauna Loa (4,170m) on Hawaii, in the Pacific Ocean. The last eruption was in 1984. Its sides slope gently, and this shape of volcano is less dangerous than other kinds.

Unlike Mauna Loa, Mount Fuji in Japan is a dormant volcano which last erupted in 1707. Mount Fuji (3,776m) is perhaps the world's most famous volcano because of its almost perfect shape – a cone with quite steep sides.

To summarise, Mauna Loa is higher than Mount Fuji but the sides of Mount Fuji are steeper. Mauna Loa is an active volcano. In contrast, Mount Fuji is dormant. Mauna Loa last erupted in 1984, whereas the last eruption of Mount Fuji was in 1707. In conclusion, we can see that these two volcanoes have more differences than similarities, but they both catch our imagination.

8a Good organisation is very important in an essay. Compare this essay with the one on page 117. Which is easier to understand? Why?

8b An essay has three main parts.

1 introduction

2 main body

3 (summary and) conclusion

Draw a line around these parts in the essay in Exercise 7.

9a **Linkers** Look at these sentences. Do they mean the same thing?

1 The River Nile is 6,670km long. In contrast, the River Thames is only 335km long.

2 The River Nile is 6,670km long but the River Thames is only 335km long.

3 The River Nile is 6,670km long, whereas the River Thames is only 335km long.

What is the difference in punctuation between them?

9b Write three sentences (like those above) about these places. Use *In contrast*, *but* and *whereas*.

1 Mount Everest: 8,848m high
  Ben Nevis: 1,343m

2 Pacific Ocean: 11,022m deep at its deepest point
  North Sea: 310m

10 Write an essay comparing and contrasting:

1 two natural features (e.g. two mountains, lakes, rivers) in your country or a country you know well OR

2 two different animals OR

3 two of the islands in lesson 5.1 (Look at Track 1.31 on page 154 to help you.)

Mauna Loa

Mount Fuji

6 Society and family

In this unit

Grammar
- *will*, *might* and *may* for predictions
- first conditional

Vocabulary
- ages
- negative adjectives (*un* and *less*)

Scenario
- Family matters

Study skills
- correcting your writing

Writing skills
- an article

6.1 FUTURE OPPORTUNITY

The spirit of truth and the spirit of freedom – these are the pillars of society.
Heinrik Ibsen, 1828–1906, Norwegian dramatist

SPEAKING

1 Are these statements true about your country?

1 More people are now making friends over the Internet.
2 People are living longer than before.
3 People are having more holidays abroad.
4 People are using robots in their homes.

READING

2a Read the advert. Who uses the institute and its services? Why?

1 politicians   2 business people   3 academics

2b Find words in the text that mean:

1 someone who studies the future
2 fashions or changes over time
3 opinions about what will happen in the future

LISTENING

3a [1.38] Listen to a meeting between Susan, a futurologist, and Patrick, a business investor. Tick (✓) the future changes she discusses.

1 domestic use of technology
2 longer lives
3 Internet friendships and relationships
4 people working from home
5 leisure activities and travel

The Institute of Future Analysis

IFA 0890 546 990
www.ifa.co.uk

**Are you planning for the future?
Do you know what's coming next?**

The world and your markets are constantly changing.
Will the elderly be the big spenders of the future?
When will middle-age begin? When will people retire?
What will tomorrow's teenagers want to buy?
Our futurologists can help you profit from the future.

We provide:
- information about future trends in society.
- predictions about future consumer needs.
- analysis of your company and its future plans.
- advice for business investors.

Call us now and improve your future opportunities.

3b Listen again and complete Patrick's notes from the meeting.

> Main trends are about ¹_____ and ²_____.
>
> In 2025, more than a ³_____ of people over 55, also people live ⁴_____.
>
> In 2025, more over-65s than ⁵_____.
>
> Fewer party and adventure holidays, more holidays on ⁶_____.
>
> Robots: to ⁷_____, to ⁸_____, to do the gardening.
>
> More divorces: Older people meet new partners ⁹_____.
>
> Invest in businesses that offer ¹⁰_____ and ¹¹_____ for the elderly and that use ¹²_____.

VOCABULARY: ages

4 What age do you think these people are?

> an adolescent   a middle-aged person
> a young adult   a thirty-something   a child
> an elderly person   a teenager   a retired person

What is life like at these ages? What responsibilities do people have? What kind of things do they spend their money on? Which is the best age to be?

GRAMMAR: *will, might* and *may* for predictions

5a [1.39] Complete these sentences from the meeting with the words in the box. Then listen and check.

> will   definitely (x2)   might
> may   won't   probably

1 These older people _____ live for much longer – we know that from the statistics.

2 They _____ live until they're 95, or even 100.

3 That _____ won't be good for business.

4 I'm sure they _____ have much money.

5 These people will _____ need things to do with this extra time, for sure.

6 They _____ also want activity holidays but that'll depend on their health.

7 They _____ won't go bungee-jumping.

5b Answer these questions about the sentences.

1 In which sentences is the speaker certain that his/her idea about the future is true?

2 In which sentences is the speaker less certain?

3 What verb form do we use after *will, might* and *may*?

4 Do we usually put adverbs (e.g. *probably*) before or after *will*? Do we put them before or after *won't*?

➡ Language reference and extra practice, pages 136–137

5c Correct the mistakes in these sentences.

1 He might lives to the age of 90.

2 Many people will probably to work from home.

3 I will live definitely in my own country.

4 There won't probably be big families.

SPEAKING

6a Choose the correct word in these predictions according to your opinion for your society twenty years from now.

1 *More / Fewer* people than now will leave their country to find work.

2 People *will definitely / may* spend more time using the Internet than watching TV.

3 *More / Fewer* people will probably live alone.

4 Most people *will / won't* retire at the age of 55.

5 The differences between rich and poor people will probably be *greater / smaller.*

6 People will have *more / less* free time.

6b Compare your ideas with a partner, and explain your predictions. Which of the predictions are positive or negative for your country?

WRITING

7 Write a short paragraph about your predictions for your society.

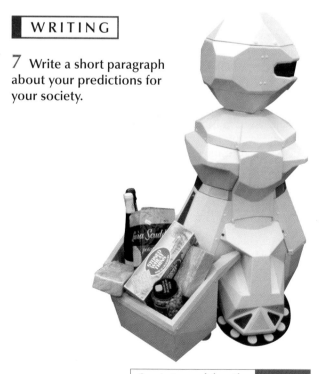

Society and family   UNIT 6   49

SPEAKING

1 Discuss these questions with a partner.

1 How important is family life in your country?

2 How many people are there in your immediate family (parents, children, brothers and sisters)?

3 What are the advantages and disadvantages of a small or big family?

READING

2a Match these words with their definitions.

> birth rate   childcare   employer
> old-fashioned   responsible   suitable

1 not modern

2 you did it or caused it

3 a person or company that pays you to work for them

4 right for a particular purpose or situation

5 when someone looks after children while the parents are at work

6 the number of births for every 100 or 1,000 people in a particular year and place

2b Read the newspaper article and complete this sentence in six or seven words.

This article is about _____ .

2c What is the organisation of the text? Put these topics in order (1–4).

a) reasons for the low birth rate ☐

b) possible solutions to the problem ☐

c) reaction to the possible solutions ☐

d) facts about the low birth rate ☐

2d Read the text again. Are these sentences true or false? Correct any false sentences.

1 Only 40% of German female graduates have had children.

2 German women have an average of 1.37 children.

3 Few parents have more than one child.

4 A university professor believes that German employers do not have modern attitudes.

5 The government will pay each parent 1,800 euros a month so the father can take time off work.

6 Ms von der Leyen's ideas are not popular with everyone.

3 What do you think of Ms von der Leyen's plan?

Germany: What future for the family?

New figures showed yesterday that Germany has the highest percentage of childless women in the world. 30% of German women have not had children, and this figure rises to 40% among female graduates. Germany's Family Minister, Ursula von der Leyen, said that if the birth rate does not go up, Germany will die.

Germany's birth rate is one of the lowest in Europe, with an average of 1.37 children per woman, compared with 1.75 in Sweden and 1.74 in the UK. German mothers are also the oldest, with an average age of thirty when they have their first child – and most parents choose to have only one child.

According to Professor Norbert Schneider of Mainz University, the reasons for Germany's low birth rate

Ursula von der Leyen with her children. She wants fathers to help more with childcare.

include poor childcare, a school day that ends at 1 p.m., and old-fashioned attitudes among employers. In addition, many German women are already in their mid-thirties when they finish university and get a good job.

Ms von der Leyen, a mother of seven, says that

another difficulty is that some women cannot find a suitable man. 'Uncertain' men (who are unsure about becoming fathers) are also responsible for the low birth rate, she claims.

The minister has developed a plan to encourage people to have more children.

First of all, if parents need private childcare, they will get help from the government, by paying less tax.

Secondly, families will get up to 1,800 euros a month from the government if men stay at home for two months after the birth of a new child.

But some men, even in the minister's own political party, are unhappy with this last idea. Professor Schneider says that in Germany it is acceptable for women to take time off to have children. However, if a man takes time off work to look after a new child, his career will be over. The typical family picture is very much alive in Germany, he said. Women look after the children while men go out to work.

VOCABULARY: negative adjectives

We can use *un-* and *-less* to show a negative or opposite, to mean 'not' and 'without'.

4a Make the negative adjectives of these words.

care   comfortable   hope   kind
lucky   use   usual

4b Write questions with four of the negative adjectives. Then ask and answer the questions with your partner.

GRAMMAR: first conditional

We can use *if* to talk about the result of a possible future action.

5a Match the beginnings and endings of these sentences.

if-clause (condition)

1 If the father stays at home for two months,
2 If parents need private childcare,
3 If the birth rate does not go up,

main clause (result)

a) they will get help from the government.
b) Germany will have a serious problem.
c) families will get 1,800 euros a month.

5b Is this grammar rule correct?

if-clause = *if* + simple present
main clause = *will / will not (won't)* + infinitive

GRAMMAR TIP

You can change the order of the *if*-clause and main clause in the sentence. Only use a comma when you start the sentence with *if*.

➡ Language reference and extra practice, pages 136–137

6a Complete these sentences with the correct form of the verbs.

1 If I _____ (see) him, I _____ (tell) him the news.
2 She _____ (be) ill if she _____ (not rest) more.
3 What _____ (you do) if you _____ (not pass) your next exam?
4 We _____ (not arrive) on time if we _____ (not hurry) up.
5 If you _____ (move) your car, I _____ (be) able to park.
6 I _____ (do) the washing up if I _____ (have) time.

GRAMMAR TIP

Use *might* instead of *will* when you are less sure that something will happen.

*If the birth rate does not go up, that country **might** die.*

6b Think of other things that you will, or might, do today / tomorrow / at the weekend, etc.

If I have time, I'll wash my hair tonight.

If I see Angelina later, I might ask her to the party.

SPEAKING

7a `1.40` You are going to role-play some situations where people discuss problems and possible solutions. Listen to this example conversation and answer these questions.

1 What is Shane and Evelyn's relationship?
2 What does Shane want to do?

7b Listen again and answer these questions.

1 What three problems does Evelyn mention?
2 What are Shane's solutions?
3 What does Evelyn think of Shane's plan?

pronunciation

8 `1.41` Contractions Listen to these sentences. How do we say *What'll ...?* Listen again and repeat.

9 Work with a partner. Turn to page 117 and consider what you will do in the situations.

PREPARATION

1 Discuss these questions with a partner.

1 Who does the cooking and cleaning in your family?

2 Could you stay out late when you were a teenager?

3 What housework did you do when you were a child or teenager?

4 Did both your parents work when you were young?

SITUATION

Speak Out is a television talk show. Robert Hughes is the presenter and the audience takes part in the discussions. This week, the topic of the show is problems and responsibilities in families.

2a `1.42` Listen to part of the show. Which of these issues do they discuss?

1 Mothers should stay at home with their young children.

2 Working men do not need to share the housework.

3 Children shouldn't watch many hours of TV a day.

4 Parents should let teenagers choose when to come home at night.

2b Look at the different points made on the show. Listen again and put them in order (1–8).

a) Some mothers can't stay at home because they need money. ☐

b) A mother's love is important for her children. 1

c) Working mothers miss the best years of their children's lives. ☐

d) Some mothers work because they want to. ☐

e) TV is an everyday thing and children should know about it. ☐

f) Parents should not let children watch TV at all. ☐

g) Only let children watch a couple of hours of TV a day. ☐

h) TV is bad for children. ☐

2c Which of the points do you agree or disagree with? Discuss in small groups.

KEY LANGUAGE: expressing opinions

3a `1.42` Listen again and complete these sentences.

1 _____ , I think mothers should stay at home.

2 Well, I understand her _____ , but sometimes mothers have no choice.

3 Well, that's a good _____ , but I think some mothers work because they want to.

4 I agree _____ Sheila.

5 Well, _____ I think is that they shouldn't watch any TV.

6 Well, personally, I _____ disagree.

7 I think it's _____ if they know that TV is a normal thing.

8 Well, that's an interesting _____ , but TV is different to phones.

3b Match the sentences in Exercise 3a to these functions.

a) agreement   b) disagreement   c) opinion

pronunciation

4a **1.43** **Word linking** Listen and repeat this phrase. Notice the link between words that end in a consonant and those that begin with a vowel.

Well, that's a good point, but …

4b **1.44** Which words do we link in these phrases? Listen and check.

1 Well, what I think is that …
2 Well, that's an interesting idea, but …
3 Well, I understand her opinion, but …

4c Practise saying the phrases in Exercises 4a and b.

5 Practise accepting an idea and then disagreeing with your partner. Use the ideas below to help you.

1 1st idea: mothers should stay at home
   2nd idea: some mothers have no choice

Personally, I think mothers should stay at home with their children.

– Well, I understand your opinion, but some mothers have no choice.

2 1st idea: TV teaches children about the world
   2nd idea: children should read books to learn things

3 1st idea: husbands should help clean the house
   2nd idea: men are tired after a day at work

TASK: speaking on a talk show

6a Complete these statements with the words and phrases in the box.

| elderly   house husband   pay |
| permission   pocket money |

1 Parents should _____ children to tidy the house.
2 It is not a good idea for a man to be a _____ .
3 A teenager can stay out late without _____ .
4 Young children should get _____ .
5 Families should look after their _____ members at home.

6b Work with a partner. Think of reasons for and against the statements above.

For: *I think parents should do that because then they won't argue.*

Against: *I don't think they should do that because children need to learn about looking after a home.*

7a Work in small groups. You are on *Speak Out*. One student is the TV presenter. He/She chooses one of the statements in Exercise 6a and asks the guests for their opinions on that topic.

7b After the first discussion, another student becomes the TV presenter and chooses a new statement for discussion.

OTHER USEFUL PHRASES
Right, the next topic is, working men should …
So, what's your name and what do you think?
Do you agree with him/her?
What do you say to that?
What's your opinion?

STUDY SKILLS: corrrecting your writing

1 Which of these sentences are true for you?

1 I always check my writing carefully when I've finished.

2 I read my teacher's comments and corrections carefully.

3 When my teacher gives back my work, the only thing I look at is my mark.

4 I look at my mistakes, but never remember them.

5 After my teacher gives back my work, I often rewrite it to make it better.

2 Match the types of mistakes in the box that learners often make with these sentences.

grammar   vocabulary   spelling   punctuation word order   leaving words out

1 That's an interesting idea.

2 If the birth rate ~~will grow~~ *grows*, the country will not die.

3 Older people will ~~robots want~~ *want robots*.

4 What will you *do* ∧ if you arrive late?

5 The situation is bad but it isn't ~~useless~~ *hopeless*.

6 Their advi*c*e was very helpf*ul* ~~helpfull~~.

3a Word order Change the position of one word in each sentence to make it correct.

1 More people will live probably alone in the future.

2 Bob hopes that there will be good opportunities business for him in the future.

3 Everyone in my family has got eyes unusual, except for me.

4 What she will do if he doesn't arrive on time?

3b Leaving words out Add one word to each sentence to make it correct.

1 People living longer than before.

2 If men spend more time at home, children might happier.

3 The majority of young people will go university.

4 Older people will meet on Internet.

Are the missing words similar in any way?

3c Punctuation Correct the punctuation in this piece of writing. Use full stops and capital letters, and take out unnecessary commas.

In my country family life is very important, we spend

a lot of time, with our families, and we always have

lunch together on sundays, there are also a lot of

family businesses

4a Look at this student's writing. The teacher has used a correction code. Correct the mistakes.

Gr = grammar	*WW* = wrong word (vocabulary)
Sp = spelling	*WO* = word order
∧ = missing word	*P* = punctuation

One problem in my *Sp* contry is that rich people *Gr* is

getting richer *Gr* poor people is getting poorer, *P* if the gap

WW among them will ∧ become *Gr* very big, it will create

WO problems serious.

4b Read the rest of the student's work. Look for mistakes and write the correct symbol above the mistake. Then check on page 117.

Violence will increase we will frightened to leave our

homes. What we can do I believe that rich people

should pay more tax and the govenment must provide

more occasions for poor people

WRITING SKILLS: an article

5a Discuss these questions with a partner.

1 Have you ever entered a competition? Have you ever written anything for a competition?

2 Have you ever won anything?

5b Read the poster below. How many people will win a prize?

UK Youth Council Competition

What makes you proud of your society today? The UK Youth Council invites young people in the UK to write about what makes them proud of British society today (maximum 200 words). The top 20 entries will receive a prize of £250 and will appear on the Council's website.

6 Read the competition entry below. What do you think the judges liked and disliked about it? Think about ideas, organisation of ideas, etc.

What makes you proud of your society today?

What to choose? It is difficult to decide, as I feel proud of many things in my society today: for example, our education system, our creativity in the arts and our science. Two things, however, make me especially proud of my society. First, our big cities are very multicultural, so you see people of many different races, colours and religions. These people all live and work side by side. I think it's a great example of how people can come together and create a mixed, peaceful society. The second thing is less obvious, as it often happens out of sight. It's the fact that every day of the year, thousands of British people do voluntary work. They give up their time to help others for nothing. They help their local hospitals, look after old people and collect money for good causes. Because of these things, I feel proud of my society and see a positive future for it. However, I also want to contribute to it. In my life, many people have helped me, so now I would like to give something back.

Silvia Hussein
20 year-old business student from Birmingham

7a **Paragraph organisation** Look at the competition entry again. It should be four paragraphs, not one. Divide it into four paragraphs.

7b What is the topic of these paragraphs?

Paragraph 2

a) big cities

b) people living and working side by side

c) a multicultural society

Paragraph 3

a) local schools and hospitals

b) unpaid work

c) old people

8 **Sentence structure** We can join these three sentences to make one sentence.

They help their local hospitals. They look after old people. They collect money for good causes.

They help their local hospitals, look after old people and collect money for good causes.

Join these sentences to make one sentence.

1 Silvia studies business at university. She lives with her parents. She helps in her parents' shop at weekends.

2 Her sister studies at school. She likes boy bands. She wants a car.

9 **Linkers** Study the use of the linking words *so, as, however* and *because of* in Silvia's article. Then use them to complete the judges' report below.

There were a very large number of entries (over 3,000) ¹_____ it took a long time to read them all. ²_____ , the judges' task was interesting ³_____ the young people wrote about a wide range of topics (e.g. the BBC, the National Health Service, popular music). The standard of entries was also very high, ⁴_____ it was extremely difficult to choose the winners. After much discussion, ⁵_____ , the judges agreed on the top 20 entries.

The judges were impressed by Silvia Hussein's article, ⁶_____ her modern vision and a feeling for other people. They also liked the style of her entry, ⁷_____ she communicated her ideas very clearly. ⁸_____ , they were not happy with her paragraph organisation.

10a Write your answer to the question: *What makes you proud of your society today?* Use the model in Exercise 6 and the useful phrases below to help you.

Two things make me proud of my society …

First … The second thing is …

10b Check your work for mistakes (e.g. grammar, spelling). Check your partner's work too!

REVIEW

GRAMMAR

1 Read the two texts about Iceland. Where is each text from?

> More dramatic than the Canary Islands, more peaceful than European cities, but only the same distance away – that's Iceland!

This island in the North Atlantic is larger than England and Wales, but few people live here – only about 290,000, with over half in the capital city, Reykjavik. Iceland has been independent from Denmark since 1944 and the capital comes alive on Independence Day (June 16), when Reykjavik feels more crowded than London.

But people don't usually visit Iceland for the city life. This is a country of amazing landscapes – blue lakes and lagoons, fast rivers and waterfalls, mountains and volcanoes that erupt frequently. Mount Hekla, in the south of the country, has erupted sixteen times in the last 1,000 years, and, in one of the most violent eruptions of recent times, the volcano on the island of Heimaey almost destroyed the town in 1973.

2 Are these sentences about the texts true or false? Correct the false ones.

1 The Canary Islands are less dramatic than Iceland.
2 Iceland is smaller than England and Wales.
3 Not many people live in Iceland.
4 London never feels less crowded than Reykjavik.
5 Iceland has been independent for less than 50 years.
6 The volcano on Heimaey has erupted sixteen times.
7 Mel has seen smaller capital cities than Reykjavik.
8 Iceland is more expensive than many other places.
9 If the weather's good, Mel will go on an excursion tomorrow.
10 They'll definitely hire a car at the weekend.

Mel's travel blog

Day 3 in Iceland

We've been here for two days now, in Reykjavik. It's the smallest capital city I've ever visited, so we've seen just about everything now. It's very pretty and has some great museums (useful for rainy days – and there are a lot of them!), but it's very expensive here, more expensive than London even, but the food's good. I've had the best lamb and fish that I've ever tasted.

We want to see more of the island, so we'll probably go on an excursion tomorrow, but it depends on the weather. If it's good weather, we'll stay here and go whale-watching in the afternoon, but if it's bad, we'll definitely take an excursion. We're also thinking of hiring a car but we might leave that till Friday and drive north over the weekend.

Time for bed! I'll write more tomorrow.

3 Complete the second sentence so that it means the same as the first sentence. Use the word in brackets.

1 Iceland is more peaceful than European cities.
European cities _____ . (less)
2 Iceland has a small population.
Few _____ . (live)
3 Iceland got its independence in 1944.
Iceland has been _____ . (since)
4 Reykjavik is the furthest north of any capital city.
Reykjavik is _____ . (further)

VOCABULARY

4 **1.45** Listen to Jane and Andrea discussing their next holiday and answer the questions.

1 What type of holiday do they want to go on?
2 Which two do they decide to think about?
Bwindi   Murchison Falls   Queen Elizabeth Mgahinga

5a Complete the names of the national parks A–D in the brochure extracts on page 57.

5b Listen again and complete the gaps 1–9 with landscape words or animals.

UNITS 4-6

KEY LANGUAGE

6 [1.46] Listen to Tom and Shula talking about a photo. Draw a sketch of the photo.

7 Complete the conversation with the words and phrases. Then listen again and check.

a) personally, I believe   e) That's a good point, but
b) look amazing   f) You should do that
c) because   g) I think it's better
d) to   h) I agree

T: ... and this photo is from my job in India, years ago. That's the clinic on the left.

S: Oh, it's lovely. Who's the little boy on the right with the two women?

T: He helped the doctors and nurses, you know, made tea, fetched things.

S: It's interesting that the photo is in black and white.

T: Yes, ¹_____ that you get better photos this way.

S: Yes, ²_____ . The mountains in the middle ³_____ – so impressive.

T: I know. I loved the mountains. In fact, I loved everything there!

S: Really, why?

T: Well, ⁴_____ the weather was good, the food was wonderful, the people were really friendly. I'd really like to go back ⁵_____ see them all again.

S: ⁶_____ ! You can take three months off from this job, you know.

T: ⁷_____ I couldn't leave my family for that long. ⁸_____ if I wait till the children are older.

LANGUAGE CHECK

8 Is there a word missing in these sentences? If so, decide where to put it. Then look back at the pages and check your answers.

have
1 I ∧had a sore throat since last Tuesday. (page 33)
2 My father worked in Brazil in 2002. (page 33)
3 There's a problem with lack motivation. (page 34)
4 I wanted to become a doctor to help people. (page 36)
5 This is least impressive part of the country. (page 41)
6 Humans have caused a lot problems to the environment. (page 42)
7 The volcano will probably erupt this year. (page 49)
8 Elderly people might healthier in the future. (page 49)
9 If we both work, we'll get childcare. (page 51)
10 I'm not sure. I think I agree Angela. (page 53)

LOOK BACK

9 Find the exercise in Units 4–6 where you:
• listen to extracts from podcasts. (Unit 4)
• learn how to give reasons for an action. (Unit 4)
• write a thank you email. (Unit 4)
• compare two places you know well. (Unit 5)
• read about animal invaders. (Unit 5)
• learn about managing your time. (Unit 5)
• talk about the different stages in life. (Unit 6)
• learn how to express conditions that affect future actions. (Unit 6)
• discuss family issues for presentation on a TV show. (Unit 6)

A _____ National Park
High above sea level, this national park has ¹_____ with a wide variety of birds and animals, including over half the world's mountain ²_____ .

B _____ National Park
On both sides of the world's longest ³_____ , the Nile, this park has some amazing animals, such as buffalo, ⁴_____ and ⁵_____ .

C _____ National Park
A mixture of open grasslands and rainforest, around the ⁶_____ in this park you can see over 100 types of animal, including elephants and big cats, such as lions and ⁷_____ .

D _____ National Park
Protecting the Ugandan part of the Virangas, nine ⁸_____ (six extinct), this park has lots of birds and animals in its forests, including the golden ⁹_____ .

7 Science

In this unit

Grammar
- *must* and *have to*
- *had to* and *could*

Vocabulary
- science and crime
- nouns, adjectives and verbs with prepositions

Scenario
- Ideas and innovations

Study skills
- making notes

Writing skills
- describing charts

7.1 CRIME LAB

There are in fact two things, science and opinion.
Hippocrates, 5th century BC, Greek physician

READING AND VOCABULARY: science and crime

1 Match these captions with the photos A–C.

1 Investigators collect important evidence at the scene of a crime.

2 Actors rehearse a scene on the set of the latest crime drama.

3 A scientist prepares DNA samples for analysis.

2a Read the two television programme reviews. Which is a documentary? Which is a drama? Which would you watch?

2b Read the texts again and answer these questions.

1 Which programme does the reviewer strongly recommend?

2 How many crimes are there in the episode of *Crime lab*?

3 What is the smallest thing that forensic scientists analyse?

Crime lab

The crime scene investigation team has to solve two murders and a burglary tonight. Senior forensic scientist Karen Warner discovers a vital clue at a crime scene, her sister's DNA. She tries to keep her discovery secret but her boss finds out and tells her she must leave the investigation. There's a burglary at the mayor's house but the burglar hasn't left any fingerprints. Because of this, laboratory assistant Dan Turner has to use a new piece of scientific equipment, with surprising results.

CSI – the reality

This new series reveals the science behind modern police investigations. Iris Battle is a forensic scientist in a government crime lab. Her team examines the material from the crime scene – furniture, bullets, knives, cigarettes – to find things you can hardly see: fingerprints, hairs and DNA molecules. This series explains how scientists analyse the evidence in order to identify who has committed a crime. It's a fascinating programme about the lives and work of the real crime scene investigators – definitely one to watch!

3 Find verbs in the texts that mean:

1 find the answer to a problem
2 find or learn something that you did not know about before
3 show something that you could not see before
4 examine something carefully in order to understand it
5 break the law

LISTENING

4a **1.47** Listen to an interview between Iris Battle (a forensic scientist) and a researcher for the documentary programme. Put these topics in the order (1–6) that they talk about them. (There is one topic that you do not need.)

a) the two teams of employees ☐
b) work in the laboratory ☐
c) the researcher's main interest ☑ 1
d) the effects of the TV dramas ☐
e) visiting the laboratory ☐
f) scientific equipment ☐
g) work at the crime scene ☐

4b Work with a partner. Complete these sentences with information that Iris Battle gives. Then listen again and check.

1 Crime scene analysts collect the evidence, whereas forensic scientists …
2 In reality, forensic scientists are experts in special areas, but on TV they …
3 In reality, most of the crimes are burglaries, whereas on TV they …
4 On TV, they get DNA test results in a few hours, but in reality …
5 Because of the TV show, the number of people applying to work in crime labs …

5 Discuss these questions in small groups.

1 Have you seen TV programmes like *Crime lab* or *CSI – the reality*? Did you enjoy them?
2 How do the police use science and technology in your country? Think about these things.
   DNA   CCTV cameras   speed cameras
   computer databases   ID cards
3 Would you like a career connected with science or technology? Why / Why not?

GRAMMAR: *must* and *have to*

6a Put sentences 1–4 from the interview into these three groups:

A It is necessary to do this (there is no choice).
B It is necessary not to do this (there is no choice).
C It is not necessary to do this (there is some choice).

1 You don't have to study law.
2 We mustn't eat or drink in the lab.
3 You must turn your phone off.
4 You have to study chemistry or biology.

6b Look at Track 1.47 on page 157 and find more examples of this language. How do we make questions with *have to*?

GRAMMAR TIP

Must and *have to* are very similar in meaning. We usually use *have to* when we talk about laws, rules, etc. We often use *must* when we give our opinion that something is important.

➡ Language reference and extra practice, pages 138–139

7a Correct the mistakes in these sentences.

1 She have to check the evidence carefully.
2 We mustn't to eat or to drink in here.
3 As I'm a DNA expert, I haven't to know about guns.
4 He must does what I say.

7b Complete these sentences with the correct form of *must* or *have to* and the verbs in the box. (Sometimes both forms are possible.)

> have (x2)   lend   make   wear (x2)

1 A forensic scientist *must have* or *has to have* a university science degree.
2 A police officer _____ a university degree.
3 A forensic scientist _____ a uniform.
4 A police officer _____ a uniform.
5 A forensic scientist _____ any mistakes.
6 A police officer _____ his gun to anyone.

SPEAKING AND WRITING

8a Write down ten things that you have to or mustn't do in your daily life. Think about work, study, home and free time activities.

8b Compare your list with a partner. Does he/she have to do things that you don't have to do? Agree on the five most annoying things that you both have to do.

SPEAKING AND VOCABULARY: science

1 Discuss these questions with a partner.

1 Which of these subjects do you consider to be the most scientific? Put them in order (1 = the most scientific; 8 = the least scientific).

Astronomy   Biology   Chemistry   Economics
History   Mathematics   Medicine   Physics

2 Is science one of the most important school subjects?

3 Are most science lessons at school boring?

READING

2a Look at this webpage about Stephen Hawking. Why is he famous?

2b Complete this summary of Hawking's life. Write one word in each gap. (The words you need are in the text.)

Stephen Hawking was [1]_____ in Oxford, in 1942. He studied at the Universities of Oxford and Cambridge. He was still a young man when he [2]_____ that he had a serious disease. However, he married Jane Wilde, finished his PhD and got a [3]_____ at Cambridge University. In 1979, he became Professor of [4]_____ . In 1985, after an operation, he started to use special equipment to help him [5]_____ . Three years later, his book A [6]_____ History of Time appeared and sold millions of copies. Hawking rewrote the book in 2005. Surprisingly, Hawking believes that he is not an [7]_____ person. He is proud of his family and his work, and grateful for the [8]_____ that many different people have given him.

3 What did you find most interesting about the text?

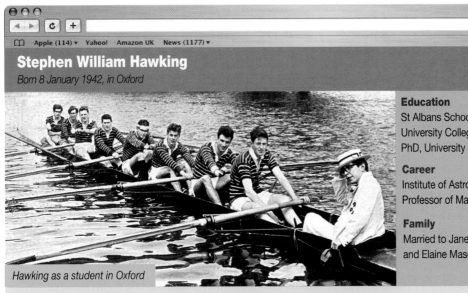

Stephen William Hawking
Born 8 January 1942, in Oxford

Hawking as a student in Oxford

Education
St Albans School (20 miles north of London)
University College, Oxford (1959–62), studied Physics
PhD, University of Cambridge (1966)

Career
Institute of Astronomy, Cambridge (1968–73)
Professor of Mathematics, Cambridge (1979–)

Family
Married to Jane Wilde (1965–1995, three children)
and Elaine Mason (1995–)

What is a black hole?
A black hole is a place in space where gravity is very strong. Anything that falls into it never comes out. Nothing can escape from it, not even light. As a result, it is impossible to see a black hole.

Work
Stephen Hawking is one of the world's most famous scientists. He is well-known for his work on black holes, and has developed a number of new ideas about them. Hawking believes that the birth of the universe (the Big Bang) created many small black holes. Hawking also thinks that there is a sort of hole in the centre of a black hole. This hole leads to another universe, completely separate from our own.

Hawking's 1988 book, *A Brief History of Time From the Big Bang to Black Holes,* sold one copy for every 750 people on Earth. However, many people could not finish the book (they found it too difficult) so Hawking decided to write an easier version, *A Briefer History of Time* (2005).

Health
Hawking discovered that he had the disease ALS (a disease that affects muscle control) at the age of 21, in his first year in Cambridge. He only expected to live a few years. However, he married Jane Wilde and found a job in Cambridge. In the early stages of his career, his illness got worse but he was fortunate that he did not have to teach. He only had to do research and this was easier for him.

Until 1985 he could talk, but in that year doctors had to operate on him and he lost his speech. Soon, however, people developed equipment that allowed him to speak. In spite of his disease, Hawking does not consider himself an unlucky man. He says it has not prevented him from having a very attractive family, and being successful in his work. He says this is thanks to the help he has received from his family and a large number of other people and organisations.

VOCABULARY: nouns, adjectives and verbs with prepositions

4a Complete these sentences with a preposition (e.g. *to, of*). Then check your answers in the text by looking for the underlined word.

1 The lab is <u>separate</u> ___ the main building.
2 He's writing a <u>history</u> ___ crime in the US.
3 She became very <u>successful</u> ___ business.
4 Communicating is much easier now, <u>thanks</u> ___ the Internet.
5 They have <u>received</u> the report ___ the police officers.

What other prepositions do you know?

4b **2.2** Can you complete these questions with a preposition? Listen and check your answers.

1 What are you interested ___ ?
2 Do you have a good relationship ___ everyone in your family?
3 What are you afraid ___ ?
4 What are you proud ___ ?
5 What's the best thing that's ever happened ___ you?
6 What do you spend your money ___ ?
7 Do you belong ___ any clubs or organisations?

4c Ask and answer the questions in Exercise 4b with a partner.

GRAMMAR: *had to* and *could*

5a Look at these sentences about the text. Then match 1–4 with a–d.

Until 1985 he **could** *talk.*

Doctors **had to** *operate on him.*

Many people **could not** *finish the book.*

He **did not have to** *teach. He only had to do research.*

1 had to	a) was/were not able to do it
2 did not have to	b) it was necessary to do it
3 could	c) it was not necessary to do it
4 could not	d) was/were able to do it

GRAMMAR TIP

There is no past form of *must*. Use *had to*.
You **must** work hard. → You **had to** work hard.

➡ Language reference and extra practice, pages 138–139

5b Complete this text from the webpage with the words in the box.

> had to   did not have to   could   could not

Stephen William Hawking

After the operation

By 1985, Stephen's speech was getting worse, and only a few people who knew him well 1 _____ understand him. But at least he 2_____ communicate. In 1985, he 3_____ have an operation on his throat. After that, he 4_____ have 24-hour care by nurses. For a time after the operation he 5_____ speak at all. The only way he 6_____ communicate was by spelling words. He 7_____ raise his eyebrows when someone pointed to the right letter on a spelling card. However, a computer expert in California (Walt Wotosz) heard of Hawking's problem and sent him a computer program. With this program, Hawking 8_____ choose words from a menu on a screen. All he 9_____ do was press a switch in his hand. But he 10_____ also control the program by making a head or eye movement. In that case, he 11 _____ press the switch. At first he 12 _____ run the program on a desktop computer, but then a man called David Mason fitted a small portable computer to his wheelchair.

His second marriage to Elaine Mason

SPEAKING

6 Discuss these statements about attitudes to science in small groups.

1 I'm interested in the latest scientific developments.
2 Science has made modern life healthier and more comfortable.
3 My government should spend more money on scientific research and less on other things.
4 Science and technology can solve any problem.
5 More women should work in the field of science.

PREPARATION

1a Match these inventions, theories and discoveries with the science subjects 1–4.

> the theory of relativity   molecules   infinity
> the printing press   vaccinations   genetics
> levers and pulleys   psychoanalysis

1 Biology and Chemistry
2 Engineering and Mechanics
3 Physics and Mathematics
4 Medicine and Psychology

1b Can you think of more inventions, theories and discoveries for the different sciences?

SITUATION

Ideas and Innovations is an intellectual discussion programme on radio. For a special programme they are choosing the most important inventions and scientific discoveries of the last thousand years.

2 [2.3] Listen to part of the discussion. Julian Blake thinks the printing press is one of the most important inventions. Which of the following reasons does he mention?

1 People could make books and communicate ideas quickly.
2 Education became possible for everyone.
3 Libraries and universities increased in number.
4 Writing became a way to earn money.

3 Listen again and complete the notes below. Write one word or number in each gap.

KEY LANGUAGE:
developing an argument

4a [2.4] In the notes in Exercise 3, each arrow (←↑↓→) shows a connection between two ideas. The arrows represent the words and phrases in the box below. Listen and complete these sentences.

> caused   is connected to   led to
> means that   meant that   so

1 I think this _____ a revolution in knowledge.
2 This _____ ideas could spread much more quickly than before.
3 It _____ education for everyone.
4 This _____ the fast production of books.
5 The written word became important at work, and _____ people had to read.
6 The printing press _____ writers can make money.

4b Look at Track 2.3 on page 157 and find more examples of this language.

5 Complete these sentences. Then compare your ideas with a partner.

1 The car means that …
2 The discovery of DNA led to …
3 Rapid global warming is connected to …
4 Television means people stay at home more, and so …
5 The discovery of nuclear energy caused …
6 The invention of the refrigerator meant that …

Guttenberg invented PP in ^{1}_____
　　　　↓
revolution in knowledge, society, etc.
　　　　Why?
The first reason:
PP ——→ *books, large* ^{2}_____ *, quickly* → *ideas spread quickly*
　　　　　　　　　　　　　　　　　　↓
　　　　　　　　　　great ^{3}_____ *in society*
The second reason:
PP ——→ ^{4}_____ *for all* ← *schools* ← *fast pdctn. of books*
　　　↑
　　reading skills v.imp. ← *written word imp. at* ^{5}_____
The third reason:
PP ——→ ^{6}_____ *can make money* →^{7}_____ *writers and journalists*
　　　　　　　　　　　　　　　　↓
　　　　　　　　　　　　good for ^{8}_____

Criticism:
Did PP → *educ. for all?* ^{9}_____ *years between PP and schools*

pronunciation

6a `2.5` **Voiced/unvoiced consonant pairs** Listen to this phrase. Can you hear the different pronunciations of the 'th'?

the theory of relativity

/ðə ˈθɪəri əv ˌreləˈtɪvəti/

To make these sounds, we use our lips and tongue in the same way. The only difference is in the way we use the vocal chords in our throat.

/ð/ is voiced. /θ/ is unvoiced.

6b `2.6` There are many pairs of consonants like this. Complete the table below with the sounds in the box. Then listen, check and repeat.

/b/	/g/	/z/	/ʒ/	/d/	/dʒ/	/v/

	1	2	3	4	5	6	7	8
Unvoiced	/p/	/t/	/k/	/f/	/θ/	/s/	/ʃ/	/tʃ/
Voiced					/ð/			

6c `2.7` Work with a partner. Which sound do the consonants in bold have? Is it voiced or unvoiced? Listen, check and repeat.

1 nuclear energy /dʒ/
2 aeroplanes
3 the car
4 DNA
5 the clock
6 the printing press
7 the telephone
8 the computer
9 television and radio
10 electricity
11 the refrigerator
12 the Internet

TASK: choosing the best invention

7a The inventions and discoveries in Exercise 6c are the top twelve from the radio programme in Exercise 2. Choose the four that you think are the most important and make notes about them. Think about these questions.

• What are your reasons for choosing the inventions or discoveries?

• What do the inventions or discoveries mean we can/could do?

• What did they lead to? What is connected to them?

7b Work with a partner. Explain and compare your choices. Agree on the top three.

7c Tell the class about your three most important inventions and discoveries. Does the class agree?

OTHER USEFUL PHRASES

The main reason I have chosen this is because …

One reason it is important is that …

Another thing is that …

I completely agree with you.

I don't agree with that point.

Which shall we choose?

STUDY SKILLS: making notes

1 When and why do you make notes?

to write an essay or report, to remember what you have learnt …

2 `2.8` Anisha is a student mentor. She is a second-year student who gives advice to first-year students. Listen to her conversation with Shannon. What advice does she give her? Does Shannon think the advice is useful? Listen two or three times if necessary.

3a You are going to read an article about problems for women in science in the UK. What kind of problems do you think the article will mention? Discuss your ideas with a partner.

3b Read the article on page 118. How many of your ideas does it mention?

4a A group of students have to write a 150-word essay on 'Problems for women in science in the UK'. Work with a partner. Look at the notes (A–C) that three different students have made from the article. Find one mistake in the facts in each set of notes.

4b Find examples of these things in the notes.

1 good and bad organisation

2 not enough details of the topic or idea

3 students using their own words – not just copying parts of the original text

4 information that will not help to do the writing task

5 words that the students have made shorter (e.g. *neg*) and symbols (e.g. +)

6 places where words (e.g. *the*, *it*) are missing

Remember: there is no right or wrong style for notes. Find a style that suits you.

5 Imagine you are going to write an essay on 'Invasive species in the UK'. Look at the text on page 43. Make notes on it. Then compare your notes with a partner.

A

Problems for women in science in the UK

1 Schools must encourage girls to study science + show them what you can do with facts

2 Male attitudes — men often make neg comments

3 Having children → hard to compete with women who have written lots of academic papers

4 S.o. has to give them more confidence, e.g. so they talk about pos things in interviews
  1—4 ↓

5 unsure about career + life

B

must change way schools teach science — can be interesting for girls if we show them how to use facts

big diff between men's and women's brains

PROBLEMS FOR WOMEN IN SCIENCE IN THE UK

male attitudes → women feel anxious: 'Where am I going?'

if women have children → don't go back to work

need to give them confidence, e.g. when applying for jobs

C

Problems for women in science in the UK

Teaching in schools. People made sexist comments about her. Worked in Paris lab – 40% women. Having children not prob for French women. Need more confidence.

WRITING SKILLS: describing charts

At the age of sixteen, British students take national exams (GCSE) in a number of subjects, including English and Maths.

6 Look at chart A on page 65. Which information 1–4 can you find in the chart?

1 students' exam success in Scotland

2 differences between boys' and girls' performance in the GCSE Chemistry exam

3 students with grades D to G in the GCSE Chemistry exam between 1997 and 2005

4 the number of students who took the GCSE Chemistry exam between 1993 and 2005

7 Complete this description of chart A.

The chart shows the number of boys and ¹_____ who took the GCSE ²_____ exam in ³_____ between 1993 and ⁴_____ , and how many of them passed the exam with the highest ⁵_____ , A to C.

8 Look carefully at chart A and choose the best answer.

1 The red bar shows the number of boys who *took the exam / passed the exam with grades A to C.*

2 The blue bar shows the number of girls who *took the exam / passed the exam with grades A to C.*

3 In 1997, about *13 / 130 / 1,300 / 13,000* girls took the exam.

4 In 2001, about *15 / 150 / 1,500 / 15,000* girls passed the exam with grades A to C.

9a Describing graphs Look at these words and answer the questions below.

an increase	fell	a rise	a decrease
decreased	rose	increased	a fall

1 Which are nouns? Which are verbs?

2 Which are about going up? Which are about going down?

3 Which words mean the same?

9b Complete this summary of the important information we get from chart A. Use the words in the box above. (For each gap, two answers are possible.)

Between 1993 and 2005, more boys than girls took the exam. Looking at the chart in more detail, we can see that between 1993 and 1995, there was ¹_____ in the number of boys who took the exam. The number of girls who took the exam also ²_____ . In contrast, from 1997 to 2005, there was ³_____ in the number of boys who took the exam and there was also ⁴_____ in the number of boys who passed the exam with grades A to C. In a similar way, the number of girls who took the exam ⁵_____ , and the number of girls who passed the exam with the highest grades also ⁶_____ . Overall, there was ⁷_____ in the total number of students who took the exam between 1997 and 2005, and passed with grades A to C.

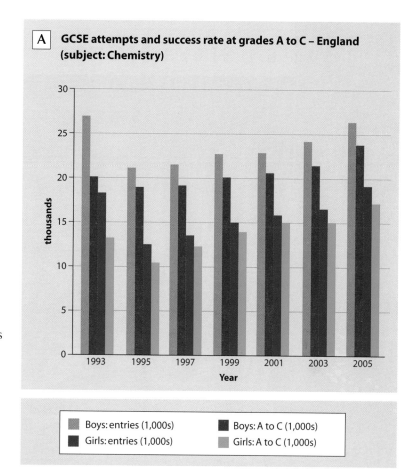

A **GCSE attempts and success rate at grades A to C – England (subject: Chemistry)**

Boys: entries (1,000s)   Boys: A to C (1,000s)
Girls: entries (1,000s)   Girls: A to C (1,000s)

10 Now write about chart B. Describe a) what it is about and b) some of the most important information.

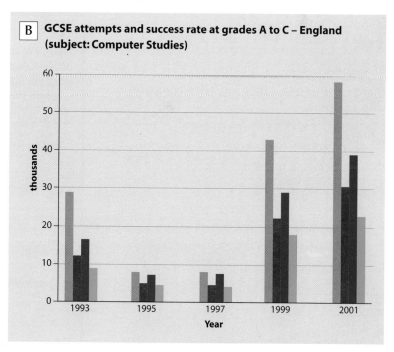

B **GCSE attempts and success rate at grades A to C – England (subject: Computer Studies)**

The night

In this unit

Grammar
- verb patterns
- future intentions

Vocabulary
- expressions with *sleep*
- *-ing/-ed* adjectives

Scenario
- A night out

Study skills
- improving your memory

Writing skills
- a story

8.1 SLEEP TIGHT!

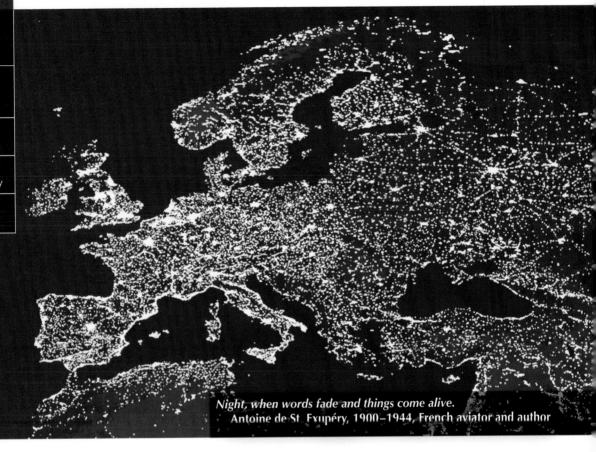

Night, when words fade and things come alive.
Antoine de St. Exupéry, 1900–1944, French aviator and author

SPEAKING AND VOCABULARY: sleep

1 Are these statements true for you? If not, change them so that they are. Then compare with a partner.

1 I sleep for about six hours a night.
2 I usually have a lot of dreams.
3 I never talk in my sleep.
4 I often have sleepless nights.
5 I can sleep through a lot of noise.
6 On Sundays, I usually sleep in.
7 When I go to bed, I fall asleep very quickly.
8 I feel sleepy or doze after a big lunch.

READING

2 Abolaji is a student on a foundation course in Manchester before starting a science degree. Read the emails and answer these questions.

1 Why has Abolaji written to Dr Wilson?
2 What is the relationship between them?
3 Do you think Dr Wilson's reply is helpful?

Dear Dr Wilson

I think I've managed to find a good subject for the end-of-course talks next month. I'm thinking about doing a presentation on sleep and the brain (how much we need to sleep, stages of sleep, dreams, etc.). What do you think about this? Could you give me some advice? Could I come and see you about it later this week?

Thanks very much.

Abolaji

Dear Abolaji

You seem to have a really interesting topic here. You might also want to look at:

1 different types of sleep
2 why people talk in their sleep
3 how modern life affects our sleep, e.g. light pollution

I'm afraid I can't see you this week as I've decided to go to the conference in Oslo that I mentioned on Tuesday. I'll be back on Monday. Perhaps we can talk after the class on Tuesday? In the meantime, keep reading about the topic!

Steve Wilson

LISTENING

3a **2.9** Listen to the first part of Abolaji's talk. According to the information in the talk, are these statements true or false, or does Abolaji not say?

1 A one-year-old baby needs to sleep for about twelve hours a day.

2 Some adults only need five hours of sleep a day.

3 REM stands for 'rapid eye movement' and NREM stands for 'non-rapid eye movement'.

4 Rapid means quick or fast.

5 The brain becomes more active in REM sleep.

6 Brain temperature increases during REM sleep.

3b **2.10** Listen to the second part of the talk and answer these questions.

1 How many stages of sleep are there?

2 What does NREM sleep do?

3 Why is it never completely dark?

4 Why can our modern way of life have a negative effect on our sleeping patterns?

3c Complete this summary of the talk with the words in the box.

| brain damage darkness dreams |
| less organising types |

As we get older, we need to sleep ¹_____ , although not everyone needs the same amount of sleep. The two ²_____ of sleep are REM and NREM. About 80% of sleep is NREM sleep, when ³_____ activity slows down. REM sleep is when ⁴_____ happen and is important for ⁵_____ our memories. One of the problems we face today is that there is less ⁶_____ than in the past and this could ⁷_____ our health.

GRAMMAR: verb patterns

4a Look at the highlighted sentences in the emails. Then put the infinitive of the verbs in the table below.

verb + infinitive with *to*	verb + *-ing*	verb + preposition + *-ing*

4b Find other examples of these verb patterns in the emails and Tracks 2.9–10 on page 158.

GRAMMAR TIP

We can use some verbs (e.g. *like, hate*) with both the infinitive with *to* and with the verb + *-ing*. Often, there is not a big difference in meaning.

➡ Language reference and extra practice, pages 140–141

4c Complete Dr Wilson's feedback comments with the correct tense and pattern of the verbs.

> Abolaji
>
> Your presentation was excellent. You ¹_____ (seem / have) a good understanding of the subject, and you ²_____ (succeed in / keep) the attention of the audience throughout. ³_____ (keep work) hard. You ⁴_____ (start / develop) into a first-class student.

> Amy
>
> Your presentation was satisfactory. The topic was interesting and you ⁵_____ (manage / cover) the key points. However, you ⁶_____ (need / say) more about each point, and give some examples. You ⁷_____ (tend / speak) rather quickly. You also ⁸_____ (keep / reading) your notes and didn't look at the audience much. I think you're an intelligent and talented student but you can do better than this.

5a Complete these questions using a correct verb pattern.

1 (What) do you want _____ ?

2 Do you like _____ ?

3 Why did you decide _____ ?

4 What do you hope _____ ?

5 Have you ever thought _____ ?

6 Do you enjoy _____ ?

5b Work with a partner. Ask and answer your questions.

SPEAKING

6 Work in small groups. How much do you know about sleep? Do the quiz on page 118.

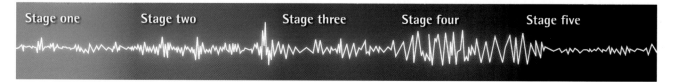

Stage one   Stage two   Stage three   Stage four   Stage five

READING

1a Which of these jobs regularly involve working when most people are asleep?

astronomer   baker   call-centre worker   cleaner engineer   lorry driver   nurse   office worker police officer   security guard   teacher

1b What do you think are the disadvantages of working at night? Make a list and compare with other students.

2 Read the first paragraph of an article about night workers. Does it mention any of your ideas from Exercise 1b?

3a Read the rest of the article about four people who work the night shift. What problem does each person have with their job?

3b Read the extracts again and match the people to these questions. (Sometimes more than one person is possible.)

1 Who couldn't get another job at first?
2 Who is doing a job that he/she loves?
3 Who wants to stop working at night?
4 Who enjoys working with his/her colleagues?
5 Who has a job helping people in another country?
6 Who talks about the money that he/she earns?
7 Who talks about people in other countries?
8 Who plans to use some of his/her work time to do something else?

3c Would you like to have any of these jobs? Why/ Why not? Would you mind working a night shift? Have you ever done that?

VOCABULARY: -ing/-ed adjectives

4a Underline the adjectives in these sentences and answer the questions below.

Night-shift work is tiring, so he is often tired.

I am bored because my job is boring.

1 Which adjectives describe how we feel, often because of something else?
2 Which adjectives describe what something is like?

4b Choose the correct adjectives.

1 We were *frightened / frightening* because the film was *frightened / frightening*.
2 The lecture was *interested / interesting*, so the students were *interested / interesting* in it.

WORKING
IN THE
DARK

9-5: the standard working day. However, for some people, it's bedtime. These people are the night workers – nurses on the night shift, lorry drivers crossing continents and bakers preparing our breakfast bread. Working at night brings particular problems: family life is difficult, social life is limited, cafés are closed, there are few buses and it's bad for your health. With all these problems, who chooses to work the night shift, and are they planning to stay in their jobs?

4c We can make *-ing/-ed* adjectives from verbs, e.g. *bore → bored/boring*. How many *-ing/-ed* adjectives can you find in the text in Exercise 3a? What are the verbs?

4d Complete these questions with the correct adjective. Then ask and answer the questions with a partner.

1 Have you seen an _____ TV programme recently? (interest)
2 What is the most _____ thing you have done? (excite)
3 When did you last feel really _____ ? (tire)
4 Is there anything that you are _____ by? (fascinate)
5 What is the most _____ thing you have seen? (amaze)
6 What is the most _____ thing that has happened to you? (embarrass)
7 When did you last feel _____ ? (surprise)
8 Is there anything you are _____ of? (frighten)

Peter Moore

I work at night because I'm fascinated by the stars, and I have been since I was a little boy. I'm happiest when I'm looking down my telescope. The stars are amazing and it's great taking pictures of them. Honestly, I'm never going to change my job – I'm an astro-photographer for life. Of course, my social life is poor, but I think I've found a solution to this problem. I'm going to bring my laptop to work and join an Internet chat room. I'm hoping to make friends with people abroad. They're the only people awake when I'm working!

Tony Baggio

My work involves repairing the railway tracks, so we have to work at night because they can't stop the trains during the day. It's not so bad, our team spirit is great and we get paid extra. However, I'm going to leave this job soon. It's tiring and I have to find a

normal job because my wife's pregnant. I haven't found a new job yet, but I'm hoping to be a builder. It's hard work, but no more nights!

John Millar

When I came to this country, the only work I could find was as a night security guard. This job is boring because it's so quiet, but I've decided to turn this problem into an advantage. Next month, I'm going to start a degree in literature by distance learning. I'm going to read my course books during the long quiet nights! I don't want to be a security guard all my life; I'd like to be a teacher. I'm going to apply for a teacher-training course when I finish my degree.

Indira Patel

I work in a call centre in India, but I answer calls from people in the UK so I have to work at night. It's a good job with a good salary. It's

also interesting because I use my English. But, to be honest, working at night is depressing – I miss my friends and family – so I'd like to leave this job soon. But well-paid jobs aren't easy to find, so I don't know what I'm going to do really.

GRAMMAR: future intentions

5a Who says these sentences in the article?

1 **I'm going to** bring my laptop to work.

2 **I'm hoping to** make friends with people abroad.

3 Next month, **I'm going to** start a degree in literature.

4 **I'd like to** leave this job soon.

5b Underline more examples of this language in the text.

5c Answer these questions about the sentences in Exercise 5a.

1 Which sentences describe a planned action in the future (i.e. a definite intention)?

2 Which sentences describe an ambition or dream for the future?

3 How do we make negatives and questions with this language?

➡ Language reference and extra practice, pages 140–141

WRITING

6 Think about your future. What plans, hopes or dreams do you have? Write five sentences. Then find out about your partner.

SPEAKING

7a Work with a partner. Make plans to solve these problems.

1 You have a lot of free time, but you don't have a lot of money. You are often bored.

2 You live in a foreign country. You have just lost your job and you have nowhere to live.

3 You have just locked yourself out of your house. You have left your keys, wallet and mobile phone inside your house. There is no one else at home.

Why don't we …   I think we should …

7b Find out what other students have decided to do to solve the problems. Are you going to do the same things?

PREPARATION

1 Do you do these things when you go out in the evening or at night? How often do you do them? What other things do you do? Discuss with other students.

go to a museum

go to the cinema

go out for dinner

go to a concert

go dancing

go to the theatre

go to a firework display

go to a sports event

go on a boat trip

SITUATION

Every year, for the month of August, there is a large arts festival in Edinburgh in Scotland. There are classical and popular music concerts, large and small theatrical productions, comedy shows, films, dance shows, talks and special events.

2a Look quickly at the festival events listing and answer these questions. At which event(s) can you:

1 see a film?

2 see a play?

3 hear some music?

4 see something from Britain?

5 see something from other countries?

2b Complete the events listing with the words in the box.

actor	around	famous	father	forget
location	plays	popcorn	songs	world

3a `2.11` Listen to Paul, Christine and Emma, three American tourists, plan a night out. Which of the events at the festival do they decide to go to?

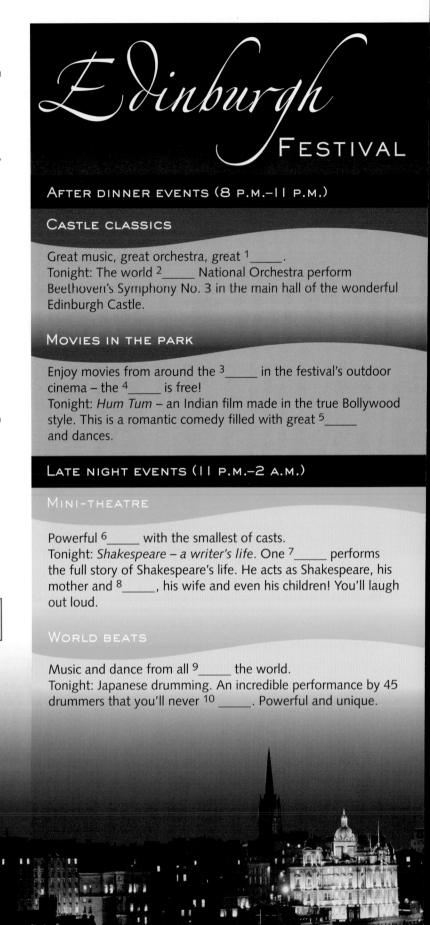

Edinburgh FESTIVAL

AFTER DINNER EVENTS (8 P.M.–11 P.M.)

CASTLE CLASSICS

Great music, great orchestra, great 1_____.
Tonight: The world 2_____ National Orchestra perform Beethoven's Symphony No. 3 in the main hall of the wonderful Edinburgh Castle.

MOVIES IN THE PARK

Enjoy movies from around the 3_____ in the festival's outdoor cinema – the 4_____ is free!
Tonight: *Hum Tum* – an Indian film made in the true Bollywood style. This is a romantic comedy filled with great 5_____ and dances.

LATE NIGHT EVENTS (11 P.M.–2 A.M.)

MINI-THEATRE

Powerful 6_____ with the smallest of casts.
Tonight: *Shakespeare – a writer's life*. One 7_____ performs the full story of Shakespeare's life. He acts as Shakespeare, his mother and 8_____, his wife and even his children! You'll laugh out loud.

WORLD BEATS

Music and dance from all 9_____ the world.
Tonight: Japanese drumming. An incredible performance by 45 drummers that you'll never 10 _____. Powerful and unique.

3b Listen again. Who has these opinions; Paul, Christine or Emma? Write *P*, *C* or *E*.

1 The film is a funny love story.

2 He/She doesn't like the Bollywood film.

3 He/She doesn't like classical music.

4 He/She likes all kinds of music.

5 He/She wants to visit the castle after dark.

6 People go to bed late during the festival.

7 A second music performance is not a good idea.

8 He/She thinks the drum show is something unusual.

KEY LANGUAGE: expressing preferences

4a 2.12 Can you complete these sentences from the conversation with the words in the box? Listen and check.

than   prefer (x2)   love   fancy
rather (x2)   keen   would   mind

1 What would you _____ to do, Christine?

2 I don't _____ that.

3 I'd _____ to go to the classical concert.

4 I'd _____ see the film.

5 I'm not that _____ on the concert.

6 What _____ you rather do?

7 Well, to be honest, I don't _____ .

8 I'm more interested in the Japanese drummers _____ the one-man theatre show.

9 I'd _____ to see the drummers.

10 I'd _____ see that than a play about Shakespeare.

4b Which sentences in Exercise 4a:

a) ask for someone's favourite thing or choice?

b) mean you like one thing more than another thing?

c) mean you don't like something?

d) mean you'd really like to do something?

e) mean you don't have a strong opinion?

5 2.13 Intonation in *Wh*- questions Listen to these questions. Does the intonation go up or down at the end? Listen again and repeat.

1 What would you like to do?

2 Where would you like to go?

3 What would you prefer to do?

4 What would you rather do?

5 What do you fancy doing?

6 Look back at the events listing in Exercise 2a and write sentences about your preferences. Use the language from Exercise 4a. Compare your preferences with a partner.

TASK: planning a night out

7a You are visiting the Edinburgh festival. Look at the events listing on page 119 and decide which of the things you would/wouldn't like to do.

7b Work in groups of three or four students. Plan your night out together. Choose three different things to do.

7c Compare your plans with another group. Do you prefer your group's plan?

First of all we're going to go to …

OTHER USEFUL PHRASES

What shall we do tonight?

What about you?

Why don't we …?

I'd like to …

What would you like to do after that?

I think we should …

I think that'll be fun/boring/tiring.

That sounds great/unusual/interesting.

MEMORY STRATEGIES

ORGANISATION

One way we can remember things is by putting them in groups or ordering them. Look at these words for one minute. Then cover them. Write the words you can remember.

> bus   star   nurse   café   bed   office worker
> brain   cinema   baby   restaurant   teacher
> railway station   children   bread

Now look at this list of words from Unit 7. Organise them into groups. Then compare your groups with your partner's. Are they the same?

> book   clock   equipment   notes   television
> car   hair   uniform   Earth   phone   lab
> black hole   computer   aeroplane

ASSOCIATION

Another way we can remember things is by imagining them in a particular place (e.g. in your house or room). Look at these words for different kinds of people.

> graduate   minister   teenager   investor
> employer   consumer   retired person

Imagine these people in different places in your house. You can add surprising or funny details, e.g. imagine the minister at a long table in your dining room, surrounded by piles of paper. These associations and connections can help your memory.

Look at the other words and think of a place in your house where you can 'see' these people. Add some details to the scene. Tell your partner about your house.

Also, it can be a good idea to make up stories using new words. Imagine you want to learn these words.

> presentation   weekend   sleepless nights
> festival   dinner   museum   engineer   cousin

You could make up a story like this:
Last week, I had a lot of sleepless nights because I had to do a presentation on Thursday. The weekend was good, though. My cousin, who's an engineer, came to stay with me. On Saturday we went to the Science Museum and then we had dinner together in the evening. On Sunday, we went to a festival in Central Park.

Find 8–10 words in this unit that are difficult or important for you. Make up a story using these words. Tell your partner your story.

1 We tend to forget things very quickly. Can you answer these questions?

1 What time did you go to bed last night?
2 What colour clothes were you wearing the day before yesterday?
3 Who was sitting next to you on your last bus or train journey?
4 What was the weather like on your last birthday?

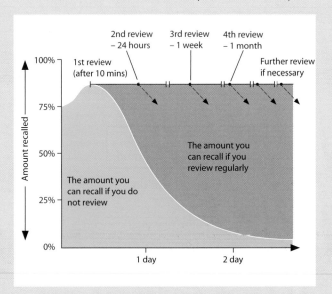

2 Work with a partner and answer these questions.
1 Look at the graph above. How much can we remember after one day? After two days?
2 When do we forget the most?
3 What can you do to remember more?

3a What methods do you use to try to remember things (e.g. information, words)? Tell your partner.

3b Quickly read the text on the left about ways to improve your memory. (Don't do the memory exercises yet.) How many different methods does it mention?

3c Work with a partner. Read through the text again and do the practice exercises together.

4a Which of the methods in the text were new ideas for you? Which do you think are effective?

4b How many of the words can you remember:
1 from the yellow box?
2 from the words in the blue box that you grouped?
3 from your house or room?
4 from the story you made up?

WRITING SKILLS: a story

5 Discuss these questions in small groups.

1 What kind of stories do you like?

2 Do you like folk stories or legends? Why / Why not?

3 Are there any stories about the beginning or discovery of your country?

6 Read the Maori story below about the discovery of New Zealand. How do you think it will end? Turn to page 119 to check your ideas.

7 Match these headings to the paragraphs 1–6 of the story. (This includes the ending on page 119.)

a) final events   d) background information

b) later events   e) result/conclusion

c) first events

8a Time expressions Underline all the time expressions in the text (e.g. *soon, after a while*).

8b Choose the best word or phrase.

1 I was lying on the beach with my eyes closed. *Soon / After some time / Suddenly* something jumped on top of me.

2 Water poured into the boat. *At last / In the end / Before long* it sank.

3 We saw an island in the distance. *At that moment / Soon / Suddenly* we reached the coast.

4 Every day he went fishing. Every day he failed to catch anything. *Soon / Finally / At that moment,* after several weeks, he caught a tiny fish.

9a We can use adjectives to make a description more interesting. Underline all the adjectives in the text.

9b Add these adjectives to the sentences. (More than one answer is sometimes possible.)

> brave   dangerous   difficult   fierce   giant

1 I saw a fish, about three metres long.

2 The king fought the dragon.

3 There was a dog at the gate.

4 Twenty men and women made the journey.

5 We looked for a bridge to cross the river.

10 Write a story about one of these topics.

• a folk story from your country

• a strange dream

• the worst night of your life

Use the paragraph structure in Exercise 7 and some of the words and phrases you underlined in Exercise 8a. Make your description interesting by using adjectives.

The discovery of New Zealand – a Maori legend

1 Kupe was a great fisherman and chief who lived on the island of Hawaiiki (Tahiti). When the moon was full, Kupe and the other fishermen went out to sea and caught fish. Usually, they caught lots of fish, of all colours and sizes.

2 One night, the fishermen did not catch a single fish. They realised that a large octopus was eating all the fish. Kupe gathered his people and told them his plan. 'Without fish we cannot live here. We're going to find this giant octopus and kill it, however long it takes!' The people built an enormous canoe. When it was ready, they loaded it with food and water and prepared for a long sea journey. In all, there were seventy-two brave people on board, including Kupe's wife and children.

3 They chased the sea monster across the endless Pacific Ocean for many days and nights, but the octopus was much faster than the canoe. The food and water were running out, and the people were suffering. Finally, one morning, Kupe's wife, Hine-te-Aparagi, saw a long cloud in the distance. Land was near! She named the land Aotearoa, land of the long white cloud. Everyone in the boat was amazed by this beautiful new country.

4 Before long, they landed the canoe on the east coast and collected fresh food and water. Then, with fresh energy, they chased the octopus down the east coast. After some time, Kupe and his friends entered a dangerous area of water between the north and south islands of Aotearoa and at last they caught the octopus. A fierce sea battle began. The octopus smashed its strong arms into the canoe and made a hole in the side of it. Then the octopus held the canoe very tightly. It seemed that the end was near for Kupe.

Work and industry

In this unit

Grammar
- used to
- present simple passive

Vocabulary
- work
- compound nouns

Scenario
- Import-export

Study skills
- giving a short talk

Writing skills
- describing a process

9.1 EMPLOYMENT

When work is a pleasure, life is a joy!
Maxim Gorky, 1868–1936, Russian writer

SPEAKING

1 What do you look for in a job? Put these things in order of importance (1 = the most important; 8 = the least important). Compare in small groups.

a well-known company	good pay
pleasant working conditions	having fun
opportunities to travel	good managers
learning new skills	friendly colleagues

READING

2a Read this company email. What do the managers of the company want to know? How will they get this information?

2b These employees all quickly read the email. Who has not understood it?

1 I'm interested, and I can do it because I started here four years ago.

2 I don't want to do it, because I don't want to discuss these matters with the company. They might use it against me later.

3 There's no point because they never tell you the results of these surveys.

4 It sounds really interesting. I'll give Melanie Chadwick a call on Wednesday 12th.

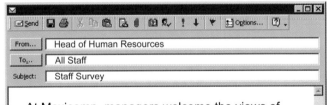

From...	Head of Human Resources
To...	All Staff
Subject:	Staff Survey

At Maxicomp, managers welcome the views of staff on a wide range of company matters. We believe that listening carefully to our employees over many years has helped us to maintain our position as the market leader.

For this reason, we would now like to find out if, and how, staff think that Maxicomp has changed in the last few years. We want to know how staff used to feel about the company and their jobs, and how they feel now.

An external organisation, Swift Consulting, will do the research, including interviews with a number of employees. All staff who have worked for the company for more than five years can take part. The discussions will be completely private, and Maxicomp will not be able to identify staff from their comments at any stage in the process. We will inform staff of the results in a future report.

If you are interested in taking part, please contact Melanie Chadwick of Swift Consulting, m.chadwick@swift.co.uk (020 6320 1244) by Friday 14th May.

LISTENING

3a [2.14–15] Listen to Swift Consulting interview two Maxicomp employees and answer these questions.

1 Who thinks that the company has changed the most, Shami or Rory?

2 Who thinks that he/she has changed the most?

3b Listen again and choose the best answer.

1 Shami thinks that she is less enthusiastic now because
   a) she started working for the company six years ago.
   b) she is older.
   c) she works longer hours.

2 The company has helped her to
   a) learn new skills.
   b) achieve more.
   c) travel.

3 Rory
   a) was more friendly in the past.
   b) ate more fifteen or sixteen years ago.
   c) doesn't have long for lunch these days.

4 Rory thinks that he is still working for the company because
   a) he can learn new skills.
   b) it is more professional.
   c) the pay is better.

3c Discuss these questions in small groups.

1 Do you think Maxicomp is a good company to work for?

2 Would you like to work for a company for a very long time, like Rory?

3 Do workers in your country work longer or shorter hours than in the past?

VOCABULARY: work

4 Find these words in Tracks 2.14–15 on page 159 and the email. Can you explain their meaning?

employee   long service   lunch break
market leader   department   promotion
staff   training course   work as a team

GRAMMAR: *used to*

We use *used to* to talk about a) past habits and b) past states.

a) Rory used to travel a lot.

b) It used to be more fun.

5a Look at Tracks 2.14–15 on page 159 and find examples of a) and b) above.

We can always use the past simple instead of *used to*, e.g. *He used to travel a lot when he was younger.* (= He travelled a lot when he was younger.)

We cannot use *used to* for single actions in the past, e.g. ~~She used to finish work early yesterday~~.

5b How do we make the negative and ask questions with *used to*? Look at Tracks 2.14–15 on page 159 and check.

➡ Language reference and extra practice, pages 142–143

5c Complete these sentences about the interviews with *used to*, *didn't use to* or *use to*.

1 Shami _____ feel the same way about the job.

2 Did she _____ go home after 7 p.m. every day?

3 Rory and his colleagues _____ use the gym together.

4 Did Rory _____ have long lunch breaks?

5 They _____ work more as a team.

6 They _____ have many opportunities to learn new skills.

6 Write six sentences about you, your family and friends. Use *used to* (x3) and *didn't use to* (x3) and the verbs in the box. Then tell your partner.

be   eat   feel   finish   go out   have
help   know   listen   think   travel   work

pronunciation

7a [2.16] *used to* Look at Track 2.16 on page 159 and listen. How does the speaker pronounce *use* and *used*?

7b Listen again and repeat.

SPEAKING

8 Work with a partner. You are going to find out what people in your class used to do.

Student A: Turn to page 119.

Student B: Turn to page 124.

WRITING

9 Compare yourself now with the past. Write three or four sentences about a) your personality and b) your likes and dislikes.

a) I used to be quite shy, but I'm not anymore. I'm more confident now.

b) I didn't use to like tomatoes, but I eat a lot of them now.

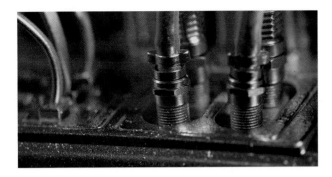

READING

1a Discuss these questions with a partner.

1 What things do people have that are gold (e.g. jewellery)?

2 Which do you prefer, gold or silver?

3 Look at the photos. Can you think of any other uses of gold in industry?

4 Which use of gold do people admire the most?

1b Read this webpage and check your answers to questions 3 and 4 above.

1c Read the text again and match the sentence beginnings 1–4 with the endings a–g. (You can use the endings more than once.)

1 Pure gold   a) is an alloy.

2 Gold wire   b) is in many electrical products.

3 Gold in teeth   c) is not very thick.

4 Gold leaf   d) is not very hard.

              e) contains 62–78% gold.

              f) lasts longer than some other materials.

              g) is not difficult to use.

1d Find words in the text that mean:

1 when something allows heat or electricity to travel along or through it (verb)

2 the places where two things join

3 you can trust someone or something to do what you want them to do

4 when you mix two or more metals together so that they combine and become a single metal

5 pretty or attractive, but not always necessary or useful

WORLD GOLD COUNCIL

[Search box] Search

USES OF GOLD IN INDUSTRY

Where is gold used in industry?

Gold is used almost everywhere, from our homes to outer space.

Why is it used?

Gold has a number of advantages over other metals. It is soft, so it is easy to use. It conducts heat well. It lasts a long time and it is not damaged by the environment. Gold connections are very reliable, so they are used where safety is important. In addition, gold is a popular material in industry because of its special appearance, colour and beauty.

How is it used?

It is used in a wide variety of ways. The main use is in electronics – computers, pocket calculators, washing machines, televisions, recordable CDs, cars, credit cards and spacecraft. The Columbia space shuttle, for example, used nearly 41 kilograms of gold. Gold is the perfect material for contacts. An ordinary telephone contains 33 gold contacts. In some electronic equipment, very fine gold wires are used to connect different parts of the equipment. Each piece of wire is made of very pure gold (99.99%) and thinner than a human hair.

The second most important use of gold is in teeth. However, pure gold is not used, as it is very soft to use on its own. It is mixed with other metals to make an 'alloy'. A typical alloy contains 62–78% gold.

Decorative uses of gold include jewellery, pens and pencils, watches and glasses. It is found in bathrooms, on plates and especially on perfume bottles. The most impressive use of gold is gold leaf. This is an extremely thin sheet of gold. Generally, it is produced by hand and is used by builders, glass makers and artists. It is applied to the roofs and ceilings of public buildings, and lasts much longer than paint.

Done   Internet

VOCABULARY: compound nouns

We can use two nouns together to make a compound noun. Sometimes we write them as one word (e.g. *bathroom*), sometimes as two words (e.g. *credit card*).

2a **Complete these sentences with a compound noun. Use a word from each box to fill the gaps.**

1 Do you read a _____ every day? If so, which one?

2 Is there a _____ near your house? If so, how often do you rent films?

3 Do you prefer _____ or apple juice?

4 Do you use Internet _____ ?

5 Has an _____ ever lost your _____ ?

air	chat	news	orange	suit	video

juice	case	shop	line	rooms	paper

2b **Ask and answer the questions with a partner.**

2c **Find examples of compound nouns in the text.**

GRAMMAR: present simple passive

3a **Look at these sentences and answer the questions below.**

a) Pure gold is not used in teeth.

b) It is mixed with other metals.

c) Gold wires are used in electronic equipment.

1 Underline the main action verb in these sentences.

2 Do the sentences say who or what does the action (the agent)?

When we use the passive, we aren't focussing on the agent of the action. The agent may be unnecessary or unknown, e.g. in sentence a), we do not need to talk about the dentists. In sentence b), we do not know who mixes it.

3b **Look at these sentences and answer the questions below.**

a) Gold is not damaged by the environment.

b) The environment does not damage gold.

1 Which sentence focuses our attention on gold?

2 Which sentence emphasises the environment?

3 Which word do we use in a passive sentence when we give the agent of the action?

3c **We form the present simple passive with *is/are* and the past participle of the verb. How do we make questions in the passive?**

3d **Find other examples of passive forms in the text on page 76.**

➡ Language reference and extra practice, pages 142–143

4 **Complete this text with the present simple passive of the verbs.**

Oil is sometimes called black gold, because it is extremely valuable. It [1]_____ (make) by very small plants and animals that died on the sea bed millions of years ago. Over 50% of the world's oil is in the Arab World. Russia and other countries that were once part of the Soviet Union also have a lot of oil. When oil [2]_____ (find) in the sea bed, a special platform called a rig [3]_____ (move) into the right position. Oil from the ground or sea bed [4]_____ (separate) into different types of oil in a special factory called a refinery. Oil [5]_____ (use) for fuel (e.g. in car engines) and to make electricity. We also make plastics with it. About 9,000 million litres (55 million barrels) of oil [6]_____ (use) every day.

Oil rig

Sea bed

Oil

SPEAKING

5 **Work with a partner. Tell each other about industry in your country.**

There are a lot of big factories around the capital. Most of them are new.

Cars are made in the north.

The products are sent all over the world.

PREPARATION

1a   Discuss these questions with a partner.

1 Do shops in your country often have sales? How much discount do they generally offer? Have you bought any bargains recently?

2 Have you ever bought things at a market? Do you ever bargain for a lower price?

1b   Complete these sentences with the words in the box. Use your dictionary if necessary.

> supply   import   buyers   exports
> manufacturers   retailers

1 We have to _____ these machines because we can't find them in our country.

2 Coffee is one of our main _____ . We sell a lot to Europe.

3 We are _____ of clothes that are sold abroad.

4 We sell car parts to Ferrari and Fiat. They are our most important _____ .

5 'Tesco' and 'Marks and Spencer' are British _____ that have shops abroad.

6 We _____ electrical items to shops and supermarkets; we don't sell to the general public.

SITUATION

2   Look at the business advert and answer these questions.

1 What does Route One do? Choose the correct answer.
  a) It manufactures electrical goods.
  b) It sells electrical goods to the public.
  c) It sells electrical goods to shops.

2 Where is it based and where does it import from?

Route One wants to import some digital music players from Guangdong Digital (an electrical goods manufacturer in China). Richard Hallows, Purchasing Manager for Route One, is making a deal with Lu Han, a Sales Representative for Guangdong Digital.

3a   Before you listen to their negotiation, look at these questions. Who says each one, the buyer or the seller?

> **1 Price**
> What's the price per item?
> How much are they per item?
> How much would you like to pay?

> **2 Delivery time**
> What's your normal delivery time?
> We need delivery in two weeks. Can you do that?
> When would you like us to deliver?

> **3 Quantity and discounts**
> How many would you like to order?
> Can you offer me a discount?
> What discount can you offer?

3b   2.17   Listen to the negotiation between Richard and Lu Han. Tick (✓) the questions in Exercise 3a you hear.

3c   Listen again and circle the correct details of the negotiation. Who do you think gets the best deal?

Starting price:	1 *$100 / $80* per item
First discounts offered:	2 *5% / 15%* (orders > 500)
	3 *10% / 15%* (orders > 1,000)
Final quantity ordered:	4 *1,800 / 800*
Final price:	5 *$87.50 / $87* per item
Final delivery time:	6 *30 days / two weeks* after order

Route One
Discount Electrical Goods Supplier

■ New brands from Asia
■ Fast delivery
■ Large orders welcome
■ Suppliers to major retailers

Route One: the fastest way to get new products into your shop

0794 8345586
www.route1r1.ca
info@route1r1.ca
Unit 57, Harbour Business Park,
Ontario, Canada

KEY LANGUAGE: negotiating

4a `2.17` **Listen again and complete these sentences.**

1 $100? That _____ rather high.
2 I see. Well, I'm not _____ that we can go that low.
3 If you order 1,000, we _____ offer 15%.
4 What about _____ we order 750?
5 That's still a _____ low.
6 _____ about 12.5%?
7 _____ we call it $87?
8 That _____ fine. $87 per item it is, then.

4b **Which of the sentences above are:**

a) suggestions, offers or proposals?
b) reactions or replies to offers and proposals?

pronunciation

5 `2.18` **Sentence stress in proposals Look at these proposals. Which words do you think are stressed? Listen, check and repeat.**

1 We can only offer a 5% discount on 500.
2 If you order 1,000, we can offer 15%.
3 What about if we order 750?

6a **Work with a partner. Write this negotiation from the prompts.**

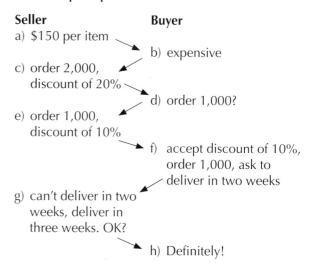

Seller
a) $150 per item
c) order 2,000, discount of 20%
e) order 1,000, discount of 10%
g) can't deliver in two weeks, deliver in three weeks. OK?

Buyer
b) expensive
d) order 1,000?
f) accept discount of 10%, order 1,000, ask to deliver in two weeks
h) Definitely!

6b **Practise the negotiation with your partner.**

TASK: making a deal

7a **Work with a partner to negotiate a deal.**
Student A: Turn to page 118.
Student B: Turn to page 110.

7b **After your first negotiation, swap roles.**

STUDY SKILLS: giving a short talk

1 Louise works for a company that makes chocolate. Part of her job is to give talks about the company. Here are four questions she always asks herself before she starts to prepare a talk.

1 What is the topic of my talk?
2 Why am I going to say it (e.g. to inform, persuade, amuse)?
3 Who am I going to talk to?
4 How much time do I have for the talk?

2.19 Listen to the beginning of her talk and answer questions 1–4 above.

2a **2.20** Listen to the second part of the talk and complete these notes. Write one or two words in each gap.

History of chocolate

Mayans discovered chocolate in about ¹_____ AD.
They made a ²_____ from roasted cocoa beans – 'chocolatl'.
Spread to Aztec civilisation (modern ³_____).
In ⁴_____, Hernán Cortés drank chocolate with Moctezuma.
Cortés returned to Spain in ⁵_____, taking cocoa beans with him.
Chocolate became popular with ⁶_____ in Spain.
It took nearly ⁷_____ to spread across Europe because the Spanish kept it a ⁸_____.
In 17th century, chocolate ⁹_____ became popular in London.
In 19th century, chocolate became ¹⁰_____ and the first eating chocolate appeared.

Moctezuma, the ninth Aztec king

2b Look at Track 2.20 on page 160 and find the phrases Louise uses to:

1 introduce the first topic
2 finish a topic
3 summarise/conclude a topic
4 start a new topic

2c Match these phrases with 1–4 above.

To summarise, …   First, I'd like to talk about …
Turning now to …   That's all I want to say about …
In conclusion, …   Let me begin by -ing …
To conclude, …   I'd like to start by -ing …

3 Look at the list of things you should do when you prepare a talk. Fill in the gaps with the words in the box.

> charts   information   notes   order
> practise   pronunciation

1 Find out some interesting _____ .
2 Put your ideas in the best _____ .
3 Make some _____ to help you to remember things in the talk.
4 Prepare some pictures or _____ to make your points clearer.
5 Check the _____ of difficult words.
6 _____ the talk.

4a Prepare a short talk of about two minutes on one of these topics.

• your life story
• the history of your … (family / university / town / city / favourite pop group)

4b Work in groups. Take turns to give your talk. When you listen, look at this list. How well does the speaker do these things: very well, OK or needs to improve?

1 He/She welcomes his/her audience.
2 He/She tells the audience what he/she is going to talk about.
3 He/She speaks slowly and clearly.
4 He/She sounds interested in what he/she is saying.
5 He/She tries to build a relationship with his/her audience.
6 He/She chooses vocabulary that he/she thinks the audience will know, and explains any difficult words.

The early stages of making *chocolate*

– a traditional family business in West Africa

To begin with, cocoa pods are cut from cocoa trees with large knives, taking care not to damage nearby flowers. The women of the family collect the pods in large baskets, which they carry on their heads. Next, the pods are split open with a knife and the beans are removed. Following this, a pile of wet cocoa beans is put on banana leaves, which are spread out in a circle on the ground. More leaves are put on top to cover the pile. After five to six days, the wet mass of beans is dried in the sun. Lastly, the beans are put into sacks for transport all over the world.

WRITING SKILLS: describing a process

5 The pictures above show the early stages of making chocolate. What do you think is the correct order? Read the text and check.

6a Linkers Sequencing phrases (e.g. *to begin with*) tell us the order in which things happen. Underline the sequencing phrases in the text.

6b Which other sequencing phrases do you know?

7 We usually use the passive when we are describing a process. Underline the examples of the passive in the text above.

8 The pictures below show the early stages of tea production. Write a paragraph describing the process, using the nouns and verbs below and some sequencing phrases.

Use these nouns: fields, leaves, machine, tea plants, special beds

Use these verbs: crush, dry, grow, pick, plant

about a year

about four years

10–20 hours

REVIEW

A GIRL'S BEST FRIEND?
Our quick guide to ... diamonds

Most people ¹___ own a diamond, but why? What exactly are these stones and why are they so special? Read our quick guide and find out!

What are diamonds?
Diamonds are the hardest natural stones on Earth. They ²___ many kilometres below the Earth's surface, and come to the surface only during volcanic eruptions. The stones that we find now have of course been near the surface for thousands of years.

Diamond history
Early references to diamonds come from India, where people ³___ they brought good luck, and from China, where people ⁴___ them as tools. There are many references to the stones in Europe in the Middle Ages. For example, in the thirteenth century the French King, Louis IX, introduced a law that said that only the king ⁵___ diamonds! But his people soon ⁶___ the law so that anyone with money could buy the jewels.

Diamond industry
The industry of mining diamonds is thousands of years old. The main diamond industry ⁷___ to be in Africa, as today, but in south India.

It stopped in the eighteenth century because there were no diamonds left, so the industry then ⁸___ a different source for the stones, and it moved first to Brazil, and then to Africa.

Diamonds in jewellery
A diamond ⁹___ very good quality to become a jewel, with high levels of clearness and colour. In fact, over 80% of diamonds are used in industry, mainly as cutting tools.

Diamonds as symbols
Diamonds are often symbols of love and eternity. Many couples exchange diamond rings when they get married. The 60th wedding anniversary ¹⁰___ as the 'diamond wedding', symbolising love forever.

GRAMMAR

1 Read the text about diamonds and choose the correct form for the gaps 1–10.

1 a) are going to   b) would like to   c) hope
2 a) form   b) are form   c) are formed
3 a) used to think   b) use to think   c) used thinking
4 a) seemed using   b) seemed to use   c) seemed use
5 a) could own   b) can own   c) own
6 a) succeed in changing   b) succeeded to change   c) succeeded in changing
7 a) wasn't used   b) didn't use   c) didn't used
8 a) had to find   b) must find   c) had to found
9 a) have to be   b) can be   c) has to be
10 a) known   b) is knowing   c) is known

2 Complete these sentences with the correct form of *used to, had to* or *could*.

1 The Indians _____ believe that diamonds brought good luck.
2 In the past, many people _____ afford to buy diamonds because they were very expensive.
3 They _____ save their money for months before they could buy any jewellery.
4 Today, people tend to insure their jewellery, but in the past they _____ do that.

VOCABULARY

3a Look at the words in the box below and find:
1 two verbs connected with crime.
2 two other words connected with crime.
3 three words for people at work.
4 two verbs connected with sleeping.

Biology   commit   colleague   doze   employee   evidence   fingerprints   staff   Mathematics   Physics   sleep in   solve

3b There are three words left in the box. What do they have in common?

4 Complete the gaps 1–6 in the film review on page 83 with one word from each box.

belong   happen   history   interested   relationship   successful

in   in   of   to   to   with

82 REVIEW 7-9

Blood Diamond

When I went to see *Blood Diamond* last weekend, I wasn't sure if it was an action movie, or a 1_____ _____ the diamond industry in Africa, and I still don't know! But it doesn't matter – it's a great film.

The film tells the story of Danny Archer (Leonardo DiCaprio), a man who is only really 2_____ _____ one thing – making money, which means smuggling diamonds from Africa. He meets Solomon Vandy, a fisherman who finds a remarkable diamond – enormous, pure and very valuable. However, when his village is attacked, he runs and leaves the diamond there. The story then follows Solomon's 3_____ _____ Archer, as they join together to find the diamond, and of course, all the frightening things that 4_____ _____ them. The film has a social side – looking at the way the First World takes things that 5_____ _____ other countries, but at the same time it's an exciting movie with an interesting storyline.

If you want to find out if the men are 6_____ _____ their search for the diamond, you'll have to go and see the film!

My rating: ★ ★ ★ ★

KEY LANGUAGE

5 2.21 **Listen to Anna and Rob talking about what to do. Who would prefer something active? Who would rather go to a concert?**

6 Put these lines from the conversation in order. Then listen again and check.

a) Mmm, I'm more interested in something active. I think I'd rather go dancing. ☐

b) There's a play by David Mamet. The tickets are £20, £25 or £30. ☐

c) I'm bored. Let's go out this evening. ☐1

d) If you go with your friends, I'll cook a really nice dinner for us on Sunday. ☐

e) Well, what would you prefer to do? ☐

f) I don't know. Look, why don't you go dancing with your friends at the weekend? ☐

g) I don't fancy dancing. I'd prefer to go to a concert. ☐

h) OK. I'd love to go to the theatre. I haven't been for ages. ☐

i) OK, that sounds fine! ☐

j) Oh, that seems a bit high to me, for a play in our local theatre. ☐

k) A concert? OK, let's see what's on. But what about if we go dancing at the weekend? ☐

l) I'm not sure about that. I'm not that keen on the theatre. What's on? ☐

m) But I'd rather go with you. ☐

LANGUAGE CHECK

7 There is a word missing in each sentence. Write it in. Then look back at the pages and check.

1 You don't have study medicine to be a psychologist. (page 59)

2 The science building is separate the main school. (page 61)

3 We belong a classical music group. (page 61)

4 They had solve the crime very quickly. (page 61)

5 I usually asleep very quickly when I go to bed. (page 66)

6 When are you going start the course? (page 69)

7 Would you prefer see a film or a play? (page 71)

8 We didn't use take long lunch breaks. (page 75)

9 Silver used in a lot of jewellery. (page 77)

10 The prices seem bit high to me. (page 79)

LOOK BACK

8 Find the exercise in Units 7–9 where you:

• listen to an interview with a forensic scientist. (Unit 7)

• learn the names of some scientific subjects. (Unit 7)

• describe a chart about UK examinations. (Unit 7)

• listen to a talk about the importance of sleep. (Unit 8)

• plan a night out. (Unit 8)

• write a short story. (Unit 8)

• talk about what classmates used to do. (Unit 9)

• read about the uses of gold. (Unit 9)

• give a short talk. (Unit 9)

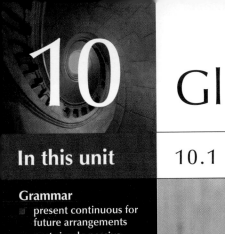

10 Global affairs

In this unit

Grammar
- present continuous for future arrangements
- past simple passive

Vocabulary
- people and organisations
- adjectives

Scenario
- An Olympic bid

Study skills
- improving your listening

Writing skills
- a for and against essay

10.1 UNITED NATIONS

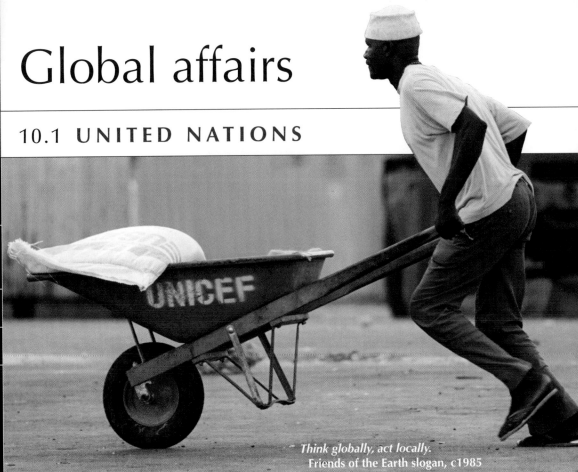

Think globally, act locally.
Friends of the Earth slogan, c1985

SPEAKING

1a **What do you know about the United Nations (the UN)? Discuss these questions with a partner.**

1 When was the UN founded?

2 How many countries are now UN members?

3 Where is the UN headquarters?

4 Where is the current Secretary General from?

5 Which of these activities is the UN not involved with?

Aid and peace keeping	Children's rights
Religious education	Economic development
International justice	Entertainment

1b 2.22 **Listen and check your answers.**

READING

2a **Read this entry from an encyclopaedia. What is the main subject of the text?**

1 the work of the United Nations

2 celebrities who work for the Secretary General

3 the Secretary General and his/her department

The United Nations is an organisation that works in many different areas. In order to carry out its work, the UN has a large department of international civil servants (the Secretariat). The head of this UN department is the Secretary General and there are about 9,000 other staff members. The Secretary General is responsible for the day-to-day organisation of the UN and its many projects.

As well as these work responsibilities, the Secretary General is a symbol or face of the United Nations. He or she is also a spokesperson for the people of the world and can ask the UN to help with difficult situations in the world.

The Secretary General also chooses the Messengers of Peace. These people publicise the work of the UN and they are chosen from the fields of arts, literature and sports. Messengers of Peace have included Luciano Pavarotti (opera singer) and Muhammad Ali (boxer).

2b **Are these statements true or false, or does the text not say?**

1 The UN helps protect endangered animals.

2 The Secretariat manages the UN's daily business.

3 The Secretary General is very well paid.

4 The Secretary General can request that the UN solves a problem.

5 The countries in the United Nations select the Messengers of Peace.

6 The Messengers of Peace tell the world about the UN's work.

7 Politicians can become Messengers of Peace.

LISTENING

The Secretary General's schedule of activities and meetings is available on the UN website.

3a `2.23` Listen to Beth tell the web designer about the Secretary General's appointments for next week. How many meetings does he definitely have?

3b Listen again and answer these questions.

1 When is he meeting the Syrian Foreign Minister?
2 Who is he meeting at 4 p.m. on Monday?
3 Which committee is he talking to on Tuesday at 10 a.m.?
4 Who is he meeting at 3 p.m. on Tuesday?
5 Where is he going on Wednesday morning? Why?
6 Who is he meeting at 12 p.m. on Wednesday?

VOCABULARY: people and organisations

4a Put these words into two groups: A for individuals and B for groups of people.

> ambassador   assistant   civil servant
> committee   department   head of a department
> minister   president   spokesperson   staff

4b Match some of the words above with these definitions. Write definitions for the other words.

1 a group of people who meet regularly and make important decisions
2 a politician with an important government job
3 one part of a company or organisation
4 someone who represents and speaks for a group of people or an organisation
5 someone who helps a more senior colleague

GRAMMAR: present continuous for future arrangements

5 Look at these sentences and answer the questions below.

a) At 11.15 he's meeting the Syrian Foreign Minister.
b) After lunch, he's seeing the President of the Security Council.
c) He might phone the British Prime Minister.

1 Are these sentences about the present or the future?
2 In which sentence is the action not certain?

We can use the present continuous to talk about fixed future arrangements and meetings. These arrangements often involve other people and we usually give the time or place of the action or event.

GRAMMAR TIP

When we talk about future plans, we can use either the present continuous or *going to* with little change in meaning. When we want to show the plan is more arranged or fixed, we use the present continuous, especially when we give the exact time of the arrangement.

➡ Language reference and extra practice, pages 144–145

6 Jane Goodall (an author) and Luciano Pavarotti (a singer) are UN Messengers of Peace. Complete their appointments diaries for next week.

Student A: Turn to page 120.
Student B: Turn to page 123.

SPEAKING AND WRITING

7a Interview your classmates to find out what they are doing in the next week. Make notes of their answers.

What are you doing tonight / this weekend?
– I'm going to the cinema on Saturday, and on Sunday I'm …

7b Write a paragraph to summarise your class's social arrangements.

SPEAKING

1 Look at this list of companies and answer the questions.

BP Coca-Cola Fiat Google Honda IBM McDonald's Nestlé Nintendo Nokia Philips Samsung Shell Sony

1 What do they do/produce?

2 In which country did they start?

3 Would you like to work for them?

READING

2a Read the text about Microsoft. How did Microsoft change between 1975 and 2007?

2b Which decade do the following statements go with?

1 People in the USA thought that Microsoft was the top company.

2 The company started making software abroad.

3 Sales of one particular product were very good.

4 Microsoft helped people after the terrible events in the Indian Ocean.

5 Gates and Allen started the company.

6 Microsoft became more interested in selling computers to people than to companies.

7 Microsoft had problems in Europe.

3 Find words in the text that mean:

1 an idea that you think is true

2 the programs that a computer uses to do different jobs

3 gave most of its time or attention to this

4 an area of land where company (or university) buildings are

5 a short, clever phrase that is used in advertising

6 made a new product available

4 What do you think were the three most important years for Microsoft?

GRAMMAR: past simple passive

We often use the past simple passive to talk about the history of something (e.g. an organisation), especially when we are more interested in 'what happened' than in 'who did it'.

*Microsoft **was set up** in 1975.*

*Windows 95 **was released**.*

*Plans **were announced** to develop the campus in Redmond.*

5a Find other examples of the past simple passive in the text.

5b We form the past simple passive with *was/were* and the past participle of the verb. How do we make negatives and questions?

➡ Language reference and extra practice, pages 144–145

Growth of a Global Giant

Today Microsoft employs more than 55,000 people in 85 countries and regions. In 2006, the company made profits of US$12.6 billion. But it wasn't always that way ...

The seventies and eighties (1975–1989)

Microsoft was set up in Albuquerque (New Mexico, USA) in 1975 by Bill Gates and his friend Paul Allen. The two men were guided by a belief that every desk in every office, and every home, should have a computer, so they started to develop software for personal computers. At first, the company concentrated on selling to businesses. In the late 1970s, Microsoft moved to the Seattle area. It is still based there today, on its own 'corporate campus' in Redmond. In the mid 1980s, Microsoft was growing rapidly and chose the Republic of Ireland as the location of its first production facility outside the USA. By the end of that decade, however, attitudes were changing in the USA, and the company was criticised for making its employees work too hard!

The nineties (1990–1999)

1994 Microsoft Encarta was launched – the first encyclopaedia that was designed to run on a computer. The company slogan was also changed to: 'Where do you want to go today?'
1995 Windows 95 was released, and more than a million copies were sold in the first four days. The company focus moved from business to the consumer. MSN, the Microsoft Network online service, was also launched, and quickly became one of the largest Internet service providers.
1996 Microsoft was named the company that Americans respected and admired the most.
1997 Microsoft opened its headquarters in India, now the second largest after its US headquarters.
1999 Gates's book *Business @ the Speed of Thought* was published. The book shows how computer technology can solve business problems in new ways. It is now published in 25 languages and is available in more than 60 countries.

The 'noughties' (since 2000)

2001 Windows XP was released worldwide.
2004 Microsoft gave $3.5 million for relief and recovery efforts after the Asian tsunami. Bill Gates himself has given over $30 billion to support projects in global health and learning. In this year Microsoft faced legal action from the European Union for unfair competition.
2006 Plans were announced to develop the campus in Redmond.
2007 Microsoft Windows Vista was launched.

6a Use these prompts to make questions about the start of the Italian company Fiat.

1 When / Fiat / set up? *When was Fiat set up?*
2 Where / cars / test / in the early years?
3 When / car adverts / aim / at women for the first time?
4 Which newspaper / buy / by Fiat in 1926, *Corriere della Sera* or *La Stampa*?
5 What / set up / in the late 1920s?
6 Where / Fiat cars / construct / in the early 1930s?

6b `2.24` Listen and check your questions.

6c `2.25` Listen again and note the answers. Then compare with a partner.

7 Complete this text with the past simple passive or active form of the verbs in brackets.

Samsung ^{1}_____ (set up) in Taegu, Korea, in 1938 by Byung-Chull Lee. At that time, Samsung General Store (its original name) ^{2}_____ (sell) dried fish, vegetables and fruit to China. Samsung (which means three stars in Korean) ^{3}_____ (grow) quickly.

In the 1970s, Samsung ^{4}_____ (move) into industry and many new Samsung companies ^{5}_____ (create), e.g. Samsung Shipbuilding. During this decade, Samsung also ^{6}_____ (develop) its home electronics business. In 1976, the one millionth black-and-white TV ^{7}_____ (produce). The next year, colour televisions ^{8}_____ (export) for the first time.

In the 1980s, Samsung ^{9}_____ (put) its energies into technology, and new products ^{10}_____ (introduce) to the global market. In 1987, Samsung's Chairman, Byung-Chull Lee, ^{11}_____ (die) after almost 50 years in charge of the company. His son, Kun-Hee Lee, ^{12}_____ (become) the new chairman of Samsung.

SPEAKING

8 Discuss these questions in small groups.

1 In what way do the companies on these pages affect your life?
2 Do you think that big companies have too much power?
3 Do you think they are good or bad for society?
4 Which do you think are more powerful, governments or big companies?

SITUATION

1a Where was the last Summer Olympic Games held? Did you watch any of it? Did your country win any medals?

1b Which three cities below have never yet hosted the Summer Olympic Games? Check your answers on page 115.

Amsterdam   Athens   Berlin   Los Angeles   Madrid   Melbourne   Mexico City   Moscow   New York   Osaka   Paris   Seoul

2a `2.26` In 2005, London won the competition to host the Olympic Games in 2012. Listen to four extracts from the presentation that was made by the British Olympic Committee and match them with the topics a–d.

a) transport

b) the sports facilities

c) accommodation for athletes

d) London's special ambition for the Games

2b Are these sentences true or false? Listen again and check.

1 The organisers want the Games to encourage children to play sport.

2 None of the sports venues already exists.

3 The Olympic park will be less than ten minutes from the city centre.

4 The Olympic stadium will have 18,000 seats.

5 Many venues will be a long way from the athletes' accommodation.

6 The athletes will stay in single rooms.

7 Ten train and underground lines go to the venues.

8 Visitors to the games don't have to pay to use the trains and buses.

KEY LANGUAGE: adding emphasis

3a `2.27` **Adverbs** Listen and complete these sentences from the extracts.

1 We'll create an Olympic park which is _____ seven minutes from the centre of London.

2 Half of the venues will be _____ five minutes from the athletes' accommodation.

3 _____ ten per cent will be more than twenty minutes away.

4 Athletes will be _____ a short walk from the main stadium.

5 The Olympic park will be _____ seven minutes from central London by train.

3b We can use *just* and *only* to emphasise how small something is. In the sentences above, is the emphasis positive or negative?

4 **Adjectives** These adjectives were used in the presentation. Can you remember what they described? Look at Track 2.26 on page 161 to check. What other adjectives can you find?

1 magical   memorable

2 world-class   magnificent

3 modern   comfortable

4 high-speed   comprehensive

pronunciation

5a `2.28` **Pausing and emphatic stress** When you give a talk or presentation, it is important to pause and to emphasise key words. Listen and mark the pauses like this //, and underline the words with extra stress.

First, we want to deliver a magical experience, an electrifying atmosphere for competitors and spectators. Our aim is to inspire young people in Britain and across the world to play sport.

5b Listen again and repeat.

5c Look at Track 2.26 on page 161. Practise saying the first sentences of each section. Experiment with the pausing and stress.

6 Work with a partner. Use adverbs, adjectives and emphatic stress to talk about your city or country. Think about the buildings, transport, facilities and events.

There is a comprehensive public transport system.

Every year there is a festival with a spectacular firework display.

| TASK: making a presentation |

7a The IOC is choosing the next city for the Olympic Games. The choices are New York, Madrid and Osaka. Work in groups of six (Pair A, B and C). Each pair is going to prepare a short presentation about one of the cities.

Pair A: Turn to page 122.

Pair B: Turn to page 125.

Pair C: Turn to page 120.

7b Take turns to give your presentation to your group and listen to the other presentations. Make notes under these headings.

Location, population and weather

Special ambition/concept   Sports venues

Athletes' accommodation   Transport

7c Which presentation do you think was the best?

OTHER USEFUL PHRASES

We are here to represent …

The special ambition for our city is …

There are four main points.

First of all, …

Secondly, …

Finally, …

Thank you for your kind attention.

---

8 Following the presentations, the IOC look in detail at each city's plans and choose the best city for the Olympics. Your group of six is now the IOC. Discuss each city and decide which one should host the next Olympic Games. Do other groups agree with you?

STUDY SKILLS:
improving your listening

1 The skill of listening There are two main kinds of listening: listening for the general idea and listening for detail. Look back at the listening exercises in this coursebook and find some for each kind.

2 Listening in English Make a list of different situations when *you* listen to English (e.g. watching films, listening to lectures). Which are the easiest / most difficult for you? Why? Do they involve listening for the general idea, listening for detail, or both?

There are a number of things we can do before we listen which can help us to understand better and get the information we need.

1 We can use our knowledge of the topic.

2 We can guess what the speaker will say.

3 We can guess the vocabulary the speaker will use.

3a Activate your knowledge You are going to listen to a talk about Interpol, the international police organisation. What do you know about it? Describe the Interpol emblem. What do you think it means?

3b Predicting content Here are some questions you can ask yourself before you listen to the talk. Can you add two or three more questions?

1 Where is Interpol based?

2 How many people work for it?

3c Predicting vocabulary Which of these words do you think the speaker will use?

accommodation boxer crime criminal databases entertainment financial fingerprints headquarters languages laws literature member police forces priorities slogan staff

4a `2.29` **Listen to the talk. Does the speaker talk about any of the things in your questions in Exercise 3b? What does he say about them?**

4b Listen again. Did you hear any of the words you chose in Exercise 3c?

5 Importance markers The speaker uses a number of phrases to show that what he is saying / going to say is important. Can you complete these sentences? Look at the underlined sentences in Track 2.29 on page 162 and check.

1 Interpol now has 184 member countries. And let me _____ out that it's those countries that pay for it!

2 Don't _____ that most Interpol officers stay in their own country.

3 But, and I must _____ your attention to this, we never break the law in any country.

4 One of our _____ is problems connected with drugs.

5 Another important _____ is trafficking in human beings.

6 Another _____ priority is financial crime.

7 The _____ important thing we do is to run a global police communication system.

8 _____ important thing we do is to provide training courses for national police forces.

6 Do you think Interpol is an important or useful organisation? Why / Why not?

Eddie (Jackie Chan) enlists the help of British Interpol agent Nicole (Claire Forlani) in the film *The Medallion*.

7 Discuss these questions in small groups.

1 Are there a lot of CCTV (closed circuit television) cameras in your town?

2 Where do you usually find them?

3 Do you think they are a good thing? Why / Why not?

4 How do they make you feel?

8a Zeina is a student in London. Read her essay about CCTV cameras. Does she mention any of the things you discussed in Exercise 7?

The advantages and disadvantages of CCTV cameras

There are now four million CCTV cameras in the UK. That means one camera for every fourteen people. If you live in London, you are caught on camera 300 times every day. This is becoming a very important issue in our lives. How is it affecting us? This essay will consider whether CCTV cameras are good or bad for us.

One serious disadvantage of CCTV cameras is that it is difficult to find private places in our cities. People are watching us everywhere we go. Another problem with them is that, because there are so many of them, the government has spent a lot of money on them.

On the other hand, a major advantage is that they help to catch criminals and prevent crimes from happening in the first place. Another advantage is that ordinary people feel safer and have more freedom to lead their lives as they wish.

To sum up, are the cameras good or bad? This is a difficult question to answer. Although we feel safer, every move we make is seen by someone, somewhere. Therefore, we might get more freedom in some ways, but we lose it in other ways. Perhaps we need more time to understand the effects of this, but I personally think that the advantages are greater than the disadvantages.

8b Do you agree with the ideas in this essay?

9a Match these headings a–d with the paragraphs of the essay.

a) advantages　　c) introduction

b) conclusion　　d) disadvantages

Which of these form the main body of the essay?

9b Where can you find these things in the text? Write *I* for introduction, *MB* for main body and *C* for conclusion.

1 a statement of the writer's opinion

2 a statement of the importance of the subject

3 development of important ideas

4 a statement of the writer's aims

5 a summary of the main points

10a Underline the phrases that are used in the text to talk about advantages and disadvantages.

10b Use the table to make sentences about Zeina's opinions.

The main advantage of		the government has spent a lot of money on them.
The main disadvantage of	CCTV cameras is that	they help to catch criminals.
One of the good points about		people are watching us all the time.
One of the bad points about		ordinary people feel safer.

11 **Linkers** Study the use of the linkers *although*, *on the other hand* and *therefore* in the text. Then complete these sentences.

1 _____ CCTV cameras can catch criminals, they are expensive.

2 There are a number of good points about this. _____ , there are many more bad points.

3 There is very little data about this. _____ , it is difficult to reach clear conclusions.

4 A career in the police force could be very interesting. _____ , it might be dangerous.

5 _____ the crime rate is going down, people sometimes feel less safe.

12a Work with a partner. Discuss the advantages and disadvantages of these topics.

1 having a lot more police officers on the streets of our cities

2 police forces having a lot more female officers

3 using plain-clothes police (i.e. police not in uniform)

4 sending criminals who are not dangerous to prison

5 Interpol

12b Write a for and against essay on one of the topics above.

11 The environment

In this unit

Grammar
- present perfect continuous
- phrasal verbs

Vocabulary
- global warning
- containers and materials

Scenario
- Local regeneration

Study skills
- exploring reading texts

Writing skills
- a report

11.1 GLOBAL WARMING

The environment is everything that isn't me.
Albert Einstein, 1879–1955, German-Swiss-US scientist

SPEAKING AND VOCABULARY: global warming

1 Discuss these questions with a partner.

1 What are the causes of global warming?

2 What are the effects of global warming? Use the words in the box.

> the Arctic   rainforests   glaciers   sea ice
> sea levels   coral reefs   temperature   drought
> extreme weather

3 Is climate change a new phenomenon?

READING

2a Read this essay and underline information that you didn't know. Compare with a partner.

2b Read the text again and answer these questions.

1 What causes natural climate change and what causes global warming?

2 Is there anything good about CO_2?

3 Why is there more CO_2 in the atmosphere than ever before?

4 What problem does a thicker CO_2 blanket cause?

During the long history of our planet, the climate has often changed for natural reasons. This is because the energy that we get from the sun changes regularly. The planet was warmer during the time of the dinosaurs, and during the ice age it was four degrees lower than today. However, nowadays the climate is changing faster than ever before. This rapid change, known as global warming, is caused by the current high levels of carbon dioxide (CO_2) in the atmosphere.

There has been CO_2 in the atmosphere for millions of years. Animals produce CO_2 when they breathe, and plants use it to make energy and oxygen. The CO_2 that is not used by plants forms a blanket in the atmosphere. In a positive way, this blanket traps the sun's energy and keeps the planet warm. However, CO_2 is also produced when we burn oil, coal and gas – the fossil fuels. Because of this, the amount of CO_2 in the atmosphere is now higher than at any time in the last 600,000 years. The CO_2 blanket is getting thicker and thicker, and this means the planet is getting hotter and hotter. This is causing the rapid climate change and it is a danger to life on this planet.

LISTENING

3a [2.30] **Listen to part of a documentary about global warming. Number these topics in order (1–6).**

a) the presenter's opinion   ☐ 1

b) rainforests   ☐

c) computer models   ☐

d) the Arctic   ☐

e) coral reefs   ☐

f) sea levels and the Pacific islands   ☐

3b Listen again and answer these questions.

1 How long has the presenter been a scientist?

2 How long has she been a documentary maker?

3 What does she now believe?

4 Where does John Watts work?

5 Why is life getting harder for the polar bears?

6 Why are the Pacific islands disappearing?

7 What is happening in the rainforests?

8 Why are coral reefs dying?

9 Look at the graph. What do the two lines show?

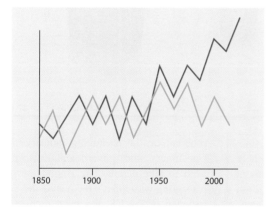

3c The presenter says we have to produce less CO_2. How can we do that? Discuss with a partner.

GRAMMAR: present perfect continuous

4 Look at these sentences and answer the questions.

a) I've been a scientist for over 40 years.

b) I've been making nature documentaries for the last twenty years.

c) I've been working here since 1980.

d) I can show how the temperature of the planet has been changing for the last 100 years.

1 Do these sentences refer to finished or unfinished time periods?

2 Which sentences describe repeated or continuous actions?

3 Which ones describe states?

We can use the present perfect continuous to describe repeated or continuous actions that continue up to now. We do not usually use it with state verbs.

➡ **Language reference and extra practice, pages 146–147**

5 Complete these sentences with the present perfect simple or continuous of the verbs. Which verbs are state verbs?

1 Sea levels _____ quickly for the last ten years. (rise)

2 We _____ about global warming for ten years. (know)

3 We _____ oil since the industrial revolution. (use)

4 How long ___ you ___ a scientist? (be)

5 How long ___ she ___ documentaries? (make)

6 Complete these questions with the present perfect simple or continuous of the verbs. Then ask and answer the questions with your partner.

1 How long ___ you ___ English? (learn)

2 How long ___ you ___ your best friend? (know)

3 How long ___ you ___ to this school? (come)

4 How long ___ you ___ your current hair style? (have)

5 Are you reading a novel at the moment? How long ___ you ___ it? (read)

6 Do you have a job? How long ___ you ___ it? (have)

SPEAKING

7 How much do you agree with these statements? Give them a mark out of 5 (1 = completely disagree; 5 = completely agree). Compare your opinions with your partner and discuss the statements.

1 We can't stop global warming. It's too late.

2 My government has been doing a lot to reduce global warming.

3 Nuclear power is the best way to replace fossil fuel power.

4 There should be an extra eco-tax on flights.

5 The way I live my life is bad for the environment.

6 Wind farms are ugly and shouldn't be built in beautiful places.

WASTE NOT, WANT NOT

VOCABULARY: containers and materials

1a Work with a partner. What do you think the photo on page 95 shows? Check your answer on page 110.

1b Match these words for containers with pictures 1–8.

> bottle box can/tin carton
> jar packet pot tube

Match these materials with the containers.

> aluminium cardboard glass metal paper plastic

1c What do you do with containers when they are empty?

READING

2a Read this email discussion that appeared in a national newspaper. Which of these best describes Kevin and Alicia?

1 Kevin is a consumer and Alicia works for a supermarket.

2 Kevin is a journalist and Alicia works in the packaging industry.

3 Kevin works for an organisation that protects the environment and Alicia works for the government.

Dear Alicia Stewart,
On my way home from work yesterday, I stopped off at my local supermarket. Among other things, I
5 wanted to buy a couple of coconuts. When I picked them up, I was amazed that each coconut was wrapped in clear, thin plastic. Isn't this the most stupid example of packaging ever?
10 Regards, *Kevin McCabe*

Dear Kevin,
You've picked an unusual example of packaging, but there is a reason for this. Supermarkets want to make sure
15 that coconuts reach the consumer in the very best condition. The packaging helps to keep the product fresh; it cuts down the damage if the product gets broken; it stops coconut hairs
20 from getting into other food during transport and it allows supermarkets to put on an information label.
Best wishes, *Alicia*

Dear Alicia,
25 I see. However, the fact is that here in the UK, we throw a huge amount of packaging away – 4.6 million tonnes every year. All those cans, jars and boxes add about £480 a year
30 to the average food bill. The main supermarkets give 17 billion plastic bags out a year. In addition, our streets are full of packaging rubbish such as water bottles, crisp packets,
35 noodle pots and plastic bags. Isn't it your responsibility to do something about this?
Yours, *Kevin*

Dear Kevin,
40 As a matter of fact, we are doing something. A lot of thought now goes into the design of packaging, so that in many cases we use the minimum amount of material. We're also using
45 more biodegradable materials and these end up mainly as water vapour. But people shouldn't just blame this problem on the packaging industry. Consumers and governments also
50 need to take action. The amount of packaging waste that's recovered and recycled in the UK has been going up for some time. It now stands at 63%, but this country's record is
55 poor compared with other European countries. What's more, even with biodegradable materials, it's not enough just to put rubbish in a hole in the ground. Without sun, air and water,
60 a rubbish bag that should break up in fifteen days could still exist hundreds of years from now. That's a problem for planners. Remember too, that changes in society are going on which
65 affect the amount of packaging that's produced. People are buying more all the time. Also, more and more people are living alone and they're eating more convenience food. So everyone
70 has to pull together on this.
Yours, *Alicia*

2b According to the text, which two sentences are correct?

1 There are no arguments to support wrapping coconuts.

2 People in the UK are paying nearly £500 a year for food packaging.

3 Kevin thinks that the packaging industry must reduce the amount of packaging waste.

4 The packaging industry is not concerned about the amount of packaging waste that is produced in the UK.

5 The UK recycles more packaging waste than many other European countries.

6 Changes in society have little effect on how much packaging we use.

2c What do these words in the text refer to?

1 this (line 8)   4 It (line 53)

2 it (line 17)   5 That (line 62)

3 these (line 46)   6 they (line 68)

GRAMMAR: phrasal verbs

A phrasal verb is formed by a verb and one or two other words (e.g. *up, down, off*). We call these other words particles. The meaning of a phrasal verb is often different from the meaning of the verb without a particle.

3 Underline the verbs in these sentences. Which two are phrasal verbs? What are the differences in meaning between the phrasal and non-phrasal verbs?

1 a) He's going to the supermarket.

  b) The amount of waste is going up.

2 a) She cut her birthday cake.

  b) Packaging cuts down damage.

➡ Language reference and extra practice, pages 146–147

4 Complete these sentences with the particles in the box. (The phrasal verbs are from the text and earlier in the coursebook.) Then ask and answer the questions with a partner.

> away   back   down (x2)
> out (x2)   up (x2)

1 Did prices go _____ or down last year?

2 What's the most interesting thing you've found _____ recently?

3 Have you ever carried _____ any research?

4 Has anyone in your family ever set _____ a company or a club?

5 Do you write _____ all the new words you learn?

6 Do you throw _____ your old clothes when you buy new ones?

7 Have you ever borrowed anything that you haven't given _____ ?

8 Why must we cut _____ the amount of packaging waste?

SPEAKING

5a Work in small groups. Discuss what you can do to cut down waste. Think about these things:
birthday cards, toys, plastic bags, fruit and vegetables, print-outs from your computer, videos and DVDs, water.

Examples:

mobile phones – recycle them

birthday presents – give cinema or concert tickets, not disposable goods

5b Turn to page 124 to check your ideas.

PREPARATION

1 Change these sentences so that they are true for the place where you live. Compare your ideas with a partner.

In my city …

1 there's a lot of ugly graffiti.
2 most of the canals and ponds aren't very clean.
3 there are many empty and derelict houses.
4 there are some scruffy areas of wasteland.
5 my local park isn't very well-kept.
6 many streets are run-down.
7 people often dump rubbish in woods and green areas.

SITUATION

Local community groups often try to improve local environments. They apply to the government for funding for their projects.

2a Read the funding proposal below and answer these questions.

1 What is the main purpose of the project?
2 Which do you think are the three most important benefits of the project?
3 How much does it cost each year?

WILD CITY

Project title Wild City

Project description The regeneration of an area of wasteland by turning it into a small, urban wildlife park.

Benefits of the project
1 It will turn a scruffy, ugly area of wasteland into an attractive nature park.
2 It will increase the number of trees and animals in this urban area.
3 It will be an educational resource for local children.
4 It might attract some visitors to the area.
5 It will bring the community together. Local people will build and look after the park.

Budget
Total cost: £60,000

Cost breakdown
Clearance of the wasteland: £10,000
Purchase of 100 trees: £40,000
Purchase of plants and seeds: £5,000
Annual running cost: £5,000

2b The government funding committee have some guidelines to help them assess a project proposal. Look at the guidelines below. Which ones does the Wild City project meet?

Good projects should …
1 improve the local environment.
2 solve a problem.
3 involve local people working together.
4 need no, or little, annual financial support.
5 offer ideas for future developments.
6 make the local area 'greener'.

3a [2.31] Listen to the funding committee discuss the project. Which of the guidelines do Rick and Poppy discuss and in what order? Do they generally agree or disagree with each other?

3b Listen again. Are these statements true or false?

1 Rick says the project is good for the environment.
2 It solves a problem because it brings local people together.
3 The project does not meet two of the guidelines.
4 The annual running costs are acceptable.
5 Projects with unpaid volunteers are often unsuccessful.

KEY LANGUAGE: question tags

4a **2.32** Complete these sentences from the conversation. Then listen and check.

1 You can't get much greener than a wildlife park, _____ you?
2 The project solves a problem, _____ it?
3 They could do it unpaid, _____ they?
4 We've seen that fail before, _____ we?

We can use question tags when we think someone will agree with what we say. We use them to check that someone has the same idea or opinion. In the sentences in Exercise 4a, the speaker expects the listener to agree.

4b Look at Track 2.31 on page 163 and find more examples of question tags.

4c Complete these sentences with question tags.

1 It costs a lot of money, _____ ?
2 We can't pay for everything, _____ ?
3 They haven't answered all the questions, _____ ?
4 It's a good idea, _____ ?
5 They could make a few changes, _____ ?

pronunciation

5a **2.32** Intonation in question tags Listen to the sentences in Exercise 4a again. Does the intonation on the question tags go up or down?

We use this intonation when we think the listener will agree with us.

5b Work with a partner. Practise saying the sentences in Exercise 4c.

TASK: allocating funds

6a Work in groups. You are the funding committee considering three projects. Look at the information about the other two projects on page 122 and assess all the projects. What are the good/bad things about all three projects? Which of the guidelines' points do/don't they meet?

6b You have a total of £100,000 available. In your group, decide which projects you will fund. You can suggest possible changes to the projects if that means you might fund them.

6c Compare your decisions with other groups.

OTHER USEFUL PHRASES
What do you think of this one?
What about the other guidelines?
What changes could they make?
Exactly. / Indeed. / Of course.
I'm not sure. / Possibly, but ...
So, which shall we support?

STUDY SKILLS: exploring reading texts

1 Here are some questions to ask yourself when you meet a new text. They will help you to understand it better.

1 **Where** did the text appear? (e.g. in a newspaper, on a poster)

2 **Who** wrote it and **who** will read it?

3 **When** was it written?

4 **What** is it about?

5 **Why** was it written?

2 Read the action group newsletter and answer the questions in Exercise 1. Then compare your ideas with a partner.

3a Below are some more questions you can ask yourself about the letter. Answer them.

Asking about the quality of information

1 In the first two paragraphs, find examples of information that is a) fact and b) opinion.

2 Is everything in the letter true?

Asking about the reasons for something

3 How many reasons does the writer give why the area is not a good location for an airport? What are they? Which do you think is the most important?

Asking about what is missing

4 Does the letter give arguments for and against the new airport?

5 Only 5,000 people live in the Finchfield area. Why doesn't the writer mention this fact in his letter?

Asking about language

6 What is the effect of the word 'attractive', which is used to describe the village?

7 What do you think the phrase 'a very long time' means in paragraph 2: five years, twenty years, 200 years, something else?

8 What does the phrase 'the majority of local people' mean in paragraph 3: 51%, 60%, 75%, more?

3b Do you think the letter will have the effect that the writer wants? Why / Why not? Imagine you live in the area. Will you go to the meeting?

NEWSLETTER

Finchfield Action Group

Dear Resident

As you may know, the government wants to build four or five new airports in this country in the next twenty years. One possible location is in our area, close to the attractive village of Finchfield.

As local residents, we do not believe that this is a good location for a new airport. It is a quiet and beautiful part of the countryside. Also, many families have been living and working in the area for a very long time. Their lives could be turned upside-down.

We already know that the majority of local people are against the plans. As a result, **we are setting up an action group** in order to fight against the government's plans for this airport. The first meeting of our group will be in **Finchfield Village Hall** on **Tuesday 5 May at 7.00 p.m.** We hope you can join us then. We will decide how we can best organise our protest. Please help us to protect our environment and way of life for yourselves and for future generations.

Barclay Smethurst
Acting President, Finchfield Action Group

WRITING SKILLS: a report

4 Discuss these questions with a partner.

1 When do people often write reports?

2 Why do they write them?

3 Have you read or written any reports recently?

5 Read the report below and choose the best title.

1 Plans for a new airport in Finchfield

2 Reactions to plans for a new airport in Finchfield

3 Opposition to plans for a new airport in Finchfield

A _____

The aim of this report is to summarise the findings of a recent survey among local residents in the Finchfield area of north Essex on plans to build a new airport in their area. PSG Research was asked to carry out the survey by a local action group. The data was collected by questionnaire and interviews with 500 local residents between 9th and 17th September.

B _____

C _____

The majority of local residents (82%) said that they were against the plans for the new airport. The main reason (mentioned by 74%) was that their area was one of great natural beauty. Another important reason (mentioned by 63%) was that many families had long connections with the area, sometimes going back hundreds of years.

D _____

A minority of residents (18%), on the other hand, felt that a new airport could bring benefits to the area. It could create new jobs and a better transport system.

E _____

However, 96% of all residents thought that one of the government's other possible locations for the airport was a better choice – this was the man-made island off the coast of Clamton.

F _____

To sum up, there was a great deal of opposition to the plan for the new airport. There was an almost universal feeling that the government should look for an alternative site. Because of the strong local feeling, we believe that the government should consider carefully the other possible locations, before they make a decision.

6 Put these headings and sub-headings in the correct place A–F in the report.

1 Conclusion

2 Arguments against building the airport in Finchfield

3 Introduction

4 An alternative location for the airport

5 Arguments for building the airport in Finchfield

6 Findings

7a Look at the questions in Exercise 1 again. How many of them can you answer about the report?

7b Write two or three questions you can ask yourself about the report. Use the questions in Exercise 3a to help you.

Is the information true?

8 Look back at the essay on page 47. What is the main difference between a report and an essay?

9a Match these phrases 1–6 with a–f below.

1 The aim of this report is to …

2 The data was collected by …

3 The majority … said that …

4 The main reason … was that …

5 A minority … felt that …

6 To sum up, there was …

a) the opinion of most people

b) the opinion of a small number of people

c) why the report was written

d) a summary of the report

e) how the information was obtained

f) why people had particular views

9b In paragraphs C, D and E of the report, which four verbs are used to report the opinions of the local residents?

10 You work for an independent market research company. The government wants to build a new terminal at a major airport. You have carried out a survey and found out what local people think about the idea. Write your report. Use the information on page 124 and your own ideas.

In this unit

Grammar
- second conditional
- *too* and *enough*

Vocabulary
- sports

Scenario
- Sports psychology

Study skills
- doing exams

Writing skills
- a formal email

12.1 MINORITY SPORTS

Running's like breathing. It's something that comes really naturally.
Cathy Freeman, 1973– , Australian 400 metre Olympic champion

VOCABULARY AND SPEAKING: sports

1a Discuss these questions in small groups.

1 What's the most popular sport in your country
a) to watch and b) to play?

2 How popular are the sports below in your country?

> gymnastics   archery   badminton   cycling
> fencing   table tennis   dragon boat racing
> hockey   judo   football   sailing

3 Which of the sports do you consider minority sports?

1b Which verbs are used with these sports: *do*, *go* or *play*?

1c How much do you know about some of these sports? Do the quiz on page 124 with a partner.

READING

2a Read this letter that appeared in a national newspaper. What is the purpose of the letter?

Dear Prime Minister

For the last few weeks, I have been travelling around the country, talking to young people about minority sports. The youngsters that I met were doing a wide variety of minority sports (e.g. fencing, judo, archery) and they were all enthusiastic and dedicated. However, they were also sad, disappointed and angry about the lack of media interest in their sports, and also about poor facilities and funding. All over the country, I heard the same comment: 'If we had more funding, we would do really well in international competitions.'

I believe it is now time for the country to show that it is truly committed to minority sports. We need proper government investment in facilities and training. We also need a sympathetic media that tells young people about less well-known sports in order to develop their interest.

Let's give the young people of this country a real chance to improve their fitness, show their talents and achieve success.

Yours sincerely
Michaela Scrivin
World Dragon Boat Champion

2b Find the following things in the text.

1 a list of minority sports
2 a reason why the media should report minority sports
3 problems faced by people who do minority sports
4 young people's feelings about doing their sports
5 information about the writer's recent activities
6 a statement about what official action is required

LISTENING

3a **2.33** Listen to this excerpt from a current affairs TV programme. There are three guests: the Minister for Sport, a journalist and an actress. Answer these questions.

1 What time of day is this programme broadcast?
2 How many emails does the presenter read out?
3 Do the guests agree or disagree with the emails?

3b Listen again and tick (✓) the ideas mentioned in the programme.

1 The government has spent a lot of money on minority sports recently.
2 British sportsmen and women have been successful in some minority sports.
3 There are a lot of articles about judo in the newspapers.
4 The TV programme *Grandstand* introduced people to minority sports.
5 There will be more minority sports on TV during the 2012 Olympics.
6 The Minister for Sport wants children to do five hours of sport a week at school.
7 The majority of children cannot do many different sports at school.

3c Are these statements true for your country? Compare with a partner.

1 Children play many different sports at school.
2 The government supports minority sports and sports players.
3 My national sports teams are often successful.
4 We can see a wide range of sports on television.

GRAMMAR: second conditional

4 Look at these sentences and answer the questions below.

a) If we had more funding, we would do really well in international competitions.
b) If the media showed more interest in other sports, kids would want to try them.
c) If they had more opportunities, they wouldn't be so unhealthy.

1 Do the sentences describe real or unreal situations?
2 In the *if*-clause, which tense do we use after *if*? Does this refer to past time?
3 In the main clause, which form of the verb follows *would*?

➡ Language reference and extra practice, pages 148–149

5 Correct the mistakes in these sentences.

1 If I knew the answer, I would to tell you.
2 Would she increased taxes if she was the Prime Minister?
3 If you have the power to change one thing in the world, what would it be?
4 They would didn't go sailing if they didn't like it.
5 I wouldn't lend him any money if I don't trust him.

GRAMMAR TIP

We can use *might* instead of *would*. *Might* is less certain than *would*.

SPEAKING

6 Work in small groups. Ask each other these questions and discuss the unusual situations.

What would you do if …

1 you (win) a million dollars?
2 you (meet) your favourite film star?
3 a stranger (stop) you in the street and (ask) you for money?
4 you urgently (need) $50?
5 you (hear) someone moving about in your house late at night?

SPEAKING

1 **What do you know about the FIFA Football World Cup? Discuss these questions with a partner.**

1 Which countries do the fans in the photos A–D support?

2 Can you name any winners and hosts of the World Cup?

3 How popular is the World Cup in your country with both men and women?

READING

2a **Read this magazine article and choose the best title.**

1 Men 1: Women 0

2 Companies spend billions on World Cup ads

3 Advertisers forget female fans

4 Record numbers of women watch World Cup

2b **According to the text, are these sentences true or false?**

1 Many women have been watching football for many years.

2 Men are the target audience of advertisers during the World Cup.

3 More than half the English audience was female during the Sweden game.

4 The advertising executive thinks there should be more adverts aimed at women.

5 An airline offered special trips to the World Cup for women.

6 Companies did not spend a lot of money on advertising during this World Cup.

7 Adidas believes that it didn't make a mistake with its advertising.

8 Women often stop watching during the advertisements.

2c **Find words in the text that mean:**

1 the places where a football match is held (paragraph 1)

2 more than 50% of a group (1 and 2)

3 a chance to do something (2)

4 in every part of the world (4)

5 usually do or be something (5)

This year, female football fans are everywhere. You can see them in the stadiums, you can see them at the big screen events and you can probably see them in front of your own television. However, despite the recent increase in the number of women watching the World Cup, the majority of the advertisements during the games are aimed at men.

This year, nearly 50 per cent of the tournament's audience has been female. In South Korea, a female majority of 51 per cent watched their match against Togo. In England, 47 per cent of the audience was female during the match against Sweden. 'We've certainly missed an opportunity,' said an advertising executive. 'There have been too many adverts for men and there haven't been enough adverts for female fans.'

There have been some adverts that have been aimed at women. However, these adverts have seen women not as fans, but as people who dislike the game. For example, one airline has been offering women-only holiday trips to escape the World Cup.

3 **Discuss these questions with a partner.**

1 Do you think that the advertisers missed an opportunity or do you agree with Adidas?

2 Do you think that women are casual watchers of sport or do you agree with Sean Gabb?

3 Who do you think watches more sport, men or women? Why?

GRAMMAR: *too* and *enough*

4a **Look at these sentences. Which three describe a problem or mistake?**

1 There have been **too many** adverts for men.

2 They've spent **too much** money on the male fans.

3 Companies have spent **enough** money on advertising.

4 There have **not** been **enough** adverts for female fans.

4b **Which of the phrases in bold above mean:**

1 you have the right amount of something?

2 you need more of something?

3 you need fewer things?

4 you need less of something?

4c We can also use *too* and *enough* with adjectives. Find the two examples in the text.

4d **Choose the correct word to complete these grammar notes.**

Too comes *before / after* nouns and *before / after* adjectives.

Enough comes *before / after* nouns and *before / after* adjectives.

➡ Language reference and extra practice, pages 148–149

'The advertisers haven't been clever enough. They've been too interested in women who hate football and they've forgotten about those who love the game,' said Sean Gabb, a business lecturer and author. 'Companies have spent enough money on advertising, nearly £1 billion worldwide, but they've spent too much money on the male fans and not enough on the female fans.'

However, some companies think they have been clever. Adidas have said that, as this is the male World Cup, it makes sense to focus on advertising to men. They plan to focus on female products during next year's women's World Cup in China. Other people have noted that women tend to be more casual watchers of TV sport than men, so it is difficult to keep their attention during the adverts. However, as Sean Gabb said, 'Perhaps this is because they don't want to waste their time watching adverts for shaving products and car tyres.'

5 Put the words in italics in order. Are the sentences true for you and your country? Tell your partner.

1 I *enough free time have* during the week.

2 I *have too homework much* each week.

3 I *earn don't money enough* to live a comfortable life.

4 The *are buses too and trains crowded* in the rush hour.

5 Cinema *expensive tickets too are* in my town.

6 There *enough sports aren't facilities* in my local area.

7 My *national good football team is enough* to win the World Cup.

8 There *too is sport much* on TV.

▌ SPEAKING

6a Think about some of these issues. What is the current situation in your country? Is there too much or too little of something? Do people do too much or not enough of something?

Football: money, TV, competitions, players

Sport and health: adults/children

Swimming pools and sports facilities

Sport on TV

6b Compare your ideas with a partner and decide how things could be different.

I think young children don't play enough sport. If we had more sports facilities, the children would be healthier.

▌ WRITING

7 Write two paragraphs about one of the issues that you discussed. Describe the situation and the solutions you suggested.

2a Look at the advert for *Sport In Mind* below and answer these questions.

1 What service does this company offer?

2 Who are its different types of client?

3 Do people think about this aspect of sport in your country? Can you study this at university?

1a Make a list of the sports you have played in your life. Put them in order of enjoyment. Compare your list with a partner.

1b Match the different personality types in the box with the descriptions below.

> competitive risk-seeking sociable non-competitive cautious/careful self-sufficient (individualistic)

1 I like meeting people and being part of a team.

2 I perform better when I challenge someone.

3 I like to work on my own, or solve problems by myself.

4 I like a little danger and pressure.

5 Enjoyment, not winning, motivates me.

6 I avoid risks – I always drive slowly.

1c Which of these personality types would or wouldn't suit the different sports in the photos? Which ones match the sport you have played? Explain your reasons.

A competitive personality wouldn't suit yoga because you don't score points in yoga.

Do you have

Sport In Mind ?

As a professional sportsperson, you train your body to win, but do you train your mind to be a winner?
As a sports coach, you train your athletes to win, but do you understand the psychology of a winner?
As a sports lover, you exercise and stay fit, but do you play sports that suit your personality?

Our psychologists work closely with you and, through scientific research and psychological analysis, they take you to greater sporting success.

Get ahead in sport, get *Sport In Mind*
www.sportinmind.com   info@sportinmind.com

Dr Sophia Mannit is a sports psychologist with *Sport In Mind*. She uses a questionnaire to analyse someone's personality and suggest suitable sports.

2b `2.34` Listen to her interview with Alex. Which of these situations do they discuss and in what order?

a) choosing a holiday ☐

b) playing sport with a friend ☐

c) buying a car ☐

d) doing an examination ☐

2c Listen again and answer these questions.

1 Which answer A–C does Alex choose for each question?

2 Which sports does Dr Mannit recommend?

3a In the questionnaire, the three questions (1–3) are related to different personality types. Match the questions to the personality types.

1 Question 1 is related to ——— a) how risk-taking you are.

2 Question 2 is related to ——— b) how sociable you are.

3 Question 3 is related to c) how competitive you are.

3b In each question, the answers are graded (i.e. *very, quite, not at all*). Look at Track 2.34 on page 164. What does each answer mean (e.g. *very sociable, quite sociable*, or *individualistic*)?

KEY LANGUAGE: conversation fillers

4a `2.35` Listen and complete Alex's answers to the questions.

1 Well, that's a _____ one, I have studied on my own for exams before.

2 Right … erm, let me _____ , I think I'd do B.

3 Hmm, let me _____ , well, to be _____ , I'd buy a Ferrari.

We can use this language when we are thinking about an answer to a question.

4b Work with a partner. Ask and answer these questions. Use fillers when you answer. How long can you 'think' for?

1 Do you think that your country should host the Olympic Games?

2 Who is your favourite sports player?

3 What great sporting moments can you remember?

4 Which sports should every young person learn to play?

5 Do you think that some sports people are paid too much?

---

pronunciation

5a `2.36` Intonation in lists Listen to this question. How are the letters at the beginning of each option (A–C) in the list pronounced? Choose the best intonation pattern.

If you could buy any car you wanted, would you buy …

A) a fast sports car, like a Ferrari?

B) a classic car, like a Rolls Royce?

C) a reliable car, like a Honda?

1 rise, fall, rise   2 fall, fall, rise   3 rise, rise, fall

5b Listen again and repeat.

TASK: doing a survey

6a Work with a partner. Prepare a short questionnaire about personality. The questionnaire should be in three sections:

Section 1: Sociable or Individualistic?

Section 2: Competitive or Non-competitive?

Section 3: Risk-taking or Cautious?

Think of one or two questions for each section. Make sure you grade the answers for each question (e.g. A = very competitive, B = quite competitive, C = non-competitive). Use the situations in the box to help you prepare your questions.

> choosing a holiday
> making a complaint
> choosing a job
> finding some money
> spending money
> doing an examination
> having a party
> giving a talk
> playing a sport or game
> saving money
> choosing a hobby

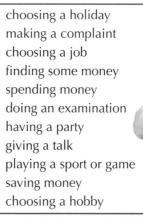

6b Interview other students in the class. Then tell your partner about the interviews.

1 Talk about your experiences of exams in small groups. What was your best/worst experience? Why?

2a **2.37** You are going to listen to a lecturer giving students advice about an English exam. Which of these pieces of advice do you think she will give? Listen and check.

1 Do lots and lots of practice tests. The more, the better.

2 Be fresh on the day.

3 Don't be late for the exam.

4 The most important thing to do in the exam is to use correct English.

5 If you don't know the answer to a multiple-choice question, don't write anything – leave it blank.

6 When you do a piece of writing, do a draft and then make a final copy.

7 Don't spend too long on one question.

8 If dictionaries are allowed, use them as much as you can.

2b Can you remember any of the reasons she gave for the advice above? Listen again and make notes.

2c Can you think of any more advice about doing exams? Think about food and drink, clothes, handwriting, checking your answers, relaxing.

3a In addition to revising, it is important to look after your health at exam time. How much do you know about health and exams? Do this quiz with your partner.

Health and Exams

1 Eating ____ before you go to bed can reduce stress and help you sleep.
a) an egg   b) a banana   c) chocolate

2 ____ increases the oxygen in your brain and encourages positive thinking.
a) Shouting   b) Yawning   c) Laughing

3 Put ____ oil on your pillow to help you sleep.
a) lavender   b) peppermint   c) rosemary

4 ____ produces new brain cells and improves memory and learning.
a) Drinking water   b) Doing exercise
c) Watching TV

5 Eat more ____ because stress destroys vitamin C.
a) pasta and rice   b) meat
c) fruit and vegetables

6 Eat more ____ because they increase brain power and concentration.
a) oily fish   b) blueberries   c) tomatoes

3b Check your answers on page 111. Can you think of any other similar advice?

4a **2.38** Listen to these interviews with four students after an exam. Match each student 1–4 with the problems that they had or mistakes that they made.

a) didn't plan a piece of writing

b) didn't have enough ideas for one question

c) ran out of time and couldn't finish a question

d) couldn't remember enough

4b Listen again and note the solutions you hear to the problems and mistakes above. Have you had problems like these when doing an exam?

5 Discuss these questions with your partner.

1 Are you going to do any exams in the near future?

2 Which four pieces of advice from this lesson might be useful for you?

3 Which of the things discussed in this lesson do you usually do anyway?

WRITING SKILLS: a formal email

6 Work in small groups. Have you ever done an English course in an English-speaking country? Talk about your experiences and ideas. If you haven't done a course, would you like to? Why / Why not?

7 Imagine you are going to do a summer course called 'English with Sport' in Belfast, in Northern Ireland. Write about six questions you would like to ask about the course and school.

How many hours a week will I study?

Is the school big or small?

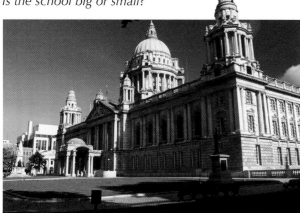

8 Read Pepa's email about the course. Are any of her questions the same as yours in Exercise 7?

Dear Sir or Madam

I would like to do a course in 'English with Sport' this summer. I am interested in visiting Northern Ireland and your college seems ideal for me. I have found a lot of the information I need from your website, but I still have some questions. Would you mind answering them for me, please?

First of all, if I stayed for four weeks, how many teachers would I have? Are there any exams at the end of the course? Could you tell me if I will get a certificate from the college when I leave?

Concerning the sports, I am especially interested in horse riding. Can I do this every afternoon and does the cost include everything? Also, is tennis available in the evening?

As I mentioned, I'm very keen on coming to Belfast and I would like to live with a local family. However, what would happen if I was not happy with the family? Would I be able to change accommodation?

I hope you can answer my questions.

I look forward to hearing from you.

Best wishes

Pepa Martinez Unamuno (Miss)

---

9 **Register** Answer these questions about the text.

1 Find examples of language that show that this email is polite and/or formal, e.g. *concerning the sports*.

2 Formal writing is well organised. What is the main topic of each paragraph?

3 Compare this email with the informal email in Unit 4 lesson 4, page 39. What differences can you find?

10 **Punctuation** Study the way commas are used in the email. Then put commas in suitable places in these sentences.

1 Would you mind sending me some information about the accommodation please?

2 If I came earlier in the summer would the course be cheaper?

3 Concerning the evening activities will our teachers come with us?

4 As I mentioned in my last email my level of English is quite good.

5 However I still have problems understanding native speakers.

11a Work with a partner. Imagine you want to go to New York to do an English course. Look at this advert and write a formal email to the academy, asking some questions about the course, school, etc. Use the email in Exercise 8 to help you.

MANHATTAN
LANGUAGE ACADEMY

*Learn English in the heart of the
Big Apple – the city that never sleeps.*

General English classes, all levels, all nationalities.

Small class sizes guaranteed.

Amazing modern facilities – all you need to study.

Special afternoon options include:
Business English, film-making, team sports,
American musicals.

Full programme of social activities.
Weekend trips available.

Accommodation service available.

11b Swap emails with another pair and write an answer to their email.

Dear . . .

Thank you for your email and enquiry . . .

REVIEW

GRAMMAR

1 Look at the photo and read the text quickly. What is dragon boat racing?

2 Complete the text with the present continuous (future meaning), present perfect continuous or past simple passive of the verbs.

3a `2.39` Listen to two people talking about the Vancouver Dragon Boat Festival. Are they both going to the festival this year?

3b Match the parts of the sentences from the conversation. Then listen again and check.

1 It's too far
2 We're leaving early and stopping
3 We haven't got
4 Several bands are
5 If we went this year,
6 If we camped,
7 Why don't I find
8 Have you got enough

a) enough spare money at the moment.
b) time for that?
c) we'd have to be very careful with money.
d) for a weekend.
e) out about some campsites in the area?
f) off to see my parents on the way.
g) then we could take our own food, too.
h) coming from south-east Asia.

4 There are grammatical mistakes in seven of these sentences. Correct them.

1 The ambassador is arrive at ten tomorrow morning.
2 Google, the Internet search engine, was founded in 1995.
3 Elizabeth Kostova's first book published last year.
4 This supermarket has using paper bags for years.
5 We need to cut the rubbish we produce.
6 How much do you throw away and how much do you recycle?
7 If kids watched less TV, they might be fitter.
8 The sports centre would be more popular if it teaches gymnastics.
9 There are too much adverts for junk food on TV.
10 My son isn't enough good for the school football team.

Annual Alcan Dragon Boat Festival
Vancouver, Canada

This year's Dragon Boat Festival 1_____ (take place) on 16 and 17 June and over 180 teams from around the world 2_____ (compete).

People 3_____ (race) dragon boats for over 2,000 years. They began in south central China and the boats were colourful and decorated with a dragon's head at the front. They 4_____ (make) of three tree trunks, which were tied together. The boats came in all sizes. They 5_____ (row) by up to 50 men and the ancient races could be extremely competitive and aggressive.

Modern dragon boat racing began in 1976 with the first Hong Kong International Boat Races, and the International Dragon Boat Federation 6_____ (set up) in 1991. Since then, the number of dragon boat festivals worldwide 7_____ (increase) and interest 8_____ (go up) steadily each year. The first races outside south-east Asia 9_____ (hold) in Canada, at the 1986 Vancouver World Fair, and they 10_____ (take place) regularly since then. Racing now tends to be in colourful boats made from wood, with about twenty rowers and a drummer at the front, who sets the pace for the rowing. Of course, it's no longer aggressive, but it's great fun for all the family!

VOCABULARY

5 Complete the newspaper advert about recycling facilities in a small town with the words in the box.

| aluminium boxes cans cardboard |
| cartons glass jars packets plastic pots |

RECYCLING FACILITIES IN KNARESFIELD
The following facilities are available for household recycling. Please recycle only between the hours of 9.00 a.m and 8.00 p.m.

Poplar Lane car park: 1_____ and plastic
Facilities here for bottles and 2_____ , and drinking glasses; also all household 3_____ , e.g. water bottles, yoghurt 4_____ and plastic bags.

Community centre: Paper and 5_____
Kitchen waste such as juice 6_____ , cereal 7_____ , egg 8_____ , also newspapers and magazines and unwanted books.

Cinema car park: Metal
All types of metal, including 9_____ , e.g. soft drink 10_____ .

6 Find nine words for people and groups in organisations. Use the clues to help you.

→3 words ↓3 words ↑1 word ↙1 word ↘1 word

C	O	M	M	I	T	T	E	E	X	O	S
F	I	N	I	J	K	N	S	Q	U	P	T
L	A	V	N	E	B	E	R	D	O	L	D
O	M	A	I	B	H	D	M	K	P	S	E
E	B	W	S	L	V	I	E	I	A	G	P
R	A	Z	T	E	S	S	T	A	F	F	A
J	S	D	E	C	P	E	S	Y	H	O	R
P	S	F	R	E	I	R	R	T	G	H	T
H	A	X	R	S	B	P	N	V	L	M	M
S	D	S	Z	H	J	V	P	I	A	D	E
I	O	Q	O	C	G	U	Z	K	R	N	N
N	R	Y	A	S	S	I	S	T	A	N	T

KEY LANGUAGE

7a **2.40** Listen to a student talking to her tutor. What day and time do they agree to meet?

7b Complete the conversation between the student and tutor with phrases a–h. Then listen again and check your answers.

a) could you   d) is it   g) to tell the truth
b) didn't you   e) Let me see   h) Well
c) are you   f) only

T: You wanted a meeting next week about your project, ¹_____ ?

S: That's right.

T: OK, let's try to arrange one. ²_____ ... I can do Tuesday at 11.00.

S: Erm, I'm in lectures all day Tuesday, I'm afraid. What about Wednesday at 9.00?

T: No, I'm not planning to come in till 11.00 on Wednesday. You couldn't do straight after lunch, ³_____ , say 2.00?

S: ⁴_____ , I could, but for ⁵_____ half an hour. I'm going to the dentist at 2.30.

T: I think we'll need more than half an hour, about an hour, I'd say. I'm free all day Friday.

S: Mmm, I'm taking the 10.30 train home on Friday, for the weekend. Nine isn't too early, ⁶_____ ?

T: Well, ⁷_____ , yes. It takes me over an hour to get here. You aren't busy on Thursday afternoon, ⁸_____ ?

S: No, well, not until 4.00.

T: Well, what about 3.00 on Thursday, then?

S: Yes, that's fine, thanks.

8 Work with a partner. You are going to arrange a meeting.

Student A: You are the student from Exercise 7a. Look at your timetable on page 110.

Student B: You are A's friend. Look at your timetable on page 115.

Use the dialogue in Exercise 7b to help you.

LANGUAGE CHECK

9 Two words in each sentence are in the wrong order. Correct them. Then look at the pages and check your answers.

1 My uncle is a servant civil in the public transport department. (page 85)

2 Plans announced were to set up a new government department. (page 87)

3 The new stadium is two only minutes from the underground. (page 88)

4 He has writing been soap operas for the last ten years. (page 93)

5 You can recycle those books. Don't throw away them. (page 95)

6 They didn't listen very carefully, they did? (page 97)

7 If had they the money, they'd send him to a sports academy. (page 101)

8 We've spent much too money on your birthday. (page 102)

9 She isn't enough talented to be an actor. (page 102)

10 That's a one difficult. I really don't know the answer. (page 105)

LOOK BACK

10 Find the exercise in Units 10–12 where you:

- talk about the United Nations. (Unit 10)
- read about the development of Microsoft. (Unit 10)
- work on predicting vocabulary when listening. (Unit 10)
- learn words for containers and materials. (Unit 11)
- listen to a funding committee discussing a project. (Unit 11)
- write a report about a building proposal. (Unit 11)
- learn how to talk about unreal situations. (Unit 12)
- read about big business in sport. (Unit 12)
- carry out a survey about personality. (Unit 12)

COMMUNICATION

Lesson 1.2 Exercise 6 (page 9)

How much do you know about winter?

1 Which parts of the world do not have winter?
2 Why does really cold weather begin late in winter, not at the beginning?
3 Where is most of the world's ice?
4 Which is heavier, ice or water?
5 What is the warmest part of a river or lake in winter – near the surface or at the bottom?
6 When does snow lie on the ground, and not melt?
   a) When the average temperature is below 0 °C.
   b) When the average temperature is below 3 °C.
7 What is the average temperature in London in January?
   a) – 14 °C   c) 4 °C   b) – 4 °C   d) 14 °C
8 How many days of snow do you think there are per year in …
   a) Moscow?   c) New York?
   b) Paris?   d) Tokyo?
9 Why do some animals in snowy places have white fur?
10 What is the fastest winter sport?

Check your answers on page 112.

Lesson 9.3 Exercise 7a (page 79)
Student B

1 You are a sales representative for Guangdong Digital. Read your company information below.

• You are selling a new digital camera, Model DC3, that costs $100.
• You want to get some big orders for this new product – up to 2,000.
• You can offer discounts – up to 20%.
• Longer delivery times are better for your company – up to eight weeks.

2 Before you begin the negotiation, look back at the lesson on pages 78 and 79 and choose more phrases for the box below.

> **USEFUL PHRASES**
> What's the price per item?   That's a deal!

3 Now have the meeting with Route One and negotiate a deal.

Lesson 11.2 Exercise 1a (page 94)

The photo shows the packaging waste for a British family in one month (20kg).

Review Units 10–12 Exercise 8 (page 109)
Student A

You want to arrange to meet Student B next week for coffee. Use this timetable to try to find a time that suits you both. Remember the tutorial you have just booked!

	Monday	Tuesday	Wednesday	Thursday	Friday
9.00		Study group		Tutorial (Art 2)	
10.00	Lecture (Art 1)	Lecture (Art 2)	Library	Study group	Train home 10.30
11.00	Tutorial (English)	Lecture (Art 2)	Library	Study group	
12.00		Lecture (Art 2)	Library	Study group	
13.00			LUNCH		
14.00	Swimming	Lecture (English)	Dentist – 2.30		
15.00	Study group	Lecture (English)	Dentist		
16.00	Study group	Lecture (Art 1)		Football practice	

ACTIVITIES

Lesson 1.3 Exercise 7 (page 11)

Student B

Answer your partner's questions about Peru. Then ask your partner questions and complete the notes for Chile.

> **USEFUL PHRASES**
>
> | | |
> |---|---|
> | What activities are there? | There's … |
> | What's the weather like? | In the winter, it's … |
> | What's the average temperature in …? | It's … |

PERU

	At the coast	In the mountains
Activities and attractions	snorkelling sea kayaking	white-water rafting horse riding
Weather		
Winter (May–October) Average temperature:	foggy and cool 15 °C	dry and sunny 20 °C
Summer (November–April) Average temperature:	sunny and hot 26 °C	cloudy and wet 20 °C

CHILE

	In the desert	In the mountains
Activities	_____ _____	_____ _____
Weather		
Winter (June–October)	_____ and _____ Daytime temperature: _____ °C Night-time temperature: 5°C	_____ and _____ June–August good for skiing Average temperature: 5°C
Summer (November–May)	_____ Daytime temperature: _____ °C Night-time temperature: _____ °C	_____ and _____ – no snow Average temperature: _____ °C

Review Units 1–3 Exercise 9 (page 31)

Student B

First, respond to Student A's suggestion. Then make a suggestion about one of the activities in the box, and agree or disagree with Student A's response.

B: Why don't we watch that new reality TV show tonight?

A: Great idea! I love reality TV.

B: So do I!

> fashion show   reality TV show   a marathon
> computer games   skiing   nature programme
> street festival   art gallery

Lesson 1.4 Exercise 3 (page 12)

> **cloud** /klaʊd/ noun
> a white or grey shape in the sky that is made of small drops of water: *There were no clouds in the sky.*

> **fog** /fɒg/ noun
> cloudy air near the ground, which is difficult to see through: *There was thick fog early in the morning.*

> **autumn** /'ɔ:təm/ noun
> the season when leaves fall off the trees; FALL AmE

> **hurricane** /'hʌrɪkən/ noun
> a violent storm with very strong fast winds

> **blizzard** /'blɪzəd/ noun
> a storm with a lot of wind and snow

> **sun** /sʌn/ noun
> the thing in the sky that gives us light and heat: *The sun's gone behind a cloud.* | *She lay in the sun reading.*

From *Longman Wordwise Dictionary*

Lesson 12.4 Exercise 3b (page 106)

1b Bananas are high in potassium. This is good for lowering stress levels.

2c All of the possible answers increase the oxygen in your brain, but only laughing encourages positive thinking.

3a Lavender oil helps you relax. Peppermint and rosemary oil both wake you up and make your mind more alert.

4b Exercise can promote the growth of new brain cells, especially in the area of the brain that is linked to memory and learning.

5c Pasta, rice and meat don't contain vitamin C.

6a The omega 3 oils in oily fish are very good for the brain. Blueberries and tomatoes contain antioxidants, which are good for fighting illness and disease.

Lesson 2.1 Exercise 8b (page 15)

Student A

Read the article about Mother Teresa and answer these questions.

1 Was she European or Indian?

2 What were the problems in Kolkata?

3 How old was she when she died?

Your article is missing some information. Make questions to get this information from your partner. Use these prompts.

1 What/teach?   4 What/win?

2 When/decide?   5 Who/give?

3 What/rent?

Ask and answer questions with your partner.

Teresa was born in Macedonia in Eastern Europe in 1910. From 1930 to 1948 she taught [1]_____ at a church school in Kolkata (originally Calcutta), India. She became **the principal of the school** in 1944.

There were many poor people in Kolkata. In [2]19 ___, she decided to help these people. She left the school and in 1948 she started **an open-air school for homeless children**. There were also many very ill people on the streets, but there were no hospitals for these poor people. Teresa rented [3]_____ and looked after these people.

There are now over 4,000 of her centres in India. In 1965 she opened **her first centre in another country**, in Venezuela. There are now centres in Asia, Africa and Europe.

Teresa gave all her time and life to the poor people of the world. In 1979 she won [4]_____ and she received **$6,000**. However, she did not keep this money; instead she gave the money to [5]_____.

Teresa died in **1997**. During her life, she inspired many people to help others. And this is still true now, many years after her death.

Lesson 1.2 Exercise 6 (page 9)

Answers

1 around the equator / in the tropics

2 because early in the winter, the air, ground and seas still have some summer heat

3 in the Arctic and Antarctic

4 water

5 at the bottom

6 b

7 c

8 a) 164 b) 4 c) 5 d) 5

9 so predators can't see them

10 speed skiing – up to 248 kph

Lesson 2.4 Exercise 3 (page 20)

Analysis of questionnaire

High scores in section A

You are probably a **visual** learner. Visual learners like to see information. A lot of learning in universities and colleges is visual learning because it involves reading.

Tips: Look again regularly at what you have learned. Write things down several times (e.g. summaries of important information from textbooks and lectures) and using your own words. Copy information from your lectures and textbooks onto the computer, then read the print-outs. Use different colours to organise and highlight information.

High scores in section B

You are probably an **auditory** learner. Auditory learners like to hear information. They understand best when they are listening or discussing.

Tips: If possible, record your lectures and listen to them later. Record things (e.g. your notes and textbook information) and listen to them later. Get information from radio programmes or sound files on the Internet. Say things aloud. Sing things to music you know. Study with other students and talk about what you're learning.

High scores in section C

You are probably a **physical** learner. Physical learners remember best by moving around and touching things.

Tips: Put information on cards that you can move around or put on the walls of your home or room. When you study, walk around with your textbook or notes in your hand and read the information aloud. In lectures, sit near the front of the room and take notes. Choose subjects where you can do practical work or research, e.g. interviews. Spend time 'in the field' (e.g. visiting a museum or working in an office).

All students

Have a look at the tips in the other sections – perhaps there is something there that can also help you.

Lesson 1.3 Exercise 7 (page 11)

Student A

Ask your partner questions and complete the notes for Peru.
Then answer your partner's questions about Chile.

USEFUL PHRASES

What activities are there?	There's …
What's the weather like?	In the winter, it's …
What's the average temperature in …?	It's …

PERU

	At the coast	In the mountains
Activities and attractions	_____ _____	_____ _____
Weather		
Winter (May–October)	_____ and _____	_____ and _____
Average temperature:	_____ °C	_____ °C
Summer (November–April)	sunny and hot	cloudy and wet
Average temperature:	_____ °C	_____ °C

CHILE

	In the desert	In the mountains
Activities	horse riding	skiing
	mountain biking	snowboarding
Weather		
Winter (June–October)	clear skies and sunny	cold and snowy
	Daytime temperature: 15 °C	June–August good for skiing
	Night-time temperature: 5°C	Average temperature: 5°C
Summer (November–May)	hot	cloudy and wet – no snow
	Daytime temperature: 25 °C	Average temperature: 15 °C
	Night-time temperature: 5 °C	

Lesson 2.3 Exercise 6a (page 19)

Student A

Isabelle

Young French woman

No job (unemployed). Looking for office work. Comes from rich family.

Personality — very friendly, cheerful, chatty, confident. Not very tidy

Likes — going out: cafes, cinema, parties. Cooking

Dislikes — washing up, sport

Appearance — not professional or smart. A bit scruffy (untidy, old clothes), short blonde hair

Other information — non-smoker, speaks extremely good English

---

Review Units 1–3 Exercise 9 (page 31)

Student A

Make a suggestion about one of the activities in the box, then agree or disagree with Student B's response.

fashion show	reality TV show	a marathon
computer games	skiing	street festival
nature programme	art gallery	

A: Let's go to the fashion show this weekend!

B: I'm not sure. I don't really like fashion shows.

A: Don't you? I love them!

Then swap roles and respond to Student B's suggestion.

Lesson 3.2 Exercise 9 (page 25)
Student A

1 Look at the crossword and prepare definitions for the words you have. (Do not include the word in the definition!)

2 Ask your partner for definitions for the missing words and complete the crossword.

USEFUL PHRASES

What's one down?   What's two across?

This is someone who …   This is a machine that …

This is something that …   It's …

This is an adjective which means …

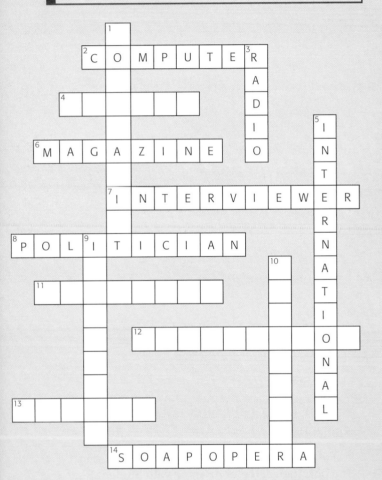

Lesson 12.1 Exercise 1c (page 100)

1	c	4	true
2	a	5	yellow
3	false (There are	6	sailing
	three higher	7	yellow
	grades: red and	8	b
	white striped, red,	9	drums
	and white belts.)	10	d

Lesson 2.3 Exercise 6a (page 19)
Student B

Toshi

Young Japanese man

Engineer (works for a big company)

Personality — friendly (nice smile), polite and clever, quite shy

Likes — sport: plays football/tennis
        going to the cinema

Dislikes — cooking (usually goes to cafés/restaurants)

Appearance — smart tidy clothes, short black hair, glasses

Other information — smokes, speaks good English

Lesson 2.1 Exercise 8b (page 15)
Student B

Read the article about Mother Teresa and answer these questions.

1 Was she European or Indian?

2 What were the problems in Kolkata?

3 How old was she when she died?

Your article is missing some information. Make questions to get this information from your partner. Use these prompts.

a) What/become?   d) How much/receive?

b) What/start?   e) When/die?

c) What/open?

Ask and answer questions with your partner.

Teresa was born in Macedonia in Eastern Europe in 1910. From 1930 to 1948 she taught **geography** at a church school in Kolkata (originally Calcutta), India. She became a) _____ in 1944.

There were many poor people in Kolkata. In **1946**, she decided to help these people. She left the school and in 1948 she started b) _____ .
There were also many very ill people on the streets but there were no hospitals for these poor people. Teresa rented **a room** and looked after these people.

There are now over 4,000 of her centres in India. In 1965 she opened c) _____ , in Venezuela. There are now centres in Asia, Africa and Europe. Teresa gave all her time and life to the poor people of the world. In 1979 she won **the Nobel Peace Prize** and she received $ d) _____ . However, she did not keep this money; instead she gave the money to **the poor people of Kolkata**.

Teresa died in e) _____ . During her life, she inspired many people to help others. And this is still true now, many years after her death.

Lesson 4.1 Exercise 6 (page 33)

1 Work with a partner. Think of more questions for this questionnaire.

In your life

1 How many countries have you visited?
2 How _____ ?
3 Have you ever ridden a horse?
4 Have you ever _____ ?

This year

5 How many exams have you done this year?
6 How _____ ?
7 Have you had a holiday this year?
8 Have _____ ?

This week

9 How much television have you watched this week?
10 How _____ ?
11 Have you been to the cinema this week?
12 Have _____ ?

Today

13 How many phone calls have you made today?
14 How _____ ?
15 Have you eaten any fruit today?
16 Have _____ ?

2 Interview different students in the class. If someone has done something, ask more questions and take notes.

Which country did you visit first? Did you like it?

3 After your interviews, tell your partner about the different students.

Review Units 10–12 Exercise 8 (page 109)

Student B

You want to arrange to meet Student A next week for coffee. Use this timetable to try to find a time that suits you both. You don't want to meet at nine o'clock!

	Monday	Tuesday	Wednesday	Thursday	Friday
9.00			Lecture (Maths)	Tutorial (Maths)	
10.00	Lecture (Maths)		Lecture (Maths)	Study group	Lecture (Physics)
11.00	Tutorial (Physics)	Library	Tutorial (Biology)	Study group	Lecture (Biology)
12.00	Lecture (Biology)	Library	Lunch with Anna	Study group	
13.00			LUNCH		
14.00		Lecture (Biology)	Hockey practice		
15.00	Study group	Lecture (Physics)	Hockey practice		
16.00	Study group			Lecture (Physics)	

Lesson 4.3 Exercise 7a (page 37)

Student C

> **Job:** Accountant
>
> **Health problems:**
> Arms and wrists hurt. Frequently get headaches. Hearing problems – a ringing sound in your ears.
>
> **Work routines/habits:**
> Work ten hours every day. Eat lunch at your desk. Use the computer a lot and read accountancy books. Have good office chair and desk.
>
> **General lifestyle:**
> Eat well – lots of fruit and vegetables. Go to gym every day – use the running machine. Enjoy listening to loud music on MP3 player (on trains and buses, and in gym).

Student D

> **Job:** Catering manager in staff café
>
> **Health problems:**
> Often have a bad back. Feel physically tired after a day's work. Often get stomach aches.
>
> **Work routines/habits:**
> Manage staff, help clear tables and clean in kitchen. Lift and carry food deliveries. Busy all day, never sit down, eat lunch standing up.
>
> **General lifestyle:**
> No time for sport or exercise. Watch TV, eat microwaved food.

Lesson 10.3 Exercise 1b (page 88)

New York, Madrid and Osaka haven't yet hosted the Summer Olympic Games.

Lesson 4.4 Exercise 2 (page 38)

This morning I felt awful. I had a bad earache and a stomach ache and a pain in my chest, so I went to the local GP. The waiting room was crowded. One man had a horrible red rash on his face. A woman was coughing all the time. A young man in a wheelchair had his leg in plaster. There were a lot of elderly people. They were probably waiting for their flu injections. I waited for ages. Finally, the doctor called my name. When I entered her room, she was sitting at the computer. She turned to face me. 'Good morning.'

'Good morning.'

'And what's the problem today?'

I explained the problem. She examined me. She looked in my ears.

She put her stethoscope around her neck and listened to my chest. She checked my pulse and my blood pressure.

'Have you lost any weight recently?' she asked.

'No,' I replied. 'I don't think so.' I said I didn't know exactly because the bathroom scales were broken.

'Well, your chest is clear,' she said, 'but you've got an ear infection. I'm putting you on a course of antibiotics. The stomach problem is probably just a bug. There's a lot going round at the moment.'

'Do I need a blood test?'

'No, not at the moment.'

She gave me a prescription for the antibiotics and we said goodbye. I took the prescription to the chemist's and got the medicine. In the evening, I phoned Abigail and told her about my visit to the doctor.

'You've had that stomach problem for some time,' she said. 'Why don't they refer you to a specialist? You need a scan. Then they can see what's going on. Make another appointment with the doctor for later this week. Ask her to send you to the hospital.'

'OK,' I said.

In the end, Abigail became cross. She thinks the National Health Service has got a lot worse. 'You need private healthcare,' she said.

Lesson 5.3 Exercise 7a (page 45)

Student A

You have photos for two of the links on the website: Animal Hunting (C1 and C2) and Animal Captivity (E1 and E2). For each pair of photos, decide which one is best for each link, and why. Telephone the Communications Director. Describe all your photos and make your recommendations. Use the words in the box to help you.

cage gun hunter lock	
police officer tiger skin	

E1

C1

C2

E2

Lesson 5.4 Exercise 8a (page 47)

Volcanoes are one of the most impressive features of the natural world. The largest active volcano in the world is Mauna Loa (4,170m) on Hawaii, in the Pacific Ocean. Everybody can recognise a volcano, but are they all the same? Mount Fuji (3,776m) is perhaps the world's most famous volcano because of its almost perfect shape – a cone with quite steep sides. This essay looks at two famous volcanoes in different countries. Unlike Mauna Loa, Mount Fuji in Japan is a dormant volcano which last erupted in 1707. To summarise, Mauna Loa is higher than Mount Fuji but the sides of Mount Fuji are steeper. Mauna Loa is an active volcano. The last eruption was in 1984. Its sides slope gently, and this shape of volcano is less dangerous than other kinds. In contrast, Mount Fuji is dormant. Mauna Loa last erupted in 1984 whereas the last eruption of Mount Fuji was in 1707. In conclusion, we can see that these two volcanoes have more differences than similarities, but they both catch our imagination.

Lesson 6.2 Exercise 9 (page 51)

Student A: You want to start your own business. With your partner, make two lists:

1 the problems you might face.

2 the solutions to those problems.

Problems	Solutions
* the bank doesn't lend you any money	borrow some from my family
* the business fails	get a job with a company / try again

Try to think of some more problems and solutions. Then role-play the situation with your partner.

What'll you do if the bank doesn't lend you any money?

– I'll borrow some from my family.

Yes, but …

**Now do the same with this situation.
Student B: You want to live on your own.**

Problems	Solutions
* feel lonely	phone my friends
* run out of money	come home

Lesson 3.2 Exercise 9 (page 25)
Student B

1 Look at the crossword and prepare definitions for the words you have. (Do not include the word in the definition!)

2 Ask your partner for definitions for the missing words and complete the crossword.

> **USEFUL PHRASES**
>
> What's one down? What's two across?
>
> This is someone who … This is a machine that …
>
> This is something that … It's …
>
> This is an adjective which means …

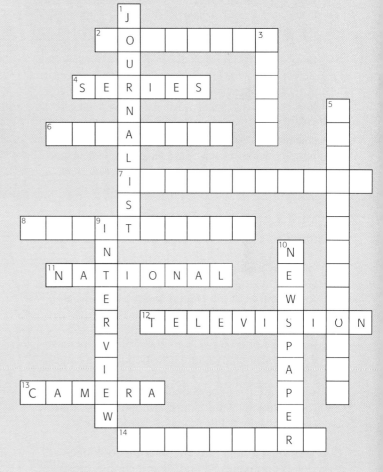

Lesson 6.4 Exercise 4b (page 54)

> P
> Violence will increase we will ∧frightened to leave our
>   wo P
> homes. What we can do I believe that rich people
>   Sp
> should pay more tax and the govenment must provide
>   WW   P
> more occasions for poor people

Now correct the mistakes.

Lesson 7.4 Exercise 3b (page 64)

Susan Greenfield is Professor of Pharmacology at the University of Oxford and Director of the Royal Institution. She is one of Britain's best-known scientists. Here she tells us about some problems facing women in science.

Schools in the UK are not doing enough to encourage girls to study science. There are no physical differences, I believe, between men's and women's brains, but there are differences in how men and women process knowledge. Most school science is about learning facts, and boys are happier about facts, and getting something right or wrong. I think that women have always had more complicated lives so they are more interested in evaluating things. Schools have to show what you can do with facts. Then girls will be more interested.

Women who want a career in science can face a number of difficulties. One of them is male attitudes. Early in my career, I was often the only woman working in my lab in Oxford. A male colleague called me simply 'the girl'. Over the years, men – and it is always men – have made comments to me such as 'You don't look like a scientist.' I realised that there was a problem in the UK when I went to France. In the lab where I worked in Paris, the atmosphere was different. This was because about 50% of the people working there were female.

The issue of children is also very important for female scientists in their late 20s or early 30s. In the lab in Paris, having children did not have a negative effect on the careers of the French women (who were also super elegant and brilliant cooks!). In Britain, if a woman takes time out to have a child at this very important stage in her career, things can be very hard for her later. If she wants to return to work after having children, it is difficult to compete with men who, meanwhile, have published a number of academic papers.

Then there is the question of confidence. I believe that, at some point in their careers, someone needs to give women scientists some confidence. They have to have more confidence in their abilities to be good scientists, to apply for jobs and to do good interviews. When women talk about their experience and skills, for example, they need to talk about the six out of ten things that they have, not to apologise for the four out of ten that they don't have.

In the end, if you are not a woman, and if you are not a scientist, the issue of women in science might not seem very important. But if you are both those things, you might feel uncertain about where your career or life is going.

Lesson 9.3 Exercise 7a (page 79)

Student A

1 You buy new products for Route One. You are interested in a new digital camera, Model DC3, that is sold by Guangdong Digital. Read your company information below.

- Your ideal order is 500 cameras. You can increase this, but you are not sure how popular the camera will be.
- You would like to pay about $80 per item.
- Your company would like a fast delivery, so that you can soon sell the cameras to the shops.

2 Before you begin the negotiation, look back at the lesson on pages 78 and 79 and choose more phrases for the box below.

> **USEFUL PHRASES**
>
> What is the price per item?   That's a deal!

3 Now have the meeting with Guangdong Digital and negotiate a deal.

Lesson 8.1 Exercise 6 (page 67)

QUIZ

1 How long should it take people to fall asleep at night?
2 How many hours sleep do parents lose a year when they have a new baby?
3 Why is it difficult to sleep on hot summer nights?
4 What is the record for the longest period of time without sleep?
5 How many hours a night did people sleep 150 years ago?
6 If you can't sleep, you should count sheep. True or false?
7 If you feel sleepy when you're driving, it is a good idea to open the window, or play loud music. True or false?
8 Losing sleep can make you fat. True or false?
9 Elephants sleep standing up during non-REM sleep, but lie down for REM sleep. True or false?
10 Fish close their eyes when they sleep. True or false?

Check your answers on page 121.

Lesson 8.4 Exercise 6 (page 73)

5 Suddenly, Kupe had an idea. He threw some big water containers into the sea. The octopus thought that the containers were people. It released the canoe and attacked the containers. At that moment, Kupe jumped onto the back of the octopus. He raised his sharp knife high into the air. He struck the octopus hard on the head and killed it.

6 Finally, after a difficult journey of thousands of miles and the defeat of the giant octopus, Kupe's people could settle on this new and wonderful land of two islands, Aotearoa.

Lesson 9.1 Exercise 8 (page 75)

Student A

Find someone in your class who used to do these things. Try to find a different person for each question. Try to continue the conversation by asking other questions.

Example

YOU: *Did you use to ride horses when you were young?*

STUDENT: *Yes, I did.*

YOU: *How old were you then?*

STUDENT: *About thirteen …*

OR

YOU: *Did you use to ride horses when you were young?*

STUDENT: *Yes, I did. And I still ride horses!*

Find someone who used to …	Name	Other information
1 ride horses		
2 have very long hair		
3 collect stamps		
4 cry a lot as a baby		
5 be shy		
6 have big birthday parties		
7 dream a lot		

Tell your partner one or two interesting things you have found out!

Lesson 8.3 Exercise 7a (page 71)

What's on?

Daily Festival Listings: Friday 24th August

EVENING (6 P.M.–8 P.M.)

Open-air theatre: A performance of Shakespeare's *Romeo and Juliet*, in the castle park.

Cinema: A remake of *Frankenstein*, including an interview with the director. Café open.

Walking tour: A tour of historic Edinburgh, with actors performing tales from Edinburgh's history.

Museum: Special evening opening, with talks by art experts. Free food and drink.

NIGHT (8 P.M.–11 P.M.)

Fireworks concert: Classical music (Beethoven, Handel, Prokofiev) with fireworks.

Theatre fun: Circus and mime performances. Stories without words, but stories with drama and laughs.

Open-air cinema: *The last dinosaur*, a documentary about Scotland's famous monster in Loch Ness. Free popcorn! (Drinks and other snacks available.)

Dance and dine: Take your partner by the hand. Learn and do traditional Scottish country dancing. A fun night out and a great way to meet new people. (Traditional Scottish food available between dances.)

LATE NIGHT (11 P.M.–2 A.M.)

Comedy: *The Best of British*. Ten top comedians make you laugh all night long.

Dance: *Bollywood Bonanza*. Incredible live performances of the dances from Indian films.

Music: *Up and Coming*. A showcase of five of Scotland's latest young rock and pop groups.

Jazz/Poetry: *Club Cool*. Jazz music, live poetry readings, an underground bar and restaurant – the recipe for a fun 1960s-style night out.

Lesson 10.1 Exercise 6 (page 85)

Student A

Luciano Pavarotti and Jane Goodall are on UN duty next week. Pavarotti has a special interest in children's rights and international peace. Goodall has a special interest in animal conservation and economic development.

Ask and answer questions with your partner to complete their appointment diaries.

Jane Goodall   Luciano Pavarotti

Jane Goodall

	Monday	Tuesday	Wednesday	Thursday	Friday
a.m.	10.00 a.m. 1 _____ about the trip to Kenya this week	2 _____ a.m. Visit an animal safari park	10.30 a.m. 3 _____	11.30 a.m. Visit a micro-credit project	9.00 a.m. Meet the Minister of Economics
p.m.	Travel to Kenya (leave at 2.00 p.m.)	1.00 p.m. Have lunch with the Animal Conservation Committee	2.00 p.m. Go to an animal hospital (meet 4 _____ at 4.00 p.m.) 6.00 p.m. 5 _____	6 _____ p.m. 7 _____	Fly back to New York (leave at 5.00 p.m.)

Luciano Pavarotti

	Monday	Tuesday	Wednesday	Thursday	Friday
a.m.	9.00 a.m. Give a TV interview about the trip to India this week	10.00 a.m. 9 _____	9.30 a.m. Go to a hospital (meet the staff who look after the children at 11.00 a.m.)	10.30 a.m. Meet the Health Minister	9.00 a.m. Hold a press conference with the president of the Peace in Africa Committee
p.m.	Travel to India (leave at 8 _____ p.m.)	1.00 p.m. Have lunch with the headmaster of the school 4.00 p.m. 10 _____	4.00 p.m. 11 _____	12 _____ p.m. Give a presentation to the UN Peace in Africa Committee	13 _____ 14 _____

Lesson 10.3 Exercise 7a (page 89)

Pair C

Your city is Madrid in Spain. Look at the information below and prepare a short presentation. Use adjectives and adverbs to emphasise the good things about your city. When your group is ready, give your presentation. Remember, emphasise that your city is the best!

City	Madrid
City facts	In the centre of the country Population: six million Weather: hot and dry, 32 °C
Special ambition / concept	**The Green Games** • The Games will pay for new green areas and wildlife parks. • We will use green electricity (from solar and wind power).
Sports venues	All the venues are in the city. • 85% already exist. • 60% of venues will be 10 mins from the village. • 39% of venues will be 20 mins from the village. • 1% of venues will be 35 mins from the village.
Athletes' accommodation	• There will be 7,000 double rooms in small blocks. • After the Games, the village will be a new residential area, a mixture of social and private housing, schools and health centres.
Transport	• We will use public transport only – there will be no extra car parks. • 90% of venues will be served by rail and metro lines. • There will be special buses and bus lanes.

Lesson 1.4 Exercise 2 (page 12)

cool /kuːl/ *adjective*
1 slightly cold, especially in a nice way ⇨ opposite WARM: *It was hot in the day, but pleasantly cool at night.* | *After his run, he had a shower and a long, cool drink.*
2 calm, rather than nervous or excited: *She tried to* **stay cool** *and not panic.*
3 *spoken informal* if you say that someone or something is cool, you like or admire them: *It was a really cool party last night.*

hot /hɑt/ *adjective* hotter, hottest
1 something that is hot has a high temperature: It was a very hot day. | *You'll feel better after a hot bath.* | *My coffee is still too hot to drink.*
2 hot food has a burning taste because it has a lot of spices in it: *a dish of hot, spicy meat and vegetables*

dark /dɑːk/ *adjective*
1 **it is dark** when it is dark, it is night time: *It's only five o'clock and* **it's already dark**. | *I want to get home before* **it gets dark** (= becomes dark). | *Come inside,* **it's dark out** (= it is dark outside).
2 a dark place is one where there is little or no light: *a dark, quiet room* | *It was very dark in the forest and we could hardly see.*
3 a dark colour is strong and closer to black than to white: *a dark blue dress* | *I'd like a carpet that's a bit darker than this one.*
4 someone who is dark or who has dark hair or eyes has black or brown skin, hair or eyes: *a beautiful dark-haired woman* | *Tony's dad was dark, but his mother had blonde hair.*

warm /wɔːm/ *adjective*
1 quite hot: *It's lovely and warm in this room.* | *Cover the bowl to keep the soup warm.* | *It was a warm day so we sat outside.*
2 warm clothes stop you from feeling cold: *I must buy a warm coat to wear this winter.*
3 friendly: *We gave the visiting students* **a warm welcome**.

From *Longman Wordwise Dictionary*

fine /faɪn/ *adjective*
1 very good: We sell fine food from around the world. | *The team gave a fine performance.*
2 very thin, or in very small pieces or amounts: *a shampoo for fine hair* | *a scarf made from very fine silk* | *The sand here is fine and soft.*
3 *spoken* good enough: *'I've only got water to drink.' 'That's fine.'*
4 *spoken* healthy and reasonably happy: *'How is your mother?' 'She's fine, thanks.'*
5 if the weather is fine, it is sunny and not raining: *I hope it stays fine for the picnic.*

clear /klɪə/ *adjective*
1 easy to see, hear, or understand: *His writing isn't very clear.* | *Some of the exam questions weren't very clear.*
2 if something is clear, it is certain and people can't doubt it: *It soon* **became clear** *that John was lying to us.* | *Sarah* **made it clear** *that she wanted to come with us.* | *It's not clear how many people were hurt.*
3 if a substance or liquid is clear, you can see through it: *clear glass*
4 a clear sky has no clouds

dry /draɪ/ *adjective* **drier, driest**
1 something that is dry has no water in it or on it: *Get a dry towel out of the cupboard.*
2 if your mouth, throat, or skin is dry, it does not have enough of the natural liquid that is usually in it: *My skin gets so dry in the winter.*
3 if the weather has been dry, there is no rain: *It's been a very dry summer.*

bright /braɪt/ *adjective*
1 something that is bright shines a lot or has a lot of light: *the bright flames of the candles* | *a nice bright room*
2 bright colours are strong and not dark: *a bunch of bright yellow flowers*
3 intelligent: *Maria is one of the brightest students in the school.*
   – brightness noun [no plural]

mild /maɪld/ *adjective*
1 not too severe, strong or serious: *Dean had a mild case of flu* | *a mild punishment*
2 not having a strong taste: *The sauce is very mild.*
3 mild weather is not too cold: *It's very mild for January.*

Lesson 8.1 Exercise 6 (page 67)

ANSWERS

1 10–15 minutes – less than five minutes means you're sleep-deprived.

2 400–750 hours

3 We need to cool down before we can sleep, and this is more difficult in summer.

4 11 days

5 9–10 hours, but this changed with the seasons.

6 False, according to some experts. They think it may be more distracting than relaxing. Relaxing imagery or thoughts may be better.

7 False. The best and safest thing to do is to stop, and take a nap.

8 True. New research shows a connection between lack of sleep and obesity.

9 True

10 False. Fish don't have eyelids.

Lesson 10.3 Exercise 7a (page 89)

Pair A

Your city is Osaka in Japan. Look at the information below and prepare a short presentation. Use adjectives and adverbs to emphasise the good things about your city. When your group is ready, give your presentation. Remember, emphasise that your city is the best!

City	Osaka
City facts	On the coast Population: three million Weather: hot and humid, 32 °C
Special ambition / concept	**The Games on the Sea** • We will use very modern technology and build magnificent islands in the sea for the Games. • We will build three artificial islands in Osaka Bay – two for the sports venues and one for the Olympic village.
Sports venues	None of the venues currently exist, so we will build the most modern sports facilities in the world. The best in the world. • 50% of the venues will be on two of the artificial islands. • 50% of the venues will be on the mainland. • 50% of venues will be 15 mins from the village (island to island). • 50% of venues will be 30–45 mins from the village (island to mainland).
Athletes' accommodation	• The Olympic village will be on the central artificial island. • There will be 14,000 single rooms. • After the games, we will sell the apartments on the private housing market.
Transport	• The mainland has an excellent rail service. • There will be ferries and train tunnels between the islands.

Lesson 11.3 Exercise 6a (page 97)

Project title Super Streets

Project description The aim of the project is to clean the streets of graffiti and litter and to reduce crime. Members of the local community will form 'Street Teams' which will be responsible for cleaning up graffiti and litter. The teams will also be in close contact with the police to help fight street crime. CCTV will mean the street teams can see anti-social/criminal behaviour easily.

Benefits of the project
1 The local area is very run-down. There is a lot of graffiti and rubbish. The street teams will be able to clean things up immediately and create a better local environment.
2 The local community will take responsibility for the local area.
3 The street teams will include children and adults, and this will bring the members of the community closer together.
4 There has been a lot of street crime. This will help reduce the crime and make the streets safer.
5 A safer and cleaner environment will attract new businesses to the area.

Budget
Total cost: £55,000

Costs breakdown
Cleaning equipment: £10,000
Purchase of ten CCTV cameras: £40,000
Management of the CCTV cameras: £5,000 per year

Project title Village of Wind

Project description The aim of the project is to create a community wind farm. It will provide electricity for local homes and we will sell extra electricity in order to raise money for other community projects.

Benefits of the project
1 It will provide green electricity for the village (and help fight global warming).
2 It will replace an ugly derelict building and it will turn an area of wasteland into a modern wind farm.
3 It will make money for the community by selling electricity to the country. This money will fund a youth club and a social centre for the elderly.
4 It will have an education/exhibition centre, so that children and adults can learn about global warming and ways to prevent it.

Budget
Total cost: £70,000

Costs breakdown
Clearance of wasteland: £10,000
Installation of ten wind turbines: £60,000
Note: There will be no annual costs because the wind farm will make money that will pay for maintenance and management.

Lesson 10.1 Exercise 6 (page 85)

Student B

Luciano Pavarotti and Jane Goodall are on UN duty next week. Pavarotti has a special interest in children's rights and international peace. Goodall has a special interest in animal conservation and economic development.

Ask and answer questions with your partner to complete their appointment diaries.

Jane Goodall

Luciano Pavarotti

Jane Goodall

	Monday	Tuesday	Wednesday	Thursday	Friday
a.m.	10.00 a.m. Hold a press conference about the trip to Kenya this week	11.00 a.m. Visit an animal safari park	10.30 a.m. Give a radio interview	11.30 a.m. 5_____	9.00 a.m. Meet 6_____
p.m.	Travel to Kenya (leave at 1_____ p.m.)	2_____ p.m. 3_____	2.00 p.m. Go to 4_____ (meet staff at 4.00 p.m.) 6.00 p.m. Have dinner with the US Ambassador	1.30 p.m. Interview some women who use micro-credit	7_____ 8_____

Luciano Pavarotti

	Monday	Tuesday	Wednesday	Thursday	Friday
a.m.	9.00a.m. 9_____	10.00 a.m. Visit a school for street children	9.30 a.m. 11_____ (meet 12_____ at 11.00 a.m.)	10.30 a.m. 13_____	9.00 a.m. 14_____
p.m.	Travel to India (leave at 3.00 p.m.)	1.00 p.m. 10_____ 4.00 p.m. Meet the head of the local UN department	4.00 p.m. Sing at a children's party at the hospital	1.30 p.m. Give a presentation to the UN Peace in Africa Committee	Fly back to New York (leave at 3.00 p.m.)

Lesson 4.3 Exercise 8 (page 37)

Student A

Job: Senior manager

Health problems:
Can't concentrate. Frequent headaches. Make simple mistakes. Sometimes get stomach aches.

Work routines/habits:
Often work late. A lot of responsibilities. Personal assistant not very good, so often also do his/her work. Often have big and long business lunches.

General lifestyle:
Eat a lot of heavy food and meat. You smoke. Play squash once a week. Take a lot of headache medicine.

Student B

Job: Personal assistant to senior manager

Health problems:
Sore throat, often lose voice. Cough and sneeze a lot. Eyes are often red and sore. Feel a little better when senior manager isn't in the office.

Work routines/habits:
Comfortable chair, but no window in office.
Office is in an old building which is difficult to clean.
Many indoor plants in office – senior manager likes them.
Don't have any of these problems at home.

General lifestyle:
Live in a large modern house.
Vegetarian. Never smoke.
Enjoy gardening, but no plants in house.
Go swimming once a week – but often have sore eyes after swimming. Do yoga.

Lesson 11.2 Exercise 5b (page 95)

Look at these ideas about cutting down waste. Then discuss these questions in your groups.

7 tips for cutting down waste – one for every day of the week

1 Send e-cards (for birthdays, etc.) and not paper or card ones. The thought is what's important, not the material.

2 Give old toys to other families.

3 Reuse plastic bags. To help you remember to do this, keep some in your pocket or bag – they don't take up much space.

4 Buy your fruit and vegetables from a local market.

5 Think before you print. How many times have you printed something and not looked at it again? If you do print, use both sides of a piece of paper.

6 Hire videos and DVDs rather than buying them.

7 Save about 40 litres of water a time by having showers instead of baths.

1 Which do you already know about? Which are new to you?

2 Which do you do? Which could you do?

3 Which are good ideas? Are there any you don't like? Why?

Lesson 11.4 Exercise 10 (page 99)

Plans for a new airport terminal
1,000 local residents interviewed (February 4–11)
- 64% against new terminal – aircraft noise, more traffic on local roads
- 25% in favour – good for local businesses
- 11% undecided – need more information about the plans
- 94% think government should pay more attention to views of local residents

Lesson 12.1 Exercise 1c (page 100)

Do this sports quiz. Then check your answers on page 114.

1 The first table tennis match was between two university students. At which university?
   a) Beijing, China
   b) Bologna, Italy
   c) Cambridge, UK

2 Which sport took the name of someone's house?
   a) badminton
   b) hockey
   c) polo

3 The highest grade of judo is the black belt. True or false?

4 In fencing, clothes must be white. True or false?

5 In archery, what colour is the centre of the target?

6 Which sport is connected with the America's Cup?

7 In cycling, what colour shirt does the leader of the *Tour de France* wear?

8 In which culture did gymnastics begin?
   a) Roman
   b) Ancient Greek
   c) Incan

9 What musical instrument is connected with dragon boat racing?

10 Where were the first football World Cup finals in 1930?
   a) Chile
   b) Sweden
   c) Switzerland
   d) Uruguay

Lesson 9.1 Exercise 8 (page 75)
Student B

Find someone in your class who used to do these things. Try to find a different person for each question. Try to continue the conversation by asking other questions.

Example

YOU: *Did you use to play the piano when you were young?*

STUDENT: *Yes, I did.*

YOU: *How old were you then?*

STUDENT: *Well, I started when I was about six …*

OR

YOU: *Did you use to play the piano when you were young?*

STUDENT: *Yes, I did. And I still play the piano!*

Find someone who used to …	Name	Other information
1 play the piano		
2 be afraid of the dark		
3 argue with his/her parents		
4 eat a lot of sweets		
5 wear black clothes all the time		
6 draw pictures of his/her teachers at school		
7 wake up very early		

Tell your partner one or two interesting things you have found out!

Lesson 10.3 Exercise 7a (page 89)

Pair B

Your city is New York in the USA. Look at the information below and prepare a short presentation. Use adjectives and adverbs to emphasise the good things about your city. When your group is ready, give your presentation. Remember, emphasise that your city is the best!

City	New York
City facts	On the coast Population: 8.5 million Weather: hot and humid, 28 °C
Special ambition / concept	**The Inner-City Games** The Games will improve poor inner-city parts of the city – there will be new housing, new sports facilities and new parks.
Sports venues	We will have the largest sports venues ever for the Olympics. All the venues will be in the city centre. • 65% already exist. • 40% of venues will be 20 mins from the village. • 30% of venues will be 30 mins from the village. • 30% of venues will be 50 mins from the village.
Athletes' accommodation	• The Olympic village will be in a poor area of the city, next to the river. • There will be 7,000 double rooms, in skyscrapers (20 floors). • The apartments will go on sale, as private housing, to the public after the Games.
Transport	• We will build extra car parks and roads for the venues. • There will be special buses for the Games.

Lesson 5.3 Exercise 7b (page 45)

Student B

You have photos for two of the links on the website: Animal Hospitals (B1 and B2) and Animal Sanctuaries (D1 and D2). For each pair of photos, decide which one is best for each link, and why. Telephone the Communications Director. Describe all your photos and make your recommendations. Use the words in the box to help you.

animal keeper hold lie down listen
neck window

D1

D2

B1

B2

Language reference

GRAMMAR

G1 Present simple

Use the present simple to talk about facts and things that are generally true.

It **rains** a lot in Britain.

Use the present simple also to talk about regular actions and habits.

We **have** a skiing holiday every winter.

Formation

With the present simple of the verb *be*, use *am*, *is* or *are* in affirmative statements, questions and negatives.

He **is** always very friendly.

Are you interested in travelling?

I**'m** not often here at the weekends.

With the present simple of other verbs, use the verb on its own in affirmative statements.

They **work** in the same office as me.

! Remember to add -*s* to the main verb after *he/she/it*.

Peter live**s** in a really big house.

Note these spelling changes after *he/she/it*:

- Verbs ending in -*s*, -*sh*, -*ch*, -*z*, -*x* or -*o*, add -*es*: wash**es**.
- Verbs ending in consonant + -*y*, change -*y* to -*ies*: carr**ies**.
- The verb *have* becomes *has* after *he/she/it*. Africa **has** a lot of problems.

Use *do/does* to form the negative and questions.

We **don't live** near here.

Does your country **have** a lot of storms?

Present simple short answers use *do/does*.

Yes, it **does**. / No, it **doesn't**.

Use *do/does* or *am/is/are* to form questions with *who, what, when, where, how, why, which*.

When does winter start here?

What is your name?

Adverbs and time expressions

We often use adverbs of frequency with the present simple, e.g. *always, often, sometimes, never*. The adverb comes after the verb *be*, but before other verbs.

It**'s never** really hot in Scotland.

It doesn't **often snow** in London.

We can also use time expressions with the present simple, e.g. *every day, once a week, every year*. We usually put these at the end of the sentence.

The news is on BBC at 6.00 **every evening**.

G2 Present continuous

Use the present continuous to describe an action happening now or around now.

We**'re having** an English lesson at the moment.

Use the present continuous also to describe a changing situation.

The weather in the UK **is** definitely **getting** hotter.

Form the present continuous with the auxiliary *be* + the -*ing* form of the main verb.

I**'m trying** to finish this exercise.

He **isn't staying** with us right now.

Is it **raining**? Yes, it **is**. / No, it **isn't**.

We usually just add -*ing* to the end of the main verb, but note these spelling changes:

- Verbs ending -*e*, remove -*e* and add -*ing*: live – liv**ing**.
- Verbs ending in vowel + most consonants, double the consonant and add -*ing*: get – get**ting**, travel – travel**ling** (but not with vowel + -*y*: play – play**ing**).

Time expressions

We often use time expressions with the present continuous, e.g. *now, today, currently, these days*.

We**'re** staying at a friend's house **at the moment**.

G3 Present simple and present continuous

Use the present simple for regular actions and the present continuous for actions in progress.

Present simple: It **rains every day** in winter.

Present continuous: It **isn't raining at the moment**.

We use both the present simple and the present continuous with verbs that describe actions (action verbs), e.g. *rain, work, play*.

The children **play** with their friends on Saturdays.

The children **are playing** football now.

Some verbs describe states (state verbs) such as feelings and situations, e.g. *be, want, believe, know, understand, like*. These verbs don't usually have a continuous form.

I want a drink. ✓   I'm wanting a drink. ✗

Some verbs can be state or action verbs, e.g. *think*.

I **think** this city is beautiful. (= this is my opinion)

I**'m thinking** about what to wear. (= deciding)

KEY LANGUAGE

KL Agreeing and disagreeing

So do I.   Neither do I.   Do you? I don't.
Don't you? I do.

VOCABULARY

V1 Types of weather

blizzard, drought, fog, hurricane, ice, rain, snow, storm, sun, wind

V2 Weather adjectives

bright, clear, cloudy, cold, cool, dark, dry, fine, foggy, hot, humid, mild, rainy, snowy, stormy, sunny, warm, wet, windy

V3 Activities

horse riding, mountain biking, scuba diving, sea kayaking, skiing, snorkelling, snowboarding, trekking, white-water rafting, wildlife watching

V4 Modifiers

extremely, quite, really, very

Extra practice

G1 **1** **Put the words in order to make sentences (affirmative or negative) or questions.**

1 snowboarding often go I in winter

_____

2 not cold in very it is the UK

_____

3 people do when in skiing your go country ?

_____

4 a lot of are in droughts Africa there

_____

5 biking like you mountain do ?

_____

6 country changeable the is your weather in ?

_____

7 you swimming do where go ?

_____

8 never the snows it jungle in

_____

G2,3 **2** **Choose the correct form.**

1 The weather in the UK *changes / is changing* these days.
2 Summers *get / are getting* hotter all the time.
3 We sometimes *have / are having* 'mini-droughts' in summer.
4 This *causes / is causing* problems every year.
5 We can't water our gardens so a lot of the plants *die / are dying*.

3 **Look at the answers. Then write the questions from these prompts in the present simple or present continuous.**

1 live / city / or / countryside?

_____

I live in the city.
2 interested in / sports?

_____

Yes, I'm very interested in tennis.
3 work hard / at the moment?

_____

Yes, I am, but I always work hard!
4 when / usually / relax?

_____

I usually relax at the weekend.
5 the weather / good / summer / your country?

_____

Yes, it is, but it rains a lot in winter.
6 rain / at the moment?

_____

No, it's sunny at the moment!

4 **Write answers for you to the questions in Exercise 3.**

KL **5** **Complete the conversation with phrases a–e.**

a) Do you?   d) OK, fine,
b) Don't you?   e) So do I,
c) No, neither do I.

A: Let's look at these brochures and find something for our summer holiday.
B: [1]___ but I don't want a beach holiday this year.
A: [2]___ I think an activity holiday would be good, for a change.
B: [3]___ but I don't like water sports.
A: [4]___ I do. But there are other sports we can look at. I like the idea of a horse-riding holiday.
B: Yes, that's a good idea. Where can we go horse riding?
A: Well, there are holidays here in South America, but I think that's a long way for two weeks.
B: [5]___ I don't agree – the flights are only about nine hours to Brazil.
A: Oh, OK then. Let's look at South America.

V1,2 **6** **Find adjectives and nouns in V1 and V2 to describe these types of weather or weather conditions.**

Adjectives
1 It isn't cold but it isn't very hot.   *warm*
2 It's hot and everything feels quite wet.
3 You can't see very far.
4 It isn't raining, but you can't see the sun.

Nouns
5 It's very hot and dry; there's almost no rain.
6 It's very, very windy.
7 It's snowing and very windy.

V3 **7** **Complete these lists with the activities in V3. (You can use the activities more than once.)**

1 We do these on or in water: *scuba diving*, _____,

_____ , _____
2 We need animals for these activities: _____, _____
3 We do these activities on snow: _____, _____
4 We do these activities on land:_____, _____, _____,

_____ , _____ , _____

V4 **8** **Complete each statement with a modifier in V4 and an adjective so that they are true for you.**

1 I think horse riding is *really relaxing*.
2 I think mountain biking is _____ _____ .
3 I think scuba diving is _____ _____ .
4 I think skiing is _____ _____ .
5 I think wildlife watching is _____ _____ .

Language reference

GRAMMAR

G1 Past simple

Use the past simple to talk about actions and situations that are finished.

David and I **trained** for the marathon last year.

We often say when the action happened,
e.g. *in* (+ year/month), *on* (+ day) or *at* (+ time).

The first modern Olympics were **in 1896**.
I watched a great documentary **on Sunday**.
We arrived **at two o'clock**.

The past form of the verb *be* is *was* or *were*.

We **were** here last night.
I **was**n't at the school this morning.

With other verbs, we use just the main verb in affirmative past simple statements. Regular past simple verbs add *-ed* to the infinitive.

train – train**ed**, watch – watch**ed**

The past simple verb does not change, i.e. it is the same after *I, you, he, she, it, we* and *they*.

! Note these spelling changes:

- Verbs ending in -e, add -d: die – di**ed**, live – liv**ed**.
- Verbs ending in consonant + -y, change -y to -ied: study – stud**ied**, marry – marr**ied**.
- Verbs ending in vowel + consonant, double the consonant and add -ed: stop – stop**ped**.

Many common verbs in the past simple are irregular.
→ irregular verb list, page 166

Use *did* to form past simple negatives and questions.

The race **didn't start** on time.
Did she **win** the London Marathon?

Past simple short answers use *did*.

Yes, she **did**. / No, she **didn't**.

Time expressions

We often use time expressions with the past simple,
e.g. *ago, last night (week/month/year), yesterday.*

We moved to this house two years **ago**.

G2 Past continuous

Use the past continuous to talk about actions in progress at a time in the past.

She **was living** in Berlin in the 1990s.

Form the past continuous with the past form of *be* + the *-ing* form of the main verb.

	Subject	be (+ not)	Verb + -ing
+	I / He / She / It	was	working.
	You / We / They	were	
–	I / He / She / It	wasn't (was not)	
	You / We / They	weren't (were not)	
?	*be*	Subject	working?
	Was	I / he / she / it	
	Were	you / we / they	

We **were travelling** to Mexico.
We **weren't travelling** to the United States.
Were you **travelling** by car?
Yes, we **were**. / No, we **weren't**.

Time expressions

We often use time expressions with the past continuous, e.g. *then, in + year (in 2005), at + time (at 9.00), at that time.*

We were living in New York **in 2005**.

G3 Past simple and past continuous

Use the past simple for a finished action or series of actions in the past.

The doorbell **rang** so I **put down** my book and **answered** the door.

To talk about an action in progress when another shorter action happened, use the past continuous for the action in progress. Use the past simple for the short action. This action can interrupt or stop the longer action.

I **was reading** my book when the doorbell rang.

Notice the difference between these two sentences:

He **was speaking** when the phone rang. (= He was speaking. Then the phone rang.)
He **spoke** when the phone rang. (= The phone rang. Then he spoke.)

KEY LANGUAGE

KL1 Asking about people

What's he/she like?
What does he/she look like?
What does he/she like?

KL2 Describing people

He seems (honest and shy).
She certainly isn't (chatty).
He's (hard-working).
She's got (short brown hair).
He looks like (that actor).
She wears (nice clothes).
He likes (watching sport on TV).

VOCABULARY

V1 Personality adjectives

chatty, cheerful, clever, confident, creative, dedicated, determined, friendly, hard-working, helpful, honest, horrible, inspirational, kind, lazy, lovely, miserable, nice, patient, polite, proud, quiet, rude, shy, sociable, stupid, talented, unfriendly

V2 Time expressions

afterwards, at first, at the moment, then, until

Extra practice

G1 **1** **Correct the mistakes in these sentences.**
1 My mother leaved school when she was fourteen.
2 Did she started a new job last year?
3 When did you born?
4 Last weekend my brother marryed his girlfriend.
5 We did not had a lot of money last year.
6 'Did they have a good holiday?' 'Yes, they had.'
7 We eated a lot of pasta last night.
8 She went to university at 2006.

G2 **2** **Complete the questions in the past continuous. Then write true answers for you. Use full sentences if you can.**
1 _Were_ you _travelling_ (travel) to the class an hour ago?
   Yes, I was. I was walking along the high street.
   No, I wasn't. I was doing my homework.
2 ___ you ___ (sleep) at 11.00 last night?

3 What ___ you ___ (do) at 8.00 yesterday evening?

4 ___ you ___ (study) English this time last year?

5 What else ___ you ___ (study) then?

6 Where ___ you ___ (live) ten years ago?

G3 **3** **Complete these sentences with the past simple or past continuous of the verbs.**
1 I ___ (have) dinner last night when the phone ___ (ring).
2 We ___ (do) some shopping when we ___ (come) home from work.
3 Sarah ___ (run) in the marathon when she ___ (fall) and ___ (break) her arm.
4 I ___ (meet) my husband while I ___ (ski) in the Pyrenees.
5 He ___ (write) a book while he ___ (recover) from an accident.

4 **Write sentences from these prompts.**
1 Iqbal / study / at university / his sister / get married
   Iqbal was studying at university when his sister got married.
2 Maria / work / the supermarket / she / receive / her exam results

3 Sam / eat / some nuts / his tooth / break

4 Angela / wait / at the station / she / find / $100

KL **5** **Match three answers from a–i for each question.**
1 What's your friend like?
2 What does your friend look like?
3 What does your friend like?

a) She's short and she's got black hair.
b) He loves mountain biking.
c) She seems really shy but she isn't.
d) Just sitting around and watching TV.
e) He looks like my brother.
f) He's very kind and patient.
g) He's quite good-looking.
h) Well, she certainly isn't stupid!
i) She likes cooking and eating good food.

V1 **6** **Match the parts of the words in A and B to make adjectives. (You can use the parts in box B more than once.)**
A

cheer creat friend hard help
inspiration love miser soci talent

B

able al ed ful ive ly working

1 _cheerful_   6 _____
2 _____   7 _____
3 _____   8 _____
4 _____   9 _____
5 _____   10 _____

7 **Use some of the adjectives from Exercise 6 to describe these people.**
1 She's always at work very early and leaves late.
2 He's never very happy.
3 She plays the guitar and she's very good at it.
4 He loves going to parties and being with people.
5 She's always prepared to do things for other people.
6 He makes other people want to be like him.

V2 **8** **Choose the correct word or phrase.**
I'm at university, in my second year, and [1]then / at the moment I'm doing film studies. I started it last year and, [2]at first / until, I hated it! I thought about changing my course, but my tutor asked me to wait [3]afterwards / until the end of the first year. I decided to follow his advice, so I waited, and [4]then / at the moment in May, I took the exams. [5]At first / Afterwards, I looked back at the year and decided it wasn't really bad, so I decided to continue with the course. Now, I'm really enjoying it.

GRAMMAR

G1 Articles

Singular nouns and jobs

Use *a/an* with a singular noun to mention something for the first time.

He works for **a** TV company.

Use *a/an* also to talk about a person's job.

He's **a** newsreader.

Use *an*, not *a*, when the noun begins with a vowel sound (*a, e, i, o, u*): **an** artist.

But note that some words that begin with the letter *-h* take **an** and we do not say the *-h*: **an** hour.

We usually say *a/an* with the schwa sound /ə/: **an** artist.

People or things in general

Use no article with plural nouns, when they refer to people or things in general.

Soap operas are boring.

Particular or known people and things

Use *the* with a singular noun to talk about a specific person or thing, or one we already know about.

The local newspaper doesn't have much news.
(= There's only one local newspaper.)
Put the flowers on **the** table. (= We know which table.)

Use *the* with plural nouns to refer to particular or known people or things.

I really like **the** photos in this magazine.
(= specific photos)
The people at the party were all very friendly.
(= We know which people.)

❗ Note the difference between general and specific use:
General = **Soap operas** are boring.
Specific = But **the soap operas** on Channel 4 are quite interesting.

We usually say *the* with the schwa /ə/: **the** journalist, but before a vowel, it is the strong form /iː/: **the** article.

First and second mention

Use *a/an* (with singular nouns) and no article (with plural nouns) to talk about something for the first time.

He works for **a** TV company.
He produces documentaries.

Use *the* when you mention the noun again.

The TV company is in the centre of London.
The documentaries he produces are historical.

Articles with the media

We usually use *the* when we talk about the media.

I heard it on **the** radio.
I use **the** Internet every day.

But note:

Did you see that programme on **TV** last night?

❗ *News* is a singular noun, not a plural noun.
The news about Beckham **was** interesting. ✓
The news about Beckham ~~were~~ interesting. ✗

G2 Relative pronouns

Use *which* and *that* to refer to things or ideas.

It's the programme **which/that** stars Katie Holmes.

Use *who* and *that* to refer to people.

She's the actress **who/that** married Tom Cruise.

Use relative pronouns to link pieces of information about a person or thing.

Marie Curie was a scientist. She discovered radium.
= Marie Curie was the scientist **who** discovered radium.

The information after the relative pronoun often defines the subject.

A search engine is a programme **that** finds information.
A newsreader is a person **who** presents the news on the TV or radio.

❗ Do not repeat the subject after a relative pronoun. The pronoun is the subject.
Bill Gates is the man **who** started Microsoft. ✓
Bill Gates is the man ~~who he~~ started Microsoft. ✗

KEY LANGUAGE

KL Making suggestions

Let's / Let's not (talk about politics).
We should (have some music on the show).
Why don't we (invite some politicians)?
What about (interviewing rich people / something on animals)?
What else shall we (do)?
Any ideas?
Anything else?

VOCABULARY

V1 TV and radio

chat show, comedy, current affairs programme, documentary, drama, game show, nature programme, news, presenter, producer, programme, reality TV show, series, sitcom, soap opera, station, variety show

V1 Newspapers and magazines

advert, article, business, celebrity, design, fashion, journalist, pop music

V3 Computers and the Internet

computer game, email, media, search engine, webcast

V4 Names for people and fields

art, artist, journalism, journalist, photographer, photography, politician, politics, psychologist, psychology, science, scientist

Extra practice

G1 **1** Complete these sentences with *a/an*, *the* or no article (write Ø).

1 Do you like ___ computer games?
2 My sister's ___ journalist.
3 There's ___ interesting programme about medicine on TV tonight. ___ programme lasts ___ hour.
4 What's the name of ___ presenter of that nature programme on Wednesday evenings?
5 Do you know ___ good Italian search engine?
6 That shop sells ___ DVDs. ___ DVDs are quite old and very cheap.
7 I don't usually like ___ comedies but I really like ___ sitcom on Mondays at 8.00.
8 My brother presents ___ news programme. He goes to the studio at 6.00 every morning to prepare for ___ programme.

2 Choose the correct meaning, a or b, for each sentence.

1 I love watching soap operas.
  a) I love all soap operas.
  b) I love only some soap operas.
2 Jason isn't here. He's at the cinema in town.
  a) We know which cinema.
  b) We don't know which cinema.
3 I like that magazine. I think the stories are interesting.
  a) I'm talking about all stories.
  b) I'm talking about particular stories.
4 Suzy works for a TV station.
  a) The listener knows which station.
  b) The listener doesn't know which station.

G2 **3** Match the two parts of the sentences and write *who/that* or *which/that*.

1 A documentary is a programme *which/that* f
2 A producer is a person _____
3 A search engine is a computer programme _____
4 A sitcom is a comedy series _____
5 A celebrity is a person _____
6 A drama is a story about things _____

a) continues a story each week.
b) happen to ordinary people.
c) is famous for appearing on TV, e.g. a presenter.
d) makes programmes.
e) looks for information on the Internet.
f) ~~tells you facts about the world~~.

4 Correct the mistakes in these sentences.

1 That's the woman which bought my car.
2 Richard Branson is the person who he started Virgin.
3 It's a word who means 'powerful'.
4 I bought a newspaper that it had the whole story.
5 It was on the programme what follows the news.

KL **5** Complete these suggestions from the prompts.

> ## Gianni's Pizzas
> ### Best pizzas in town!
> Try our fantastic vegetarian pizza.
> **Special offer**
> Monday evenings all pizzas half-price.

1 Why don't we _____ ? (have / pizza)
2 Let's _____ . (try / vegetarian pizza)
3 We should _____ . (go / Monday)

> ## STOKE
> ### LEISURE CENTRE
> All facilities:
> ● 25m swimming pool
> ● gym with modern equipment
> ● aerobics and dance
> ● Membership half-price this month

4 Why don't we _____ ? (go / leisure centre)
5 What about _____ ? (go / swimming)
6 We should _____ . (join / this month)
7 Let's not _____ . (do / aerobics)

V1,2,3 **6** Choose the correct words.

1 My sister works for a TV *programme / station*.
2 I'm interested in international affairs so I like newspapers with serious *adverts / articles*.
3 This magazine has a lot of information about *celebrities / producers*.
4 I like a good story so I prefer to watch *documentaries / dramas*.
5 Her last job was as a *presenter / journalist* on a reality TV show.
6 The children love animals so they watch lots of *nature / current affairs* programmes.

V4 **7** Complete these definitions with words from V4.

1 A _____ is someone who does experiments to understand the world.
2 _____ is the study of the mind and behaviour.
3 A _____ is someone who works in parliament.
4 _____ is taking pictures with a camera.
5 An _____ is someone that paints pictures and makes sculptures.
6 _____ is finding out about the news and presenting it in newspapers or on TV.

GRAMMAR

G1 Present perfect

We use the present perfect to talk about experiences in the past. We usually don't say when we had the experience.

We've **trained** hundreds of nurses.
They've **built** a new clinic.

Form the present perfect with *have* + the past participle of the main verb.

	Subject	*have* (+ *not*)	Past participle
+	I / You / We / They	've (have)	worked.
	He / She / It	's (has)	
–	I / You / We / They	haven't (have not)	
	He / She / It	hasn't (has not)	
?	*have* + subject		(ever) worked ...?
	Have I / we / you / they		
	Has he / she / it		

Regular past participles are the same as the past simple form of the verb, i.e. add -*ed* to the infinitive.

I've **visited** a lot of countries.
She **hasn't recovered** from her illness.
Has the surgeon **finished** the operation?

Many common verbs are irregular: *be – was/were – been, go – went – gone, write – wrote – written, drive – drove – driven.*

→ irregular verb list, page 166

! Note the difference between *been* and *gone*:
I've **been** to France. (= I've gone to France and I've come back.)
He's **gone** to France. (= He's gone and he is still in France at the moment.)

We often ask questions in the present perfect with *Have you ever ...?* to ask about experiences.

Have you ever been to Japan?
Have you ever stayed in a really good hotel?

Present perfect short answers use *have/haven't*.

Yes, I **have**. / No, I **haven't**.

G2 Present perfect and past simple

We use the present perfect when we do not give (or do not know) the exact time we did something. We use the past simple when we give (or know) the exact time we did something.

He's **travelled** to a lot of different countries.
In 1990, he **travelled** around the world.

We often start asking questions about a person's experiences in the present perfect, but then use the past simple to ask for more details.

Have you ever been to the United States?
– Yes, I have.
When **did** you **go** there?
– Two years ago.

Use the present perfect to talk about **finished** actions or situations in an **unfinished** period of time.

The surgeon **has done** four operations so far today.
(= the operations are finished but the time period – today – isn't.)

Common adverbs with this use of the present perfect are *today, this week/month/year, so far, to date, in the last hour/week/year*.

When the time period is finished, we use the past simple.

The surgeon **did** four operations yesterday.

Use the present perfect to talk about experiences in our lives, because 'in my life' is an unfinished period of time. Note the difference between:

Agatha Christie **wrote** a lot of crime novels. (She is dead = past simple)
P D James **has written** a lot of crime novels. (She is still alive = present perfect)

G3 Present perfect with *for* and *since*

Use the present perfect with *for* and *since* with state verbs (e.g. *be, have, know*) to talk about situations that began in the past and are still continuing.

My brother **has had** high blood pressure for years.
I've **been** in a bad mood all day!

Use *for* to give a period of time.

We've had the same English teacher **for two years**.

Use *since* to say when the situation began.

I've known my girlfriend **since March 2004**.

KEY LANGUAGE

KL1 Giving advice

You should (go to the optician's).
You shouldn't (drink coffee at night).

KL2 Giving reasons

(You should eat garlic) **because** it fights colds.
(You should do exercise) **in order to** lose weight.
(You should eat a lot of fruit) **to** stay healthy.
(You should go to bed early) **so that** you have enough sleep.

VOCABULARY

V1 Health and wellbeing

clinic, dentist, depression, disease, doctor, health insurance, heart disease, high blood pressure, illness, injury, insomnia, lack of motivation, local doctor, medicine, nurse, operation, poor concentration, poor memory, prevent, private hospital, state hospital, surgeon, surgery, treatment

V2 Food and nutrition

carbohydrate, junk food, malnutrition, nuts, salmon, seeds, vitamins

Extra practice

4

G1 **1** Complete the text with the present perfect of the verbs in the box.

| be (x2) not finish go employ save |
| start teach train not visit |

Our medical organisation came to Bangladesh three years ago and I ¹_____ here since the beginning. We ²_____ about 80 men and women to become nurses, and they ³_____ to different parts of the country so that they can help people. We ⁴_____ a number of doctors and managers, too, and together they ⁵_____ smaller clinics in other parts of the country. We certainly ⁶_____ all our work here. There are a lot of small towns and villages that we ⁷_____ but I'm sure we ⁸_____ a lot of lives. It ⁹_____ a wonderful experience so far and it ¹⁰_____ me a lot of new things!

G2 **2** Choose the correct form.
1 I *visited / have visited* a lot of countries in Asia.
2 Last year I *went / have been* to China.
3 The government *built / has built* ten new hospitals in the last five years.
4 *Did you ever / Have you ever* been to the USA?
5 My mother *phoned / has phoned* me every week when I worked in London.
6 Jake *didn't see / hasn't seen* me yesterday.
7 I *didn't finish / haven't finished* my essay last night.
8 I *wrote / have written* about 5,000 words on the essay so far.

G3 **3** Complete these sentences with a verb in the present perfect and *for* or *since* with one of the phrases in the box.

| five days   four years   I got up |
| two years   ~~ten years~~   1981 |

1 Ines became a doctor in 1998. It's now 2008.
   She's *been a doctor for ten years*.
2 I got a cold on Sunday. It's now Thursday.
   I've *had* _____
3 Alice met her husband in 1981.
   Alice *has known* _____
4 Mark got married two years ago.
   Mark _____
5 We bought this house in 2004. It's now 2008.
   We _____
6 This toothache started when I got up at 8.30.
   I _____

KL1,2 **4** Complete the advice for these problems. Use *should/shouldn't* and a way of giving a reason from KL2.

> I've had about three colds this winter – I'm getting really fed up with it!

1 You *should* take vitamin C *to* keep your immune system healthy.
2 You _____ close all the windows _____ you need fresh air.

> I'm studying and I also do a part-time job in a restaurant. I get up really early to study, but I don't go to bed until about 1.00 in the morning. I always feel really tired.

3 You _____ work so late _____ you need your sleep.
4 You _____ speak to your tutors _____ they understand your problem.

> I sit at my desk for hours every day. Now I find that my back hurts nearly all the time.

5 You _____ stay in the same position at your desk _____ your body needs to move.
6 You _____ get up and stretch every 20 minutes _____ reduce the tension in your back.

5 Can you think of another piece of advice for each person?

_____

_____

_____

V1,2 **6** Find the following people, places or health problems from V1 and V2.
1 a person who performs operations
2 the result of not eating enough
3 a problem with sleeping
4 the place where you usually see your doctor
5 the person who looks after your teeth
6 a physical problem, often the result of an accident
7 when you feel sad all the time
8 a medical building where you stay, and pay for your treatment
9 when you don't want to do anything
10 when you can't remember things very well

Language reference

GRAMMAR

G1 Comparative and superlative adjectives

Use comparative and superlative adjectives to make comparisons between people or things. Comparative adjectives compare one person/thing with another.

The Apennine Mountains in Italy are quite **high**. The Carpathians in Romania are **higher**.

We usually make comparisons with *than*.

The Carpathians are **higher than** the Apennines.

Superlative adjectives compare one person/thing with several other people/things (more than two). Use *the* before the superlative adjective.

The Alps are **the highest** mountains in Europe.

Note the different ways of forming the comparative and superlative adjectives:

	Adjective	Comparative	Superlative
one-syllable adjectives • ending in -e • ending in -y • ending in vowel + consonant	cheap strange dry flat	cheap**er** strang**er** dri**er** flat**ter**	cheap**est** strang**est** dri**est** flat**test**
most two-syllable adjectives • ending in -y • ending in -ow • ending in -er	peaceful pretty narrow clever	**more** peaceful prett**ier** narrow**er** clever**er**	**most** peaceful prett**iest** narrow**est** clever**est**
adjectives of three or more syllables	popular mysterious	**more** popular **more** mysterious	**most** popular **most** mysterious
irregular adjectives	good bad far	better worse farther/further	best worst farthest/furthest

G2 *less/least*

Adding -er/-est or *more* to an adjective makes the adjective stronger. If we want to make the adjective weaker, we use *less/least*. The comparative form is *less*.

London is **less beautiful than** Paris. (= Paris is more beautiful than London.)

The superlative form is *the least*.

Alaska is **the least populated** state in the United States. (= All the other states are more populated.)

Use *less* and *least* with all adjectives; it doesn't matter how many syllables the adjective has.

The Atlantic Ocean is **less calm than** the Mediterranean.
This lake is **the least impressive**, I think.

G3 Expressions of quantity

Use *a lot of*, *many* and *much* to talk about large quantities and amounts. We use *many* with countable plural nouns and *much* with uncountable nouns.

Many animals are in danger because there isn't **much food** for them.

We use *a lot of* with both countable and uncountable nouns.

A lot of animals are in danger because there isn't **a lot of food** left for them.

We use *many* in both affirmative and negative statements, but we use *much* in negative statements only.

There are many grey squirrels in the UK but **there aren't many** red squirrels now.
There isn't much damage to the environment here.

! It is quite formal to use *many* in affirmative sentences. In informal English we use *a lot of*.
I have **a lot of** squirrels in my garden.

Use *few* and *little* in affirmative statements to talk about small quantities and amounts. They mean 'not many / not much'. Use *few* with countable plural nouns and *little* with uncountable nouns.

There are **few tigers** in the world.
There's **little hope** for some animals.

We do not usually use *few* and *little* with questions and negative statements. We use *not many / not much*.

We **haven't got many** trees in the garden.
Is there much rain in the desert?

! Remember that we can use *(not) a lot of* instead of *much, many, few* and *little*.
I haven't got **much money**. / I haven't got **a lot of money**.

KEY LANGUAGE

KL Describing photographs

In the photograph, some people are watching …
In the first/second photograph, a man is showing …
There are (a lot of people) in the background.
On the right/left of the picture, (someone is walking …)
In the middle …
They look (very professional).

VOCABULARY

V1 Landscapes

beach, cliff, coast, forest, hill, island, lagoon, lake, mountain, river, rock, sand, sea, wave

V2 Animals

crab, deer, elephant, giraffe, gorilla, hedgehog, leopard, monkey, panda, rabbit, snail, squirrel, tiger

V3 Words that are nouns and verbs

cause, damage, harm, hope, plant, ship, shop

V4 Contrast

but, in contrast, whereas

Extra practice

G1 **1** Complete these sentences with the comparative or superlative form of the adjectives.

1 Samira is _____ girl in the class. (clever)
2 Paris is _____ Sydney. (romantic)
3 The Canary Islands are _____ other places in Spain. (tropical)
4 The _____ way to see the countryside is to go trekking. (good)
5 The pollution in Bangkok is _____ in London. (bad)
6 Moscow is _____ city in the world at the moment. (expensive)

2 Write a) a comparative and b) a superlative sentence about each set of figures.

1 Lewis 175cm / Kevin 185cm / Jason 166cm (tall)
   a) Jason / Lewis Lewis is _____ .
   b) _____ the tallest boy.

2 Lake Erie 19m / Lake Ontario 86m / Lake Superior 147m (deep)
   a) Lake Ontario / Lake Erie _____
   _____
   b) _____
   _____

3 a Porsche £35,000 / a Hyundai £18,000 / a Smart car £7,000 (expensive)
   a) a Smart car / a Hyundai _____
   _____
   b) _____
   _____

G2 **3** Rewrite these sentences so that they mean the same. Use *less* or *least*.

1 Nottingham is more dangerous than Oxford.
   Oxford is _____ .
2 London is more expensive than New York.
   New York is _____ .
3 All the other lakes are more impressive than this one.
   This lake is _____ .
4 Carnac is more mysterious than Stonehenge.
   Stonehenge is _____ .
5 The north of France is flatter than the south.
   The south _____ .
6 All the other Greek islands are more popular than this one.
   This island is _____ .
7 The Mediterranean is calmer than the Atlantic.
   The Atlantic is _____ .
8 All other sports are more exciting than cricket.
   Cricket is _____ .

G3 **4** Cross out the incorrect words.

1 *Many / Much / A lot of* animals are in danger of extinction.
2 We *don't have much / don't have many / have little* hope for these animals.
3 There is *few / little / not much* snow in this part of the country.
4 We haven't got *much / many / a lot of* time to save the planet!
5 There's *not much / little / few* life on this island.
6 There are *not many / little / few* tigers in the world.

KL **5** Correct the mistakes in these sentences.

1 I can see mountains at the background.
2 In this photo, a man waits at a bus stop.
3 On right of the picture there's a river.
4 The people all talk about something.
5 In second photograph, a woman is going into a shop.
6 On the left on the photo there's a sports car.
7 It looks like very fast.

V1,2 **6** Circle the odd one out in each group.

1 squirrel / hedgehog / (snail) / rabbit
2 sea / forest / river / lake
3 beach / coast / hill / sand
4 lagoon / lake / river / rock
5 mountain / hill / wave / coast
6 crab / giraffe / gorilla / monkey

V3 **7** Use the words in V3 to complete these questions. Change the form if necessary.

1 What problems does the world face? What are the _____ of these problems?
2 What do you _____ to do in the future?
3 Do you have any house _____ ? Have you got green fingers?
4 In what ways does junk food _____ your health?
5 Do you have a favourite clothes or music _____ ?
6 Have you ever sailed on a large _____ ?
7 Where do you _____ for most of your food?
8 Have you ever _____ any big items to another country?

8 Work with a partner. Ask and answer the questions in Exercise 7.

V4 **9** Add commas if necessary to these sentences.

1 I like the sea but I don't like mountains.
2 My sisters all have brown eyes. In contrast my eyes are blue.
3 Red squirrels come from the UK whereas grey squirrels come from North America.
4 Madrid is very hot in summer but very cold in winter.

Language reference

GRAMMAR

G1 | *will, might* and *may* for predictions

Use *will* ('*ll*), *won't* (*will not*), *might (not)* and *may (not)* to make predictions, i.e. to say what we think about the future.

> People **will retire** later in the future.
> They **won't have** big families.
> We **might** use the Internet for a lot more things.
> It **may not be** good for business.

Use contractions '*ll*, *won't* and *mightn't* for speaking and informal English.

> We'**ll live** longer in the future because there'**ll be** better medicine.
> There **won't be** many serious illnesses.
> But we **mightn't** find a cure for cancer.

! We do not use the contraction *mayn't*; we use *may not* instead.

> I ~~mayn't be~~ at work tomorrow. ✗
> I **may not be** at work tomorrow. ✓

We often use *I think / I don't think* to introduce a prediction:

> **I think there'll be** problems with pensions in the future.

We often say *I don't think + will* instead of *I think + will not*.

> **I don't think** the government **will have** the money for pensions.

We use *will* when we are more certain about the future. We use *might* or *may* when we are less certain.

> Older people **will work** for longer in the future, and young adults **might start** working later.

! *Might* is more common than *may* to make predictions, especially in informal English.

We usually use *will* when we ask for predictions about the future, not *might* or *may*, and we often start with *Do you think ...?*

> **Do you think** we **will live** longer in the future?
> **Will** people **have** cars in the future?
> What **do you think** the future **will be** like?

Adverbs of certainty

We often use adverbs with *will/won't* for predictions, to say how certain we are. In affirmative sentences we usually put the adverb after *will*; in negative sentences we put it before *won't*.

> We **definitely won't** use petrol in the future.
> We'**ll probably use** a biological fuel.

The adverbs *definitely* and *certainly* mean we are very certain; the adverbs *probably* and *possibly* mean we are less certain.

> People **will certainly have** smaller families in the future, so they **probably won't live** in big houses.

! We don't use these adverbs with *might* or *may*.

G2 | First conditional

Use the first conditional to talk about the result of a possible future action.

Possible future action	Result
If I get a better job,	we'll have more money.
If I don't get a better job,	we won't have a holiday.

Note the formation of the first conditional:

If-clause (condition),	Main clause (result)
If + present simple,	*will / won't* + infinitive
If you **go** to university,	you'**ll find** a good job.
If you **don't go** to university,	you **won't get** a qualification.

! We usually put a comma after the *if*-clause. We can put the main clause first. If we do this, we don't use a comma.

> You'll find a good job if you go to university.

We can also use *might* and *may* in the main clause. Then the action in the main clause is less certain than when we use *will*.

> If I get a good degree, I **might apply** to work for Microsoft. (= I'm not sure about this.)

KEY LANGUAGE

KL1 | Expressing opinions

Personally, I think (that) ...
What I think is that ...
I think it's (better if ...)
Why not just (turn the TV off)?

KL2 | Expressing agreement/disagreement

I agree with (him/her).
I understand his/her opinion, but ...
Personally, I completely disagree.
That's a good/interesting idea/point, but ...

VOCABULARY

V1 | Ages

adolescent, adult, child, elderly, middle-aged, retired, teenager, thirty-something

V2 | Negative adjectives

careless, hopeless, uncomfortable, unhappy, unkind, unlucky, unusual, useless

V3 | Population

birth rate, childcare, employer, graduate, old-fashioned, responsible, suitable

V4 | Linkers

as, because of, however, so

Extra practice

6

G1 **1** **Correct the mistakes in these sentences.**
1 I think people might to live longer in the future.
2 Doctors won't definitely find cures for a lot of diseases.
3 May people retire later in twenty years' time?
4 People mayn't take holidays a long way from home.
5 We won't to fly as much as now.
6 Families might probably get smaller.
7 Definitely I will retire when I'm 60.
8 The number of students at university will increases.

2 **Rewrite these sentences without changing the meaning. Use the phrases in the box.**

| probably won't   might   'll definitely |
| definitely won't   'll probably |

1 I'm 100% certain that we will find a better fuel than petrol.
  We _____
2 I'm almost sure that we'll get our news only from the Internet.
  _____
3 I'm not sure if couples will divorce more.
  _____
4 I don't think humans will go back to the Moon.
  _____
5 I'm 100% certain we won't have more leisure time!
  _____

G2 **3** **Match the two halves of these first conditional sentences.**
1 If people live longer,
2 We might see the late film tonight
3 If more students go to university,
4 If parents don't earn much money,
5 We'll need a bigger house

a) they won't be able to afford childcare.
b) they might get more diseases when they're older.
c) if we have more children.
d) if the children go to bed early.
e) they might not all find good jobs when they leave.

4 **Complete these first conditional sentences so that they are true for you. Then compare your sentences with a partner.**
1 If the class finishes a bit early today, …
2 If the weather's good at the weekend, …
3 If I have some spare money at the end of the month, …
4 If I get a good/better job, …
5 If I earn a lot of money in the future, …
6 If I retire early, …

KL1,2 **5** **Complete the conversation with a–f.**
a) I agree with   d) Personally, I think
b) I think it's better   e) That's a good point,
c) I understand her idea, f) what I think is that

A: I saw Jo and Steve earlier. They're looking for some childcare for Amy so that Jo can go back to work.
B: Childcare? [1]___ if the mother stays at home.
A: Really, Matt! Jo's got a good job. [2]___ that women need to get back to work.
B: [3]___ you – if they need the money, but Jo and Steve don't need the money.
A: Well, [4]___ it's better when young children can play with other children in childcare.
B: [5]___ but maybe for a couple of hours a day, not all the time.
A: Mmm. Jo feels that if she finds childcare, she'll have the choice of working or not, anyway.
B: [6]___ but I think she'll go back to work.
A: Yes, so do I.

V1 **6** **Find words in V1 for these people.**
1 someone who is over about 60 and doesn't work anymore
2 a young person between 13 and 19
3 someone between about 35 and 60
4 a person over the age of about 20
5 a very young person
6 an old person (a polite adjective)
7 a young person who is no longer definition 5 but not yet definition 4

V2 **7** **Complete these sentences with a negative adjective from V2.**
1 My brother is very _____ so he makes a lot of mistakes.
2 His father was very _____ and treated him badly.
3 Maria's very _____ because her boyfriend has gone away.
4 I never win any competitions – I'm very _____ .
5 It's a very _____ film – you've never seen anything like it!
6 I can't do this homework. I'm _____ at Maths!

V3,4 **8** **Choose the correct words.**
1 Keira can't go out this evening *as / because of* she needs to finish her History essay.
2 I don't think Chris is *suitable / responsible* to be a teacher – he isn't very patient.
3 The advert says they only want *employers / graduates* who left university last year.
4 I hate housework, *so / however* I don't often do it.
5 It's difficult to find *birth rate / childcare* in this city.
6 Alana studied very hard *as / so* she passed her exams.

Language reference

GRAMMAR

G1 Obligation

must and mustn't

Use *must* to say that it is necessary to do something.
> You **must switch** your phone **off** during the lesson.

The negative *mustn't* means that it is necessary NOT to do something.
> We **mustn't bring** food or drink into the classroom.
> You **mustn't take** anything from the crime scene.

Must is a modal verb. We use modal verbs with other verbs to talk about obligation, ability, possibility, etc. *Must* expresses obligation.

A modal verb always comes before an infinitive without *to*.
> I **must phone** my mother this evening.

The form *must* does not change after *he/she/it*.
> James **must visit** his family this weekend.

Form questions with modal verbs by putting the verb before the subject of the question.
> What time **must we get** the bus?

(don't) have to

We can also use *have to / has to* to say that it is necessary to do something.
> Forensic scientists **have to be** very careful in their work.

The negative *don't have to / doesn't have to* means that it is NOT necessary to do something.
> You **don't have to study** law to be a scientist.

It is possible to use *must* to ask a question, but we often prefer *do/does … have to …?*
> **Must I sign** the form too?
> **Do you have to leave** now?
> **Does he have to analyse** the evidence?

must and have to

Must and *have to* have very similar meanings. They both mean something is necessary.

We usually use *must* when we believe that something is important (it is our opinion).
> I **must get up** early tomorrow.

We usually use *have to* to talk about rules and laws (i.e. someone else thinks it is important).
> We **have to get** a visa to visit the United States.

❗ Remember that the negative of *must* (*mustn't*) and *have to* (*don't/doesn't have to*) are very different.
> You **mustn't use** your mobile phone in the cinema. (= it is not allowed)
> You **don't have to use** your mobile phone – use my office phone. (= it is not necessary)

G2 had to and could

Must does not have a past form. To talk about something that was necessary in the past, use *had to*.
> The doctors **had to operate** to save his life.

In negative statements, to say that something was not necessary, use *didn't have to*.
> We **didn't have to pay** for the tickets – they were free.

Use *did … have to …?* to ask if something was necessary.
> **Did you have to wear** a uniform to school?

Use the modal verb *could* to talk about ability in the past.
> I **could run** fast when I was younger.

We use *couldn't* to say that we were not able to do something or that it was not possible.
> I **couldn't finish** the book – it was really difficult.
> We **couldn't study** astronomy at our university.

Use *could …?* to ask about ability in the past.
> **Could you understand** that lecture on physics yesterday?

KEY LANGUAGE

KL Developing an argument

This **caused** a revolution in knowledge.
It **meant that** ideas could spread.
It **led to** education for everyone.
It's **connected to** the production of books.
… **so** people had to learn to read.
This **means that** society is more literate.

VOCABULARY

V1 Subjects

Astronomy, Biology, Chemistry, Economics, History, Mathematics, Medicine, Physics

V2 Crime

analyse, analysis, analyst, burglary, commit, crime, discover, DNA, evidence, fingerprints, investigator, reveal, scene, solve (a crime)

V3 Nouns, adjectives and verbs with prepositions

afraid of, belong to, connected to, happen to, history of, interested in, lead to, proud of, receive from, relationship with, separate from, spend (money) on, successful in, thanks to

Extra practice

G1 **1** Complete these sentences about what police officers *have to do*, *don't have to do* and *mustn't do*.

1 They *have to* arrive on time to work every day.
2 They _____ be rude to the public.
3 They _____ wear a uniform.
4 They _____ be very careful when they're at a crime scene.
5 They _____ damage the evidence.
6 They _____ study science.

2 Choose the correct verbs.

1 You *mustn't / don't have to* study law to be a forensic scientist.
2 I *must / mustn't* spend some time with my parents. I haven't seen them for ages.
3 We *mustn't / have to* commit crimes – it's against the law.
4 You *must / don't have to* turn off your mobile phone in class so that it doesn't interrupt the lesson.
5 We *mustn't / have to* have a passport to travel outside the UK.
6 I *must / don't have to* join the gym again – my membership has run out.
7 You *have to / don't have to* check your essays carefully when you've written them.
8 We *mustn't / don't have to* get up early today as it's a public holiday.

G2 **3** Rewrite these sentences without changing the meaning. Use *had to* or *could*.

1 Was it necessary to tell the police everything?
Did you have to tell the police everything?
2 He wasn't able to walk after the accident.
_____
3 Were you able to understand that lecture?
_____
4 They weren't able to collect all the evidence at the scene.
_____
5 It wasn't necessary to study Economics at school.
_____
6 I was able to speak Russian when I was a child.
_____
7 It was necessary to study Latin at our school.
_____
8 Was it necessary to spend all that money yesterday?
_____

KL **4** Complete the text with the phrases in the box.

| causes   so   This has led   This means |

We've had a lot of trouble in our town recently. A few months ago, one of the biggest supermarket companies in the country opened a huge shop in the centre of the town. [1]_____ to all kinds of problems: smaller shops have closed [2]_____ there isn't a choice of shops anymore, and a lot of people come from villages around the town to shop at the supermarket. [3]_____ that there are a lot more cars on the road, which [4]_____ a lot more noise in the town.

V1 **5** Find words in V1 for these definitions.

1 the study of living things
2 the study of the past
3 the study of illnesses and injuries
4 the study of the stars and planets
5 the study of natural forces, e.g. light and movement
6 the work of chemicals and how they change and combine
7 the science of numbers and shapes
8 the study of the production and use of money

V2 **6** Complete these sentences with words from V2.

1 Someone _____ a crime.
2 _____ go to the crime scene.
3 They take _____ from objects at the scene.
4 They collect other _____ and take it all to the crime lab.
5 The scientists at the lab _____ the evidence ...
6 ... and they _____ information about the criminals.
7 The investigators _____ the crime.

V3 **7** Match the two parts of these sentences.

1 I've always been afraid
2 He's studying the history
3 The police are interested
4 They received the report
5 The chemistry lab is separate
6 She's always been successful

a) from the rest of the school.
b) in talking to a man at the crime scene.
c) of flying.
d) of the United States.
e) in solving difficult crimes.
f) from the forensic lab.

GRAMMAR

G1 Verb patterns

We sometimes put two verbs together. When we do this, the second verb is often in the infinitive with *to*.

I **seemed to sleep** well last night.
Older people **tend to need** less sleep.

The second verb can also be in the *-ing* form.

Do you **like having** a doze after lunch?
These days, we **keep hearing** about light pollution.

When the first verb is a verb + preposition, the second verb is in the *-ing* form (because a verb after a preposition is always in the *-ing* form).

Have you **thought about changing** your job?

Here are some common verbs that follow these patterns:

Verb + infinitive with *to*	Verb + *-ing* form	Verb + preposition + *-ing* form
hope manage tend want decide need seem	keep enjoy suggest try	think about succeed in look forward to talk about

Some verbs can have either an infinitive with *to* or an *-ing* form after them, e.g. *like, hate, love*. When we use the *-ing* form with these verbs, we mean '(not) enjoy'.

I **love skiing.**
I **hate lying awake** all night.

When we use the infinitive with *to*, we say what we (don't) prefer.

I **like to go to bed** early.
I **hate to fall asleep** in the living room.

G2 Future intentions

There are different ways of talking about our plans for the future. We use the form *be going to* when we have a definite intention to do something, i.e. we are sure that we will do it, but it is not 100% fixed.

I**'m going to study** astronomy at university.
When Liam finishes the night shift, he**'s going to meet** some friends for breakfast.
I**'m not going to do** a distance-learning course.

	Subject + *be* (+ *not*)		Verb
+	I'm		
	He's / She's / It's		
	You're / We're / They're	going to	start …
–	I'm not		
	He / She / It isn't		
	You / We / They aren't		
?	*be* + subject		
	Am I		
	Is he / she / it	going to	start …?
	Are you / we / they		

We can also talk about plans with *hope to* and *would like to*. These are less certain than *going to* – we use them for ambitions and desires.

Sandra **would like to leave** the post office and find another job.
We **hope to buy** a new house next year.

Note how we form the questions and negatives of these verbs.

Would you like to travel round the world?
Do you hope to have children one day?

I **wouldn't like to work** at night.
I **hope not to be** late tomorrow. ✓
I ~~**don't hope to be**~~ late tomorrow. ✗

KEY LANGUAGE

KL1 Asking about preferences

What would you prefer to do?
What would you rather do?

KL2 Expressing preferences

I'd rather (go to the concert).
I'd prefer to (see a film).
I'm more interested in (the cinema) than (the theatre).
I'd love to (see the drummers).
I don't fancy (that film).
I don't mind.
I'm not keen (on concerts).

VOCABULARY

V1 Sleep

doze, dream, fall asleep, feel sleepy, sleep in, sleep through, sleepless

V2 -ed/-ing adjectives

amazed/amazing, bored/boring, depressed/depressing, embarrassed/embarrassing, excited/exciting, fascinated/fascinating, frightened/frightening, interested/interesting, tired/tiring

V3 Social activities

boat trip, cinema, concert, dancing, dinner, firework display, museum, sports event, theatre

V4 Time expressions

after some time, at last, at that moment, before long, finally, in the end, soon, suddenly

Extra practice

G1 **1** Choose the correct form.

1 I tend *to dream / dreaming* a lot when I'm away from home.
2 Karen really enjoys *to study / studying* literature.
3 You seem *to have / having* a high temperature.
4 You should think about *to be / being* more active.
5 I keep *to fall / falling* asleep after lunch.
6 She wants *to get / getting* a job with a TV company.
7 We're really looking forward to *go / going* on the boat trip.
8 What did the doctor suggest *to do / doing*?
9 The children were at a friend's so we managed *to sleep / sleeping* in on Sunday.
10 We're talking about *to go / going* to the firework display. Do you want to come?

G2 **2** Complete Janine's list of hopes, desires and intentions for the next year. Use the correct form of *hope, would like* or *going to*.

✓✓✓ = intention   ✓✓ = desire   ✓ = hope
1 I'm going to read 'A Brief History of Time'. ✓✓✓
2 _____ pass my final exams in June. ✓
3 _____ save money for a summer holiday. ✓✓✓
4 _____ spend the summer in France. ✓✓
5 _____ watch the tennis at Wimbledon in June. ✓
6 _____ find a really good job after the summer. ✓✓
7 _____ be nicer to my little brother. ✓✓✓
8 _____ move to a different city. ✓

3 Write three sentences about your hopes, desires and intentions for the future.

1 I hope _____ .
2 I would _____ .
3 I'm (not) going to _____ .

KL1,2 **4** Complete the conversation at a job centre with the words in the box.

fancy   interested   mind   prefer   rather

A: So, you want a job that you can do at night.
B: That's right.
A: OK, well, there's a job here as a security guard.
B: On, no, I don't ¹_____ that. It sounds dangerous.
A: Right. Something less dangerous … let's see. What about working in a call centre?
B: Mmm, no. Boring.
A: Well, what kind of job would you ²_____ to do?
B: I don't ³_____ , really, but I'm more ⁴_____ in working outside.
A: Outside? Do you drive?
B: Yes, I do.
A: OK … lorry driver?
B: Well … I think I'd ⁵_____ drive a car …

V1 **5** Complete these sentences with words and phrases from V1.

1 When you're in a deep sleep, you can _____ most noises.
2 It's very depressing if you have a completely _____ night.
3 It can be very good for you to _____ for half an hour after lunch.
4 If you can't _____ at first, it's a good idea to get up and have a hot drink.
5 I always _____ when I watch TV late at night.

V2 **6** The underlined adjectives are all in the wrong sentences. Correct them.

1 Playing tennis for three hours is really <u>bored</u>!   *tiring*
2 I'm always very <u>embarrassed</u> after a long meeting.
3 I'm sure that working in a call centre is extremely <u>frightening</u>.
4 Forgetting an old friend's birthday is very <s>tiring</s>.
5 Being alone in a strange town at night can be <u>embarrassing</u>.
6 Children get <u>frightened</u> when they don't have anything to do.
7 I was <u>tired</u> and didn't want to go to sleep after the horror film.
8 I was so <u>boring</u> when I fell over in the street the other day.

V3 **7** Which activity in V3 would be good for:

1 a family who like doing things on water?
2 someone who likes stories and cultural events?
3 a couple who want to be active?
4 a teenager who likes pop groups?
5 someone who wants to learn about the past?
6 people who like good food?

V4 **8** Complete the text with the time expressions in the box.

after some time   at that moment   before long   Finally   suddenly

In my last year at university, I shared a small flat with a friend. One night I was sleeping when ¹_____ I woke up, feeling frightened. I didn't know why I was feeling frightened, but ²_____ , I heard a loud crash from the living room. I waited and waited, and ³_____ ,
I decided to find out what was happening. I went to the living room but I didn't want to go in, so I stood behind the door for ages. ⁴_____ , I stepped into the room and switched the light on. My friend was on the floor, asleep. I spoke to him and shook him, and, ⁵_____ , he woke up. Then he told me that he often walked in his sleep and fell over chairs or tables without even noticing!

Language reference

GRAMMAR

G1 used to

Use *used to* + infinitive to talk about habits and states that happened in the past, and which usually do not happen now.

> We **used to have** long lunch breaks but now we have short breaks.
>
> I **used to enjoy** working here, but I don't now.

! There is no present form of *used to*.

> I ~~use to~~ work late every day in this job. ✗
>
> I work late every day in this job. ✔

We can always use the past simple instead of *used to* but we do not use *used to* for single past actions (i.e. that happened only once).

> I travelled to China for work once. ✔
>
> I ~~used to travel~~ to China for work once. ✗
>
> I used to travel to China for work. (= a lot of times)

Form the negative and questions with *did*.

		Subject	(*not*) *used to*	Main verb
+		I / you / he / she / it / we / they	used to	work.
–			didn't (did not) use to	
?	Did		use to	work?

! Note the spelling of *use to* in negatives and questions.

> We **didn't use to have** many employees then.
>
> **Did** you **use to have** a big office?

Form short answers with *did*.

> Yes, we **did**. / No, we **didn't**.

! Do not confuse the past simple and past participle of the verb *use* with *used to*.

> We **used to spend** our summer holidays by the sea. (= *used to*)
>
> I **used** the phone while you were out. (= past simple of *use*)

G2 Present simple passive

We often use the passive when we want to focus on the object of an active sentence. We do this by putting the object at the beginning of the sentence.

> **A lot of jewellery** is made from gold.

The subject of an active sentence becomes the agent of the passive sentence, and we use *by* to introduce it.

active
subject   object
↓   ↓

Children in India make these clothes.

passive
subject   agent
↓   ↓

These clothes are made by children in India.

We often use the passive when the agent is unknown or when it is unnecessary (because it is obvious).

> The gold **is brought** to Europe. (= We don't know the agent.)
>
> Silver **is used** in jewellery a lot too. (= The agent is obvious.)

Form the passive with the auxiliary verb *be* + past participle.

	(*be*)	Subject	*be* + *not*	Past participle
+		I	am	
		He / She / It	is	
		You / We / They	are	employed.
–		I	'm not (am not)	
		He / She / It	isn't (is not)	
		You / We / They	aren't (are not)	
?	Am	I		
	Is	he / she / it		employed?
	Are	you / we / they		

KEY LANGUAGE

KL Negotiating

That seems a bit/rather (high/low).
I'm not sure we can (pay that much).
How about ($100 each)?
If you order (1,000), we can (offer 15%).
What about if we (order 750)?
That sounds fine.
Shall we call it ($87)?

VOCABULARY

V1 Work

colleague, department, employee, industry, long service, lunch break, market leader, promotion, report, staff, training course, work as a team

V2 Import-export

buyer, delivery, discount, export, import, manufacturer, price, quantity, retailer, supply

V3 Compound nouns

airline, chat room, newspaper, orange juice, suitcase, video shop

V4 Sequencing phrases

after (five) to (six) days, following that, lastly, next, to begin with

Extra practice

9

G1 **1 Read this short text about a company. Then complete the sentences 1–5 with the correct form of *used to*.**

When I was younger, I worked for a really good company, for a few weeks a year. I wanted to work for it after I left university, but it closed a few years ago. The business was importing books from the USA – only educational books. I worked there in the holidays when I was at college, so the books were very useful for me. We could take copies of any book we wanted, but I only took about three or four while I was there. The only problem was that the money wasn't very good, but it helped to get me through my studies!

1 The writer _____ work for an import company.
2 It _____ import books from Europe.
3 It _____ import educational books.
4 The writer _____ take lots of books.
5 The money _____ be very good.

2 There are mistakes in six of these sentences. Find the mistakes and correct them.

1 We used to work very late but we don't now.
2 The company use to pay very good money.
3 I didn't used to work very hard.
4 I used to go on a long business trip to Korea last year.
5 I also went to Hong Kong several times.
6 Did you used to travel a lot on business?
7 We used have longer holidays than we do now.
8 'Did you use to work harder?' 'Yes, we used.'

G2 **3 Choose the correct form.**

1 This company *imports / is imported* diamonds. Most of the diamonds *import / are imported* from the Netherlands.
2 One of the shops in the village *sells / is sold* lovely chocolates. The chocolates *make / are made* by hand.
3 We can *book / is booked* hotels and flights for you. All the booking *does / is done* online.
4 The offices *clean / are cleaned* every evening. The cleaners *come / are come* at eight o'clock.

4 Look at these pairs of sentences. Which is better, the active or passive version?

1 a) Mum makes dinner for the family every evening.
  b) Dinner is made for the family every evening.
2 a) Oil is very important. Dead plants and animals make it.
  b) Oil is very important. It is made from dead plants and animals.
3 a) The cleaners don't clean the office on Sundays.
  b) The office isn't cleaned on Sundays.

KL **5 Complete these mini-dialogues with phrases from KL.**

1 A: We'd like $50.00 for each camera.
  B: _____ . They're only $70.00 in the shops!
2 A: _____ 200, we can offer 20%.
  B: That isn't possible. We only want 100 of them.
3 A: Can you offer a 25% discount?
  B: No, I'm afraid not. _____ 15%?
4 A: If you order 500, we can sell them at $5.00 each.
  B: No, _____ . We can't afford more than $3.50 each.
5 A: _____ $250 each?
  B: _____ . We accept that offer.

V1,2 **6 Find words in V1 and V2 for these definitions.**

1 the person or people who make the products
2 the people that you work with
3 one person who works for a company
4 the person who sells the products
5 the person who finds the products for a shop to sell

V1,2,3 **7 Complete the puzzle with the first part of the compound nouns below.**

(crossword puzzle)

Across	Down
3 ____ room	1 ____ shop
4 ____ service	2 ____ leader
5 ____ course	4 ____ break

V4 **8 Choose the correct phrase 1–5.**

It's easy to make your own paper. [1]*To begin with / Lastly*, take some ordinary paper and tear it into small pieces. Put it in water until it is soft. [2]*Following this / To begin with*, change the water and mix the paper and water in a food processor until the mixture is thick (the pulp). [3]*Lastly / Next*, put the pulp in a bowl with more clean water and mix it well. Put the mixture on a square mould, like a shallow box, and add any 'personal' decorations to your paper, e.g. leaves. Put heavy books on top of the mould. [4]*After / Next* about 30 minutes, take the books off. [5]*Lastly / Next*, put the paper in a warm place until it is completely dry.

10 Language reference

GRAMMAR

G1 Present continuous for future arrangements

We can use the present continuous to talk about the future.

What **are** you **doing** on Friday evening?
We**'re having dinner** with my husband's boss.
We **aren't meeting** him until 9.00.

→ irregular verb list, page 166

When we use the present continuous for the future, we are certain that the action will happen.

The taxi**'s coming** at six o'clock. (= We've booked the taxi.)
The minister **is giving** a speech tomorrow morning. (= It's organised.)

We often use the present continuous when we have made arrangements, so we usually give a time or mention other people.

I**'m meeting** Melanie at the theatre this evening.

There is very little difference between the present continuous and *going to*.

I**'m having** a tennis lesson tomorrow afternoon.
We**'re going to spend** the weekend by the sea.

G2 Past simple passive

We use the passive when we want to focus on the object of an active sentence.

→ present simple passive, page 142

We often use the past simple passive to talk about the history of something.

The first car **was designed** in Germany, but the first car for the general public **was made** in the USA.

The important information is what happened, not who did the action. If we want to mention the agent, we use *by*.

The Sony Walkman **was produced** in Japan. It **was invented by** Akio Morita.

We often use the passive when the agent is not known, not important or obvious.

The book **wasn't published** on time.
The new James Bond film **was released** last month.
The new Microsoft software **was launched** in May.

Form the past simple passive with *was/were* + past participle.

When **was** the first Harry Potter book **published**?
It **was published** in 1997.

Was the new car a success?
No, it **wasn't liked** by the public at all.

KEY LANGUAGE

KL Adding emphasis

Adverbs
It's just a few minutes from the centre.
We're only a few days from the start.

Adjectives
It will be a magical experience.
The village will have magnificent facilities and world-class hotels.
There will be a spectacular opening ceremony.

VOCABULARY

V1 People and organisations
ambassador, assistant, civil servant, committee, department, head of department, minister, president, spokesperson, staff

V2 Adjectives
comfortable, comprehensive, easy, electrifying, fantastic, high-speed, magical, magnificent, memorable, modern, quick, spacious, spectacular, world-class

V3 Linkers
although, on the other hand, therefore

Extra practice

10

G1 **1** Write present continuous sentences from these prompts.

1 minister / fly / Geneva tomorrow

_____

2 you / stay / at / Hilton Hotel / this week?

_____

3 I / give / talk / on education this afternoon

_____

4 situation / get / worse

_____

5 they / not / build / new stadium / next year's Olympics

_____

6 the president / come / to / conference?

_____

2 Now decide whether the sentences in Exercise 1 refer to the future or the present. Write *F* or *P*.

G2 **3** Complete these sentences with the past simple active or passive of the verbs.

1 The Internet company lastminute.com _____ in 1997. (set up)

2 It _____ by two business partners: Martha Lane-Fox and Brent Hoberman. (start)

3 The company _____ by finding last-minute holidays for people. (begin)

4 But it soon _____ into finding hotels, theatre tickets and even restaurants for people. (move)

5 Martha Lane-Fox _____ the company at the end of 2003. (leave)

6 She _____ in a car crash in Morocco in 2004. (almost kill)

7 She _____ from her injuries over the next year. (recover)

8 Lastminute.com _____ to Travelocity, another Internet travel company, in 2005. (sell)

4 Is the agent necessary in these sentences? If not, cross it out.

1 The company was started in 1999 ~~by its founders~~.

2 Microsoft Vista was launched in 2007 by Microsoft.

3 'Guernica' was painted by Picasso.

4 The name of the new Secretary General was announced yesterday by the present Secretary General.

5 The story was published by a popular newspaper.

6 The new building was finished in time for the conference by builders.

KL **5** Put these words in the correct order.

1 will   tickets   £30.00   cost   only

_____

2 hotels   built   world-class   they   six   have

_____

3 the   minutes   hotel   new   a   just   station   is   few   the   from

_____

4 was   experience   a   it   memorable

_____

5 only   walk   the   a   station   short   stadium   is   from   the

_____

6 new   view   give   a   will   stadium   magnificent   of   events   the   the

_____

V1 **6** Which job has each of the new members of the government got? Match these descriptions with the jobs below.

1 Marcus Antrim will work for the government in New York.

2 Geraldine Smith has the top job in economics.

3 Alistair Frank helps Geraldine Smith.

4 John Wilson has the most important job in the department that works with schools and universities.

5 Janet Laurence has a desk job, working for John Wilson.

6 Alison MacDonald gives the government's opinions to the newspapers.

a) Minister of Education
b) Civil Servant in Education Department
c) Head of Finance Department
d) Assistant to Head of Finance
e) Press spokesperson
f) Ambassador

V2 **7** The underlined adjectives are all in the wrong sentences. Correct them.

1 Your report was excellent. It covered everything and was really <u>spacious</u>.

2 The French <u>world-class</u> train is much faster than the British one.

3 I'm sure I'll sleep better in our new bed – it's much more <u>fantastic</u> than the old one.

4 A capital city needs lot of <u>high-speed</u> hotels these days.

5 Karen's new apartment is very <u>comprehensive</u>.

6 Thanks for inviting us to your party – we had a <u>comfortable</u> time.

V3 **8** Complete these sentences with *although*, *on the other hand* or *therefore*.

1 It was very cold yesterday, _____ it was very sunny.

2 My job is not very challenging. _____, I have decided to find something more suitable.

3 In some ways Julian is very pleasant. _____, he is sometimes aggressive.

4 _____ my new flat has only two rooms, it's very spacious.

GRAMMAR

G1 Present perfect continuous

Use the continuous form of the present perfect to talk about actions that began in the past and are still continuing.

I've **been working** in this company since 2002.

The action can be continuous or repeated.

The climate **has been changing** recently.
We've **been taking** measurements of sea ice.

We often use *for* and *since* with the present perfect continuous with action verbs.

He's **been making** TV programmes for ten years.
I've **been watching** his documentary series since January.

→ present perfect with *for* and *since*, page 132

Do not use the present perfect continuous with state verbs, i.e. verbs that describe feelings and situations. Use the present perfect simple with these verbs.

I've **known** my friend in New York for ages. ✓
I've **been knowing** my friend in New York for ages. ✗

Other verbs like this are *be, have, want, understand.*

There **has been** a drought in east Africa all year.
I've **had** this job for a long time now.

! The verb *have* can be a state verb (meaning *own*) or an action verb (meaning *experience* or *take*).
We've **been having** problems with floods recently.

Form the present perfect continuous with the verb *have* + *been* + *-ing* form of the main verb.

(have)	Subject	have (+ not)	been	-ing form
+	I / You / We / They	've (have)		working.
	He / She / It	's (has)		
−	I / you / we / they	haven't (have not)	been	
	He / She / It	hasn't (has not)		
?	Have	I / you / we / they		working?
	Has	he / she / it		

G2 Phrasal verbs

Phrasal verbs are combinations of a verb and one or two other words, often prepositions. These other words are called particles. Here are some common phrasal verbs:

verb	particle
cut	down
find	out
give	back
throw	away

I really must **cut down** my smoking!
We don't **throw** any paper **away**.

Phrasal verbs often have a different meaning from the verb on its own.

cut down = reduce
find out = discover

Phrasal verbs can be intransitive or transitive. Intransitive verbs do not need an object, e.g. *go up.*

Prices **have been going up.**

Transitive verbs, e.g. *give out, throw away,* need an object.

The man was **giving out leaflets** in the high street.
Don't **throw that book away**!

When a phrasal verb has a noun as the object, we can put the noun after the verb or after the particle.

Supermarkets **give out** a lot of plastic bags.
Supermarkets **give** a lot of plastic bags **out**.

When the object is a pronoun, it goes after the verb.

Can you **give** these **out**?

KEY LANGUAGE

KL Asking for confirmation: question tags

That's quite normal, isn't it?
There are a couple of other problems, aren't there?
The project solves a problem, doesn't it?
We haven't seen that before, have we?
You can't get greener than that, can you?
They could do it unpaid, couldn't they?

VOCABULARY

V1 Global and local environment

Arctic, coral reef, derelict, drought, dump, extreme weather, glacier, global warming, graffiti, rainforest, rubbish, run-down, scruffy, sea ice, sea levels, temperature, wasteland, well-kept

V2 Containers

bottle, box, can, carton, jar, packet, pot, tin, tube

V3 Materials

aluminium, cardboard, glass, metal, paper, plastic

Extra practice

11

G1 **1** Write sentences from these prompts, using the present perfect continuous and *for* or *since*.

1 sea levels / rise / many years.
   Sea levels have been rising for many years.

2 we / recycle / plastic / 1995
   _____

3 Arctic ice / melt quickly / the last few years
   _____

4 I / reuse / plastic bags / a few years
   _____

5 the car industry / reduce / fuel pollution / the 1980s
   _____

6 global warming / harm / the Earth / a long time
   _____

2 Choose the correct form.

1 We've *had / been having* solar panels for five years.

2 Phil doesn't have a car – he's *hired / been hiring* cars since he passed his test.

3 Maria hasn't *been / been being* happy since she left her last job.

4 I've *saved / been saving* money for my holiday since March.

5 How long have you *known / been knowing* your teacher?

6 The forest has *burnt / been burning* for ten days.

7 I've *used / been using* the Internet a lot recently.

8 I haven't *understood / been understanding* anything in this documentary so far.

3 Complete these sentences so that they are true for you.

1 I've been learning _____ *for / since* _____ .

2 I've known _____ *for / since* _____ .

3 I've been coming to this school *for/since* _____ .

4 I've had _____ *for / since* _____ .

5 I've been reading _____ *for / since* _____ .

6 I've been working _____ *for / since* _____ .

4 Compare your sentences with a partner.

G2 **5** Complete these sentences with the verbs and particles in the boxes. Change the form where necessary.

Verbs: carry   cut   find   ~~go~~   pick   set   throw   write

Particles: away   down   down   ~~into~~   out   out   up   up

1 A lot of thought *goes into* food packaging.

2 They _____ _____ research into global warming at the moment.

3 Supermarkets should _____ _____ the quantity of packaging that they use.

4 My friends want to _____ _____ a paper recycling business.

5 Can you _____ _____ some information about nuclear power for me?

6 We _____ _____ so much rubbish when we were younger – now we recycle more.

7 _____ that litter _____ ! We don't want rubbish on the streets here.

8 I know I _____ _____ your phone number but I can't find it anywhere.

6 Correct the mistakes in these sentences.

1 Are those your socks on the floor? Pick up them!

2 The price of petrol has been up going recently.

3 Can you give back me that book on recycling?

4 The founders of IBM have up set a new business.

5 Do you away throw old things?

KL **7** Match these statements and question tags.

1 The train's going to leave on time,

2 You can't recycle glass bottles here,

3 They've rebuilt the community centre,

4 Recycled paper doesn't cost more than ordinary paper,

5 They haven't burnt the evidence,

6 This isn't the cause of the problem,

7 Your idea really solves the problem,

8 You can get a discount if you return the bottles,

a) can you?	e) have they?
b) can't you?	f) haven't they?
c) does it?	g) is it?
d) doesn't it?	h) isn't it?

V1 **8** Circle the odd one out.

1 drought   glacier   extreme weather

2 Arctic   rainforest   rubbish

3 sea ice   graffiti   rubbish

4 coral reef   wasteland   glacier

5 well-kept   run-down   derelict

6 sea ice   sea level   rainforest

V2,3 **9** Unjumble the anagrams to make containers and materials.

1 Soft drinks usually come in MNAIIMLUU SNAC.

2 ARJS are usually made of SLASG.

3 REPPA has a lot of uses.

4 We can buy milk in TOTLEBS or CRANOTS.

5 A lot of BEXOS are made from DRACDRABO.

6 I'd like a BUTE of toothpaste.

GRAMMAR

G1 Second conditional

We use the second conditional to talk about the result of an action. The action is unreal, i.e. it can't happen or is very unlikely to happen.

If we practised more, we would be better at hockey. (= We don't practice, so we aren't good at hockey.)
If we had more time, we would practise. (= We don't have the time, so we don't practise.)
If I was rich, I'd buy a sailing boat. (= I'm not rich, so I can't buy a sailing boat.)

! It is also possible to use *If I / he / she* **were** in the second conditional.
If **she were** younger, she'd become a sports teacher.
If **I were** you, I'd start taking some exercise.

We can also use the second conditional to talk about possible future actions, but the actions are unlikely to happen.
What would you do if you won a million dollars?
If I won a million dollars, I wouldn't go to work any more!

If-clause (condition),	main clause (result)
If + past simple,	*would / wouldn't +* infinitive without *to*
If they **showed** more interest,	they'**d** (*would*) get more help.
If I **didn't** get the job,	I'**d** (*would*) be really unhappy.

! We usually put a comma after the *if*-clause.

We can also use *might* or *could* in the main clause.
If they spent more money on sports, we **might win** more medals.
If you stayed with me in the summer, we **could visit** Athens together.

We can put the main clause first. If we do this, we don't use a comma.
They'd spend more money if people showed more interest.

G2 *too* and *enough*

Use *too much/many* + noun to mean 'more than we need or want'.
We've spent **too much money**.
There are **too many adverts** on TV.

Use *enough* + noun to mean 'the correct amount'.
I've had **enough chocolate cake** for now, thank you.

Use *not enough* + noun to mean 'less/fewer than we need/want'.
There aren't **enough opportunities** for women. (= fewer than we want)

Use *too much* with uncountable nouns and *too many* with countable nouns.
I've got **too much work** at the moment.
This company has got **too many problems**!

Use *(not) enough* with both countable and uncountable nouns.
We didn't have **enough good sportspeople** at the last games.
Have you got **enough time**?

We can also use *too* and *(not) ... enough* with adjectives.
Mark doesn't do any sport. He's **too lazy**.
James will win the race. He's **fast enough**.
Gill won't pass the exam. She's **not clever enough**.

! Be careful of the word order with *too* and *enough*.
too much / too many / enough + noun: We haven't got **enough people** for the team.
too + adjective: I'm **too tired**.
adjective + *enough*: You aren't **quick enough**.

KEY LANGUAGE

KL Conversation fillers

Let me see/think, ...
Well, ...
I think I'd ...
That's a difficult one.
To be honest, I'd ...

VOCABULARY

V1 Sports
archery, badminton, cycling, dragon boat racing, fencing, football, gymnastics, hockey, judo, sailing, table tennis

V2 Personality types
careful, cautious, competitive, individualistic, non-competitive, risk-seeking, self-sufficient, sociable

G1 **1** Match the two halves of the second conditional sentences.

1 If I needed more money for my sport,
2 I would get a lot fitter,
3 Our players might win more matches,
4 If more people were interested in this sport,
5 We would host a dragon boat festival
6 What would you do

a) I'd try to get funding from a company.
b) it would receive more funding.
c) if they practised more seriously.
d) if you won a lot of money?
e) if I played more sport.
f) if we thought enough boats would enter.

2 Complete the text with the correct form of the verbs.

What ¹___ you ___ (do) if you ²___ (not have) enough money to continue your sports club?

I'm in that position now. I run a badminton club and we're in danger of closing because we don't have enough members. If we ³___ (have) more members, we ⁴___ (get) enough money to pay the sports centre that we play in. They've put their prices up – if their prices ⁵___ (not be) so high, we ⁶___ (be) in a better position. If we ⁷___ (not have to) spend all our money on paying for the club, we ⁸___ (have) enough money to advertise for more members. The other problem is insurance – we have to have insurance and that costs money too. If we ⁹___ (not have) insurance, we ¹⁰___ (have to) pay a lot of money if someone had an accident.

One way of getting more members would be to accept any players into the club, but if we ¹¹___ (do) that, we ¹²___ (get) people who can't play well enough. Can you give me any advice?

G2 **3** There are mistakes in four of these sentences. Find the mistakes and correct them.

1 We can't get funding enough for our club.
2 There are too much aspects to this problem.
3 They aren't showing enough interest in our idea.
4 Most of our players aren't enough competitive to win.
5 I can't play another game. I'm too tired.
6 There are too many adverts for expensive trainers on TV.
7 It costs much too money to do this sport.
8 My sports psychologist told me I wasn't risk-seeking enough.

KL **4** Complete the conversation with the phrases in the box.

> I think I'd   Let me   to be honest,
> That's a difficult one.   Well,

A: My doctor thinks I should do more sport, to get fitter. What do you think I should do?
B: ¹___ You're not really sporty, are you?
A: ²___ I'm not sure about that! I walk to work.
B: It's five minutes away! What would you like to try?
A: ³___ see. I was thinking about sailing.
B: Sailing?
A: Don't you think it's a good idea?
B: Well, ⁴___ I'd try something a bit easier at first.
A: What would you suggest?
B: ⁵___ prefer to learn something like archery.
A: Oh, I don't think so! I wouldn't get enough exercise from that!
B: I know! What about cycling? It's really good exercise and you can do it anywhere …
A: Yes, but I haven't got a bike!

V1 **5** Find the sports in V1 for these descriptions.

1 It's played by two teams of eleven people.
2 This involves a lot of people on a river.
3 This can be played with two or four people. It's very fast.
4 This is like a fight between two people, with no equipment.
5 This is usually done on the sea. You can do it alone or with other people.
6 You can do this alone or with others. You have to have bikes.

V2 **6** Choose the correct adjectives 1–4 in this job advert for a tennis instructor.

> **We are looking for the right person to teach the tennis stars of the future.**
>
> You will work on your own and be responsible for all the tennis instruction at the club so you must be ¹*competitive / self-sufficient*. We need a ²*sociable / risk-seeking* person who will spend a lot of time with our young people, both playing tennis and socially. You will need all your skills to teach the children to be ³*competitive / non-competitive* in their matches. You will need to try new ways of teaching and take risks in this job, so we can't accept candidates who are too ⁴*risk-seeking / cautious*.

AUDIOSCRIPTS

CD 1

Lesson 1.1 Track 1.2

Reporter, Man, Woman, Chief of police

R: Only two things are happening in Florida right now, waiting or leaving. The people of Florida are either waiting for Hurricane Helen, or they're leaving in their cars.

M: I'm staying here. I have a lot of food in my house and, at the moment, I'm covering the windows with wood. I know about the danger, especially after Hurricane Katrina, but, well, I'm not leaving.

W: I'm getting out of here. They're saying that this is a really dangerous hurricane and I don't want to meet it. Of course, the roads are really busy because many people are leaving.

R: The hurricane's moving north across the Caribbean Sea and it's coming towards Florida. Strong winds and heavy rain are hitting the coast, and the hurricane is getting bigger and faster. It's now a category four hurricane, which means the wind speed is 100 kilometres per hour … I'm now in the police station with the chief of police.

C: Our emergency plan's going well. As you know, we often get hurricanes in Florida so we know what to do. We do this kind of thing every year, and this summer is no different. On the streets, my men are doing their jobs and they're checking that people are safe. Each year some people leave the area, and others stay. Either way, we always help everyone.

R: Hurricane Helen is a very strong hurricane. And the question is – why are there more strong hurricanes every year? Research shows that the number of strong hurricanes is increasing and that they're getting stronger. Some scientists say this is because of global warming. The sea's getting hotter and warm seas cause hurricanes. The American government doesn't agree with this connection between global warming and hurricanes. Right now though, the people of Florida are just trying to save their houses and their lives. This is Joanne Webb, live from Florida. Back to Nick in the studio.

Lesson 1.3 Track 1.3

Simon, Diana

S: So, Diana, any thoughts?

D: Well, I like the sound of Argentina. I think the Antarctic wildlife cruise is a great idea.

S: Mmm, so do I. It's unusual and everyone loves penguins. Em, any problems with this trip?

D: Well, I suppose the season for the Antarctic trips is short; November to February – that's only about four months long.

S: Yeah, I agree, and I don't like the weather in the mountains.

D: No, neither do I. It's windy and changeable in the summer. But is that a problem for our customers? They like adventure after all!

S: True, but it's not nice walking in the wind all the time. In fact I don't like the activities – they're very ordinary.

D: Don't you? I do. Horse riding is always popular and everyone can go trekking. I think those activities are fine, especially if we want to attract first-timers.

S: Well, I'm not sure. I think our customers want new activities, or unusual ones. Anyway, what about Belize?

D: Well, I think this is excellent because the activities look interesting.

S: And exciting.

D: Exactly. Diving in clear blue water, white-water rafting. In fact, I don't think there are any problems with the activities.

S: Neither do I. But what about the weather? When's the best time to go?

D: Well, I think the trips should be in the dry season.

S: Yes, so do I, especially because of the hurricanes in the rainy season.

D: Yes, and also it's a little cooler from November to May.

S: So, how long is the holiday season? Let's see, er, November, December, January, February, March, April, May … How many's that?

D: Seven months. I think that's good.

S: Do you? I'm not sure. In the USA, the holiday seasons are longer. And also, I don't want to offer trips anywhere near the hurricane season. You know that hurricanes are getting stronger and stronger and, well, we don't know what's happening really.

D: Sure, so, let's say the holiday season is six months long.

S: OK. Fine. So, which do you prefer?

D: Personally, I prefer Belize to Argentina.

S: Mmm, so do I, but the Antarctic cruise is a great idea. Let's look at the other two, and then decide.

Lesson 2.1 Track 1.6

Journalist, Interpreter

J: Chimokel, did you want to become an athlete when you left school?

I: Oh, no, I didn't. I come from a very poor place and my mother died when I was sixteen, so I left school and then I married Benjamin a year later, in 1995. I didn't think about running or sport at that time. I had a lovely husband, a home, and then I became a mother. I have four beautiful boys.

J: So, why did you start running?

I: We are a poor family: we have just a few animals – three sheep and seven chickens, in fact – and a little land for potatoes. We're a hard-working family, but in our local area most people earn under a dollar a day. So, we didn't have any money, but we wanted to send our boys to school. Then, last year, my neighbour told me about the running races and the prize money. So, I decided to start running, and here I am now!

J: How did you train and look after the children at the same time?

I: My husband Benjamin was very helpful. I trained every morning; I ran in the hills and Benjamin made breakfast for the boys. They're very young – the oldest is only nine – so it wasn't easy for my husband. But he didn't get angry; he always smiled! He's a patient, friendly man. And last week he sold one of his sheep and a chicken to pay for my ticket to come to Nairobi. He helped me very much – he's very kind.

J: Did you win much money yesterday?

I: Oh, yes, I did. Oh, a lot, a lot. A lot for me and my family. I won $12,000. It's incredible. I still can't believe that I won the race. Now we can send our children to a good school. When we were young, we didn't have the chance to finish our education, but perhaps our children can go to university.

J: Was this marathon your last race?

I: Oh, I don't think so! They want me to race in Europe next year! Can you imagine? I live in a tiny village in the Kenyan countryside, and they want me to run in Paris and London. I hope I can take my family, and that we don't need to sell any more sheep and chickens.

Lesson 2.2 Track 1.9

1 I was singing.
2 – Was she eating?
    – Yes, she was.
3 We were studying.
4 – Were they running?
    – Yes, they were.
5 He was painting.
6 – Was she working?
    – Yes, she was.
7 Where was he living?
8 – Were they telling jokes?
    – Yes, they were.
9 Why were they helping him?
10 What were you reading?

AUDIOSCRIPTS

Track 1.10

I'd like to invite Louis Armstrong because I think he was the greatest musician ever. I know that his early life was very hard – he came from a very poor family in New Orleans. But he had amazing energy and abilities. He could sing, play instruments and dance. He made many records and he changed jazz – he made it into an art. So, he had a big influence on the history of jazz, blues and pop. Erm … he was also a generous man. For example, later in his life, when he was rich, he gave a lot of money to poor children – so they could learn music. Er … so, I'd like to invite Louis Armstrong because he brought happiness and pleasure to millions of people. What would I like to ask him? Well, erm, perhaps this: How did you feel when you were eight years old, and you were singing in the streets of New Orleans for money?

Lesson 2.3 Track 1.14

Stephanie, Xu Ming

s: Hello.

x: Hi Stephanie, it's Xu Ming.

s: Oh, hi. How are you? How did the interviews go?

x: Oh, I'm fine. The interviews were fine too. Have you got ten minutes or are you busy?

s: I'm fine for time. Tell me about the people. Who did you see first?

x: Well, the first person was a guy called Martin. He's a young doctor and he's Canadian.

s: Oh, that's sounds good. What's he like?

x: Well, I'm not sure. At first he wasn't very friendly and he certainly isn't chatty. He works long hours, so he's hard-working, I guess. He seems honest and tidy.

s: I see, so erm … what does he like? What are his interests?

x: Well, he likes watching sport on TV, but he doesn't play any. Er, what else? He doesn't smoke, in fact he hates smoking. Oh, he said he likes cooking, when he's got time.

s: OK, so perhaps he's a bit quiet. What does he look like? Does he look tidy and smart?

x: Well, he's a doctor, so he looks professional. He wears nice clothes. He's got short brown hair. In fact, he looks like that Hollywood actor, you know, Tom Cruise.

s: Really? I'm not sure that's a good thing! So, what do you think? Would you like to live with him?

x: Mmm, yes, I think so. I'm happy to live with a quiet person.

s: What, like me?!

x: Yeah, exactly! And I'd like to live with a Canadian, you know, my sister lives in Toronto. Also, doctors are usually honest and responsible. What about you?

s: Well … erm … he sounds quite quiet … tell me about the others first …

Lesson 2.4 Track 1.16

1

I started learning to drive when I was eighteen. I had my first lessons with my father, but he was very impatient with me. He always shouted at me when I made a mistake. So I went to a driving school instead. I wasn't a confident driver and I can still hear the words of the instructor: 'More gas! More gas!' He always wanted me to go faster. Learning to drive wasn't especially easy or difficult, but I didn't enjoy it very much. I was living in a big city and there was a lot of traffic – everyone was driving fast too. It wasn't much fun. I failed my test the first time, but I passed the second time. I didn't feel proud or excited – I was just happy it was finished.

2

I learned Russian at school. There was a teacher who taught Latin, but he also knew Russian. It was funny because I was the only student in the class – it was really a private lesson. I had an excellent coursebook. I can't remember much about it … erm … the front cover was red and it was very modern. Learning Russian was quite easy. I was surprised. The teacher was good so that helped a lot. Also, I'm quite good at learning languages. It was really enjoyable too. I loved the sound of the words. I felt really proud when I could read a short story in Russian and when I passed my exam.

Lesson 3.1 Track 1.17

Callum, Helen

c: Hi, Callum Robertson.

h: Hello Callum. Helen Francis, from *The Nation*.

c: Hi. How are you? Thanks for the email.

h: I'm fine. Thanks for agreeing to do the interview. As I mentioned in the email, it's pretty simple really. Just a few questions about the media. You can say as much or as little as you like.

c: Fine, go ahead.

h: OK … first question: which newspapers do you read?

c: I don't buy a newspaper every day because I don't really have time to read one. I cycle to work every day and it's a bit difficult to read a newspaper while you're cycling. If I travel by train, I get one of the free newspapers, like the *Metro* that we have here in London. But when I get to work we have the daily papers here, so at lunchtime, I read *The Guardian* or I have a look at one of the tabloids.

h: What about magazines?

c: I subscribe to a computer magazine, *Mac World*, because I have a Mac at home and I like to keep up with what's going on with Macs. And at work I look at some of the trade magazines and some other computer and Internet magazines, but apart from that I don't spend a lot of time with magazines.

h: Uh-huh. What do you watch on TV?

c: I watch a great deal of television. I probably watch too much television. I like documentaries and comedies. I like American drama series like *The Sopranos* and *ER* and things like that. But I do have square eyes, I think.

h: Do you ever listen to the radio, apart from the programmes you make?

c: I listen to the radio a lot. I think it's a great medium. When I'm cooking in the kitchen, I always have the radio on. When I'm in the bath, I have the radio on and when I go to sleep at night I have the radio on. And it's actually on throughout the night, and when I wake up in the morning I have the radio on. It's mainly talk radio; news station BBC Five Live is the station I tend to listen to, that or Radio 4, another BBC station. I don't listen to very much music on the radio, but I love the radio – it's great.

h: Can I ask you how you use the Internet?

c: I use the Internet a great deal. At work it's part of my job, and at home I use it a lot, obviously for email. And these days I use it for all of my banking and a lot of my shopping and so it's an indispensable tool for me now, the Internet, for business use and for personal use.

h: OK, finally, do you think the Internet is changing the way we use media? For example, do you think newspapers have a future?

c: I think the Internet allows people to get their news from different places and do research. Er, but I don't think the Internet will destroy newspapers, because having something physical in your hand, for reading and turning, is important. You can write on it, you can do the crossword on it. So, the Internet can give us a lot, but I don't think it can ever replace newspapers.

h: Great! That's it. Thanks very much.

C: My pleasure. I'm looking forward to the article!

H: Well, we can send you a copy when it's ready.

C: Thanks, Helen. Goodbye.

H: Goodbye.

Lesson 3.3 Track 1.18

Hello and welcome to *Fame and Fortune*, the programme that brings you the freshest news and views from the worlds of politics, business and entertainment. In today's programme, we interview the deputy prime minister about her sporting past and her current family life, we meet the hottest young film directors in Ireland and there's music from the chart-topping band The Hoodies. Our business specialist, Tony Cotton, visits the Google offices in the States, and Lynne Miller brings you the latest celebrity gossip. First of all, over to the news studio for the headlines of the week …

Track 1.20

Jeff, Kylie, Bill

J: OK then, Bill, Kylie, you've read the brief for the new programme. To summarise, it's a magazine-style programme with a young adult audience and it's for the early Friday evening slot. The working title is *Fame and Fortune*. Now's the time to sort out some details. Any ideas? Kylie?

K: Well Jeff, I think we should include some politics in the programme.

J: Politics? Really?

K: Yeah, I know politics is usually a turn-off for this audience, but I think we can do it in a new way.

J: Oh yes, and how do we do that?

K: Well, why don't we get some politicians on the programme? However, let's not interview them about politics. Instead, let's ask them about their lives – you know, interests, family, perhaps their life before politics.

J: OK, so er, politicians without politics.

K: Exactly.

B: I like it.

J: So do I. Anything else? Bill?

B: What about music? We should have a live band on the programme.

J: I agree, but, then again, so many programmes do that.

B: That's true, but why don't we get the band to perform three or four songs, rather than just one?

J: Nice idea, that way we get a much better idea about the band.

K: Fine, but what about the fortune part of the programme? What about interviewing rich people?

J: No, I … I don't think that's a good idea. We don't need more interviews, and rich people are often really boring. I think we should do something about high profile businesses, you know, er, like Google, Sony, Apple. You know, the big businesses that have all the exciting new ideas and products.

K: Great idea. So, we've got some politics, music and business, all with a fresh angle. I think these things are good for the target audience, but the programme is an hour long. What else shall we put in the programme?

B: What about something with animals?

K/J: Animals!?

J: And, just how are animals connected to fame and fortune exactly?

B: Well, I thought that perhaps we could find pets that have unusual talents, you know, cats that can sing. And then we could have a competition, and, you know, make them famous.

K: And you really think that young adults, after a hard week at work, are interested in that?

B: Well, I don't know, erm, well, perhaps not, erm, perhaps that's not a good idea. Why don't we …

Lesson 3.4 Track 1.22

One of the ways we like to work is by asking you to do things in pairs or small groups. Some students think this is a waste of time. They don't want to listen and talk to other students; they want to communicate with the teacher.

However, here at the York Language Centre, we believe there are many advantages to working in pairs or small groups. First, it increases the amount of time each student can talk; you can't all have long conversations with the teacher, but it is possible to have quite long conversations with your partner, and that speaking practice is important. Number two: it helps students become more confident, especially if they're a little shy about speaking in front of the whole class. Reason number three: it encourages students to become more independent learners – they're not always waiting for the teacher to tell them what to do. Number four: it provides variety in the lesson – sometimes the teacher is talking, sometimes you work in pairs or in groups, and sometimes you have a big class discussion – this makes the class more interesting. The fifth reason is that you can learn interesting things from other students, not only from the teacher! Last but not least, it gives the teacher the chance to see how everybody is working and

communicating. The teacher can go round the class and listen carefully to students and make helpful comments.

And there are probably many more reasons I haven't mentioned. So we hope that you will appreciate and enjoy working in pairs and small groups, even if you haven't learned in this way before.

Track 1.23

Roberta, Ilwoo

R: OK, so the question is: *Do you always believe the news?* Right … do you want to start?

I: Yes, alright. Er, well … it depends. I believe most of the news on TV, especially the BBC or CNN news. They're big, international organisations and a lot of people trust them, including me! I believe their websites too.

R: What do you think about newspapers? Do you believe them?

I: No, I don't believe newspapers so much. I think some of them write anything – just to sell. You know, stories about celebrities …

R: Yes, but that can be interesting sometimes when you don't want really serious news.

I: Mmm, you're right actually. It *is* sometimes interesting to read those kinds of news stories. Anyway, another thing is … the newspapers are often very political. Some are for the government, and others are against the government.

R: Absolutely. And they try to influence you.

I: I think TV news is fairer. It's more balanced. Anyway, what do you think? Do you believe the news?

R: Well, I think I agree with you, basically. I trust TV news more. But there's a special problem here in Britain, even on the TV news … you know … it's the way they talk about Europe … they seem to tell British people what they want to hear …

I: Sorry, I don't really understand. What do you mean exactly?

R: Well … when they talk about Europe in the media … it's … like it's a bad thing, you know, like it's us and them … Britain's good and Europe's bad. I'm Italian so that makes me angry.

I: So, are you saying that the British feel that they aren't really part of Europe?

R: Yes, exactly.

I: Mmm, that's an interesting point. I'm not sure I agree with you, though. Anyway, at least the British media say *something* about Europe. I never see any news about South Korea at all. My country doesn't really exist for them.

AUDIOSCRIPTS

Review Units 1–3 Track 1.24

Sally, Geoff

S: Hi, Geoff. Can I talk to you for a minute?

G: Sure, what is it?

S: Well, yesterday I met that guy Steve Giles – you know, the one I thought was a possible presenter for our new reality TV show.

G: Oh, yes. What's he like?

S: Nice. He's very polite, and cheerful ...

G: Hold on, Sally, can he present a reality TV show? I don't think we want a nice, polite person for that!

S: Don't you? Well, I'm not sure. I think the presenter has to be friendly so that people want to watch him. He's really confident too.

G: OK. What does he look like?

S: He's good-looking. He's got short dark hair, lovely eyes. He's not very smart, though, his clothes, I mean.

G: What, is he scruffy?

S: No, no, not scruffy, casual. You know, he was wearing jeans and a T-shirt. But we don't need a really smart person for this show. I think we need someone young and relaxed.

G: Yes, so do I. A lot of young people will watch it.

S: Exactly. Why don't we invite him to meet the celebrities in the show? You know, see how they all get on. I think we should arrange a meeting.

G: I don't agree, Sally. It's too soon. We don't know enough about Steve yet. What about getting him to the studio for a camera test – see how he looks on screen?

S: Oh, good idea. Let's do that. I'll ...

Lesson 4.1 Track 1.25

Extract 1

Sad news from head office concerning our work in Africa. Unfortunately, we've closed our mobile clinics in Ethiopia because of severe financial problems. Last year, we ran ten health centres in Africa but, this year, we've received very little money and we can't continue to offer medical services across the continent. We've decided to close the two Ethiopian centres and we hope to raise more money ...

Extract 2

Working here is the best thing I've ever done. When I worked in the UK I got bored with the daily routine, but out here I find every day interesting and demanding. I'm working in a small clinic in the middle of the jungle and I've never done such important work before. The villagers in this region can't get to government hospitals, so this clinic is the only hope they have. I usually do about two operations a day and, so far, in my time here, I've probably saved about a hundred lives. When your work is very important, you ...

Extract 3

The lack of food and poor diet in this region cause many of the health problems for the local people. We wanted to reduce their need for doctors like us so, on 1st January 2004, we decided to educate the local people about the effects of malnutrition. Finally, after many years of planning and raising money, in January of this year, we started a training programme. So far, we've trained 500 people. By the end of the year, that number will be 1,000. Vera is doing the course at the moment. 'This course has given me many new skills. Before, I didn't know how to help people in my village. Now, I'm sure I can make a difference.' Vera finishes the course next week and then she'll return to her village ...

Extract 4

I often work for IMA and I've worked in Kenya, Nepal and Peru. However, my current position, here in Sri Lanka, is perhaps the most difficult job I've had so far. Last year, an earthquake hit this area and this caused a massive amount of damage. I've never seen so much destruction before. I help the doctors in a couple of clinics – one here and another in a smaller village about ten kilometres away. I see people with diseases and serious injuries. Today I've seen forty patients, and I don't finish work for another four hours. These are busy days indeed. I started work at seven ...

Lesson 4.3 Track 1.26

Mary, Lucy

M: Right, now Lucy, I need to ask you a few questions. Have you seen a doctor recently?

L: No, I haven't.

M: OK. Have you had any days off sick in the last two years?

L: Erm, yes, I have ... about five, I think.

M: Right, could you tell me why?

L: Oh, just for minor things – colds and 'flu, you know the kind of thing.

M: Sure, that's fine for now, but I want to give you some advice later. OK? Do you have a back problem?

L: Er, yes, I do, actually. It's not very serious though.

M: OK, well, that's your opinion. How long have you had this problem?

L: Well, for about three years. I had a minor car accident, and since then, well, I've had this problem with my lower back.

M: I see. Well, let me know if it gets worse at work here. Do you suffer from neck pain?

L: No, I don't. The problem is just with my lower back.

M: Right. Do you have good eyesight?

L: No, I don't actually, but I wear contact lenses so there aren't any problems.

M: Fine. When did you last go to the optician's?

L: Oh, six months ago, more or less.

M: OK, the last few questions now. Do you often get headaches?

L: No, I don't.

M: Do you often get colds or 'flu?

L: No, not very often. Perhaps a couple of times a year.

M: But that means you sometimes take time off work, doesn't it?

L: Erm, yes, but not very often.

M: I know, but we can still improve things, can't we? I can give you some advice about preventing these minor illnesses.

L: OK, well, any more questions?

M: Yes, the last one. Do you sometimes get stressed by work?

L: Yes, I do! I was stressed all the time in my last job, that's why I've changed jobs, in order to reduce my stress. I hope things are better here ...

Track 1.29

Mary, David

M: So then, David, what's the matter?

D: Well, er, the thing is that, at the end of a day at work, my neck really hurts.

M: I see. Do you do a lot of computer work?

D: Well, yes, I do. I spend all day at the computer, but I take regular breaks.

M: OK, that's good, but do you stretch your arms?

D: Sorry?

M: Well, every half hour, you should stretch your arms to reduce the tension in your neck.

D: I see. Well, I can do that, I guess. Every 30 minutes?

M: Yes, and make sure you do that. Now, I see from your records that you're often off sick.

D: Well, not very often, but, yes, I seem to get a lot of colds and things.

M: I see. Can I ask about your general lifestyle? Do you eat well? Do you smoke?

D: Well, er, I don't smoke and I eat quite well.

M: That's good that you don't smoke. Do you eat a lot of fruit and vegetables?

D: Not really, especially not fruit.

M: Right, well, because you don't eat a lot of fruit, I think you should take some vitamins. You know vitamins help fight colds, don't you?

D: Sure, OK.

M: Well, if you know, why don't you take them already?

D: Well, you know, I'm very busy and …

M: No excuses, please, David. Now, you should also eat garlic because it helps fight colds too. And it should be raw when you have it, don't cook it.

D: Really? Erm, I don't really like garlic but well, er, perhaps …

M: There's no perhaps about it. The company doesn't welcome days off for colds. Now, finally, in order to improve your general health, you should do some exercise.

D: Oh, I do already. Er, I go swimming once a week.

M: Well, that's good, but you should go swimming three times a week so that it really helps your health.

D: I know, but, well, I don't really have a lot of free time, you know, we work long hours here.

M: I know, but the healthier you are, the more time you will have.

D: Er, I guess so. Er, anyway, time to get back to the computer – er, don't worry, I'll … I'll do some stretches!

M: And eat some fruit, and don't forget the garlic …

Lesson 5.1 Track 1.31

Islands have their own kind of magic, and Greenland is one of the most magical of them all. During the summer months, it's daylight a lot of the time – and it's hard to sleep! But that gives you more time to see this strange, wild and enormous place. Greenland is the biggest island in the world. It lies between the North Atlantic and Arctic Oceans, off the coast of North America. It's almost two-thirds the size of Australia; 2,655 kilometres from north to south, and 1,290 kilometres from east to west. So there's a lot of land, but it's not very green. In fact, Greenland is the least green of all the islands in today's programme. And that's because an icecap – a thick layer of ice – covers 85 per cent of Greenland. Snow falls on Greenland in every month of the year. The snow gets deeper and deeper and turns to ice. As a result, Greenland has the second largest icecap in the world, after Antarctica. On average, the ice is one and a half kilometres thick, but in some places it's thicker than that – more than three kilometres thick, in fact. And it's always moving. In large parts of the island, there are no people at all. About 55,000 people live around the coast, where the climate is less cold than in the centre. Their main work is fishing.

Madagascar is a world apart. It's the fourth largest island in the world, and lies in the Indian Ocean, off the coast of Africa. It split away from the rest of Africa about 100 million years ago. It's a land of contrasts and surprises. There's rainforest on the east coast of Madagascar. In the south it's hot and dry, but the climate is cooler in the mountains that run down the middle of the island. So some parts are less tropical than others. Most of the people are farmers, and rice is the main food. The population is about 18 million. But what makes Madagascar special is that there are unusual types of animals and plants that you can't find anywhere else in the world. The island's most famous animals are the lemurs – they look a little like monkeys and they've got long tails. But they're in danger now because people have destroyed the forests where they live. In all, about 50 kinds of wildlife are at risk on Madagascar.

Yes, it probably looks familiar … and of course it is. I'm in Trafalgar Square, in the heart of London. Sometimes it's easy to forget that Great Britain is an island, too. In fact, Great Britain is the eighth largest island in the world, and the largest in Europe. It's interesting, too, because it's actually three countries: England, Scotland and Wales. It's rich in history, and people come from all over the world to visit famous churches, museums and castles. Great Britain is more crowded than many of its European neighbours, and has a population of 60 million. But in parts it's also very beautiful. Mountains cover a lot of Scotland, where there are many long, deep lakes, called lochs. Wales and the north of England are hilly, while the south and east of England are flatter. The area around London is probably the least impressive part of Great Britain. In 1994, the Channel Tunnel opened. This rail tunnel is almost 50 kilometres long, and links England with France. It's the second longest tunnel in the world, after the Seikan tunnel in Japan. Because of the Channel Tunnel, some people think that Great Britain is no longer an island!

Lesson 5.3 Track 1.32

Katie, Neil

K: Hi Neil. Thanks for calling. Can you hear me?

N: Yes, I can. Loud and clear. How's it going over there? Having fun at the animal sanctuary?

K: Sure am, but it's hard work. But everyone's looking after me, and it's great to see the work in action. Anyway, you want to talk about the photos? I'm sorry there's no Internet connection here.

N: That's OK. Yeah, basically, I need to choose the pictures now, and I wanted to discuss my ideas with you first.

K: Fine. Fire away. Which section are you talking about?

N: Well, it's the home page link to the animal rescue page. Basically, I've got two photos of whale rescues and two of bird rescues.

K: OK.

N: So, first of all the whale rescue photos. In the first one, there are four whales that are close to the beach. Two men are pulling one of the whales off the beach, and there are loads of people in the background who are watching the rescue.

K: Fine, and the second one?

N: Well, in that one, on the left of the picture, we can see the large head of a whale. On the right, there are two people who are throwing water on the whale. I guess they're trying to keep it alive. It's a very unusual picture, the whale's head is massive. But, well, I think the first picture is the best one for the website because it shows a team of people that are working together. They look very professional and it's also more dramatic.

K: It certainly sounds good. What about the bird rescue pictures?

Track 1.33

K: What about the bird rescue pictures?

N: Sure. The first one is on the beach, and there's a man in the water. He's passing a bird to someone who's standing on the beach. The second one shows some people who are cleaning a bird. On the right, there's a woman in a blue shirt who's holding the bird. So the bird's in the middle of the picture. Then, there's another woman on the left who's cleaning the bird. She's wearing a yellow coat.

K: OK, so in the first one, are the men rescuing the bird from oily water?

N: Uh-huh. And I like that picture, I think it's more powerful than the one about the cleaning. I think it really makes you feel the terrible situation.

K: Yes, I guess so, although it's hard for me to say without seeing it. What's good about the second one?

N: Well, it shows the work that our experts do, but it's not a very interesting picture. Overall, I recommend that we use the whale rescue picture.

K: The one of the team working together?

N: Uh-huh.

K: Well, that sounds OK. Go ahead with that for the moment. We could change it quite easily in the future, couldn't we?

N: Well, we could, but I need to get something up on the site today.

K: Sure, I understand. Use the whale one and when I get back to the office, I'll let you know if there's a problem.

N: OK. You're the boss. I think you'll like this one anyway.

K: I'm sure I will. Your choices are usually spot on. Anyway, gotta go now, there's a monkey that's waiting to meet me.

N: Lucky monkey. Say hello from me! Bye for now.

K: Bye.

Lesson 5.4 Track 1.37

Tutor, Students

T: Yes, that's a very good point, Nicole. OK, now, let's have a look at the next problem. OK, it says here: 'I'm often late for appointments, or sometimes I miss appointments completely.' Would anyone like to say something about this?

S1: Yes, keep a diary which clearly shows all your appointments … and classes.

S2: That's right, but it's not enough just to have a diary. We need to make sure we look at it. Check your diary last thing at night and first thing in the morning.

T: Absolutely. You should also write all the homework you have to do in the diary – not on pieces of paper that you can lose easily. Good. Now, next problem: 'I spend a lot of time looking for my notes. I can never find anything.'

S1: Yeah, I was like that last year. The best thing is to organise your files, using colour codes and labels – so you can find things easily. I don't have any trouble anymore.

T: Thanks, Riz. So … these things show how important it is to be well-organised. OK, let's take another problem. This one says: 'I sometimes study for a long time, but I don't feel I'm learning anything. I read the material but nothing's happening – it's not going in.' Right. Has anyone got any suggestions? Yes, Tim.

S3: Basically, it isn't a good idea to study for long periods at a time without a break. It's better to do a little at a time.

T: That's right. Be nice to yourselves! When you finish something, an essay, for example, give yourselves a break, do something for fun: go for a walk, or watch a film. This can make you work better before and after the break. And another thing – it's important that you can concentrate on your studies. You can't work well when the phone's ringing every five minutes. Don't forget too, it's important to know when you study best. Do you study best in the morning, in the afternoon, in the evening or late at night? Everybody's different. We need to study at a time that suits us.

S4: Oh, that's interesting. I've never thought of that.

S5: Yeah, maybe some people study at the wrong time of day for their body clock.

T: OK, let's take another one … 'I can't finish all the things I need to do in the day.'

S1&4: Prioritise!

S4: Yes, decide what you need to do now, or later today, and what you can leave until tomorrow, or even next week.

T: Yes, good. Remember too: maybe there are some things that aren't important at all. It's a bad idea to waste time on them. And it's important to allow time for things you don't expect, and for emergencies. Perhaps this is the moment to say something about making lists. You probably make shopping lists of things you need to buy. Make a list of things you need to do as well. When you reduce all the things to one piece of paper, it doesn't seem so difficult. When you've done the things on your list, cross them off. It's a nice feeling! However, be realistic! Don't put a lot of big things on your list when you know you can't do them all. So, read one chapter of your textbook, instead of three chapters. Putting smaller things on your list means that you can achieve them, and this makes you feel good. Alright, what's the next question …?

Lesson 6.1 Track 1.38

Patrick, Susan

P: Hello, Susan. Good to see you again.

S: Hi Patrick. How are you?

P: I'm fine. Can I get you a drink? Coffee? Tea?

S: Oh, a coffee would be lovely, thanks.

P: Sure, I'll just ask Bob to do that. Bob, could you get us two coffees, please? So, what does the future hold for me?

S: Well, hopefully, good business opportunities. I've got the full report here, but I'll go through the main points first.

P: Fine. Go ahead.

S: Well, I think the two most important trends for you are about technology and age.

P: Age?

S: Yes, basically Britain is getting older. By 2025, more than a third of the UK's population will be over 55 years old. And these older people will live for much longer – we know that from the statistics. They might live until they're 95, or even 100.

P: But that definitely won't be good for business. They won't have jobs, so I'm sure they won't have much money.

S: Oh, it'll definitely be good for business. First of all, they'll retire a bit later than now, but the main point is that these people will definitely need things to do with this extra time, for sure, *and* they'll need things that improve the quality of their lives.

P: OK. Any examples?

S: Well, we predict that older people will travel more, so there'll be more companies that specialise in holidays for them. At the moment, holiday companies focus on families or young adults. But, in 2025, there'll be more elderly people, the over-65s, than under 25s. So, the party and adventure holiday market may get smaller but, for example, holidays on cruise ships will increase. They may also want activity holidays, but that'll depend on their health and on how demanding the activities are – they probably won't go bungee-jumping, but they might go hiking and sailing.

P: OK. Er, what about daily life?

S: Well, this connects to the other trend I mentioned, technology.

P: You mean the Internet?

S: Yes, indeed, and not only that, but also robots.

P: Robots?

S: Exactly. Older people want things that make life easier. In the future, they might have a robot that cleans the house, they might have a robot that drives the car, they might have a robot that does the gardening.

P: You say might, rather than will. Why's that?

S: Well, we can't be definite about this because it all depends on the technology. At the moment, robots are very basic.

P: Yes, I think there's a robot vacuum cleaner and that's about it. Oh, and robot pets.

S: Exactly, so the technology needs to improve. Perhaps it will, perhaps it won't. But, older people will definitely want robots.

AUDIOSCRIPTS

P: Mmm, that's interesting. I guess the Internet will be important.

S: Of course, or something like it. And this is the other possible area for investment. In general people will order goods and services over the Internet, and they'll meet people over the Internet. In the future, people might have more cyber friends than real friends. So, for example, we think that there'll be many companies that'll offer Internet dating services for elderly people.

P: Internet dating? For the elderly?

S: Oh yes. Love is important, however old you are. People will definitely live for longer, and they'll have more relationships in their later years. Older people will get divorced more often, and they'll probably meet new partners online, or perhaps on their cruise holidays.

P: Really?

S: Why not? You're 60 years old, your children are adults, you have 40 more years to live, a new life will be just a click away.

P: Interesting. So, basically, I should look for companies that provide goods and services for the elderly.

S: Exactly, especially those businesses that are planning to use technology in some way. The middle-aged people of today are happy to use technology, and they'll be even happier to use it in twenty years' time.

P: Well, that's all very interesting. Now, where have those coffees got to? Perhaps I need a coffee robot!

Lesson 6.2 Track 1.40

Shane, Evelyn

S: You know, Evelyn, I'm thinking about doing a course in the United States.

E: What, you want to study in America?

S: Yeah, I think it'll help my career.

E: What kind of course?

S: International Business.

E: Oh. Well … what'll you do if Mum and Dad don't like the idea?

S: Oh, it's OK. I'll persuade them.

E: Really? I don't think Dad will like the idea.

S: Oh, he'll be OK about it. You wait and see.

E: I hope you're right. And what'll you do if the course is really difficult?

S: Easy. I'll get some help from my teachers and other students.

E: You seem very confident. What'll you do if you don't like the other students?

S: I'm sure I'll find a nice American girl!

E: Oh really! Shane, I don't think this is a good idea, you know. There are lots of good courses here in Australia …

Track 1.41

1 What'll you do if your parents don't like the idea?
2 What'll you do if the course is really difficult?
3 What'll you do if you don't like the other students?

Lesson 6.3 Track 1.42

Robert, Sheila, Grace, Brian, Henry, Kate

R: OK, so that's the expert's view, let's see what you, the public, think. Now, what's your name?

S: Sheila.

R: OK, Sheila, are you a mother?

S: Yes, I am. I've got two young girls.

R: Great, so what do you think?

S: Personally, I think mothers should stay at home. I look after my kids and I think that's best for them and for me.

R: In what way?

S: Well, you know, kids should be with their mother, they need my love and, well, I know what they like and don't like. You know, it's natural.

R: OK, so does anyone disagree? Yes, you, what's your opinion?

G: Well, I understand her opinion, but sometimes mothers have no choice. They have to work. Surely it's better for the family to have money to buy food and stuff. I mean, what's the point of staying at home with your kids if you can't put food on the table? We're not all in happy families with two parents, are we?

R: Indeed. What do you say to that, Sheila?

S: Well, that's a good point, but I think some mothers work because they want to, not because they need to. They prefer to work rather than look after their children, and I think that's wrong, I really do.

R: OK. Does anyone else have anything to say on this?

B: Er, I do, Robert.

R: Yes?

B: I agree with Sheila. I know loads of mothers who work just because they like to have a job, not because they need to. And that's a real pity, because they're missing out on the best time in their children's lives. You can work anytime, but your children are only young once.

R: OK, well, while we're on the subject of children, let's look at another question. Basically, should we limit the amount of TV young kids watch? Are they watching too much TV these days? What's your name and what's your opinion?

H: Hi, I'm Henry and I'm a dad.

R: OK, then Henry, what's your view?

H: Well, what I think is that they shouldn't watch any TV.

R: What, none at all?

H: None at all. I never watched TV when I was a kid, and I don't think my kids need to watch it now, especially when they're young.

R: Right, well, I'm sure many people will disagree with you. Let's see. Yes, madam, yes, you in the red dress.

K: Well, personally, I completely disagree. TV is part of the modern world, like computers and phones. We can't hide TV from our kids. I think it's better if they know that TV is a normal thing, as normal as having dinner, or whatever.

R: Henry?

H: Well, that's an interesting idea, but TV is different to phones, and having dinner. The kids just sit there, like vegetables. It's not good for them, not good at all.

K: But why not just control how much they watch? You know, have a maximum of two hours a day or something.

H: Well, I know we won't agree, but the best control is to sell your TV. If you do that, they'll do something else.

S: That's just silly.

H: You're the one that's silly.

R: OK, OK, calm down everyone. Let's take a break now, and after the ads we'll look at the role of the father in the family.

Review Units 4–6 Track 1.45

Jane, Andrea

J: Hello, Jane Barton here.

A: Jane, it's Andrea. Listen, you know we were talking about an environmentally-friendly holiday this year?

J: Yes, why?

A: Well, I've got some details from a great company – holidays in Africa, Uganda. Shall I tell you about them?

J: Yeah … but I'm working, so I can't talk for too long.

A: OK, no problem. Right, I've looked at the information and there are four tours that look good. Oh, they're all in national parks. I think we should get more details on a couple of them.

J: OK, good idea.

A: First one, mmm, I don't know how to pronounce this. It's Mgahinga National Park – there are about nine volcanoes in …

J: Volcanoes!

A: … six are extinct, so don't worry.

J: I am worried!

A: Anyway, it's mainly forest, with lots of different plants and birds …

J: And animals?

A: It mentions the golden monkey, that's all.

J: No, I don't like the sound of that one.

A: OK, number two, Bwindi National Park. Listen ... 'over half the world's population of mountain gorillas live in Bwindi's forests ...'

J: That sounds good.

A: Yes, but the others are too. Number three, Queen Elizabeth National Park – open grassland, rainforest, lakes, with over 100 types of animal including elephants, leopards, lions and buffalo.

J: I like that one.

A: OK, and the last one, the Murchison Falls National Park. This one's by the River Nile, and there are river animals and birds, and other animals like elephants, giraffes and buffalo again. I like this one.

J: OK, well, why don't we get details on the last two – Queen Elizabeth and Murchison Falls?

A: Yes, I'll do that ... and shall I ...

J: My boss is coming – I have to go. Bye, I'll speak to you later.

Track 1.46

Tom, Shula

T: ... and this photo is from my job in India, years ago. That's the clinic on the left.

S: Oh, it's lovely. Who's the little boy on the right with the two women?

T: He helped the doctors and nurses, you know, made tea, fetched things.

S: It's interesting that the photo is in black and white.

T: Yes, personally, I believe that you get better photos this way.

S: Yes, I agree. The mountains in the middle look amazing – so impressive.

T: I know. I loved the mountains. In fact, I loved everything there!

S: Really, why?

T: Well, because the weather was good, the food was wonderful, the people were really friendly. I'd really like to go back to see them all again.

S: You should do that! You can take three months off from this job, you know.

T: That's a good point, but I couldn't leave my family for that long. I think it's better if I wait till the children are older.

Lesson 7.1 Track 1.47

Researcher, Iris

R: Well, first of all, thank you for meeting me.

I: Not at all. I hope I can help.

R: Well, as you know, we're doing some research for a documentary series about forensic science – we want to call it *CSI – the reality*. I must tell you that, at the moment, we're most interested in the differences between the TV dramas and the reality of a crime lab.

I: That's fine, I can talk about that.

R: Great. So, first of all, how do you organise the work here?

I: Well, basically, we work in two teams. In the first team, we have the crime scene analysts. They're the people who collect the evidence from the crime scene. In the second team, we have the forensic scientists, people like me, who actually do the scientific tests in the lab. The important thing is that these forensic scientists are experts in different fields, so, for example, we have an expert on guns and bullets, a fingerprints expert, and so on. I'm a DNA expert.

R: I see. That seems a little different to the TV show.

I: Yes, you're right. On the show, the crime scene analysts also work in the lab, and they often know about everything, from bullets to fingerprints.

R: Exactly. So, when the crime scene analysts are at the crime scene, what do they have to do?

I: Well, first of all, the photographer takes hundreds of pictures of the crime scene, and at the same time someone interviews any witnesses. Then, they collect any evidence, and this is when they have to be very careful. They have to wear rubber gloves because they mustn't damage any of the evidence. Basically, they look for fingerprints, hairs, perhaps blood. It all depends on the crime, really. Also, they have to take very careful notes. This is important because we, the scientists in the lab, have to know exactly where all the evidence has come from.

R: Right. Now, on TV, most of the crimes are murders. Is that true for you?

I: Oh, no, not at all. Ninety per cent of our work is with burglaries or stolen cars, you know the kind of thing.

R: Really? OK, so what about the lab work? Do you have to do anything special?

I: Well, first of all, we always tell the police that they must be patient because our work in the lab takes time. On TV, a police officer doesn't have to wait very long to get test results, perhaps just a few hours. In reality, an officer has to wait twenty days to get a DNA test result.

Secondly, we work in a lab, so there are certain lab rules. We have to turn our mobile phones off, and we mustn't eat or drink in the lab, that kind of thing.

R: OK. Any more differences?

I: Well, I must be honest here, unfortunately, scientists sometimes make mistakes, but, on TV, the scientists never make mistakes! Amazing!

R: Indeed. And, now that we have these dramas about forensic scientists, have there been any changes in your work?

I: Well, there's been a positive change in our image. For once, science is an interesting or glamorous profession. It's incredible really, so many young people are now applying to work in crime labs. There's been a 500 per cent increase in applications to university courses, for example. And many of these people are young women. And the thing is, we're scientists not police officers, so you don't have to study law. Instead you have to study chemistry or biology. So, although the TV shows are basically police dramas, more people are now studying science subjects, which is great.

R: Interesting. So, erm, can I have a look around your lab?

I: Well, I'm not sure. My boss says all visits must only be for work reasons.

R: Well, this is kind of work related. I mean, we must get the documentary right.

I: I suppose so. Well, OK, but you must turn your phone off and you must be quiet, or my boss will kill me!

R: Hmm ... murder in the crime lab. Could be a good story for the TV show ...

CD 2

Lesson 7.3 Track 2.3

Presenter, Julian

P: So, Julian, could you tell us about one of your choices please, and please just give a few reasons for your choice? Unfortunately our time is limited ...

J: Right, well, one of my choices is the printing press. Now, Guttenberg invented the modern printing press in 1457 and I think this caused a revolution in knowledge, society ... and, well, in everything really.

P: In what way?

J: Well, the main reason I think it's important is that the printing press meant we could produce books and newspapers in large numbers and very quickly. Before then, writing was a slow process and each copy

AUDIOSCRIPTS

of each book took weeks to make. Suddenly, we could make a hundred copies of a book in a day. This meant that ideas could spread much more quickly than before. This caused great changes in society, too many changes to talk about now. Another reason the printing press is important is that it led to education for everyone. This is connected to the fast production of books because if you have books, you can have a school. As well as that, the idea of education for all is also connected to the demand for reading skills. The written word became important at work, and so people had to read, and so they needed education.

P: OK then. A key reason for choosing the printing press is that it meant that ideas could spread quickly and this caused many changes in society. Secondly, you claim that it led to education for all. Anything else?

J: Well, yes. The other thing is that the printing press means that writers can make money, which, as I'm a writer, is something I'm rather pleased about. But seriously, without the printing press, you can't make thousands of copies and therefore you can't make any money. The printing press meant that people could become professional writers and journalists, which I think has been very good for society, don't you?

P: Well, yes I do, I suppose. However, I'm not completely convinced by your argument about education. After all, we didn't have general schools until about 400 years after the invention of the printing press. Is there really a connection?

J: Well, er, that's a fair point, although I still say that the mass production of books caused changes in the way people worked and this led to wider education.

P: Mmm. OK, we'll leave that discussion there for the moment and let's move on. Sandra, what have you chosen?

Lesson 7.4 Track 2.8

Shannon, Anisha
S: Morning Anisha.
A: Hi, Shannon! How's it going? Everything alright?
S: Well, I suppose so.
A: You don't sound very happy.
S: Well, I'm having a bit of trouble with my reading and note-taking.
A: Oh. Why?
S: Well, I can't take very good notes. They're usually very long. I write down a lot of stuff – pages and pages.

It takes me ages. And sometimes I think I write down the wrong information too. I don't really know what I'm doing wrong.

A: OK. Well, I can tell you what's worked for me. First of all, you should remember why you're reading and making notes. What will you use the notes for? Are they for an essay? a presentation? an exam? If they're for an essay, what's the essay question? Only make notes if the information can help you to answer the essay question. Don't make any notes if the information is about another topic. If you keep that in mind, it'll help you. You know what I mean?

S: Yeah, sure.

A: Right, let's imagine I'm reading an academic paper. It's about eight pages long. If I've got time, this is what I do. The first time I read the text, I don't make any notes. I just … read it – straight through. I just try to understand it, you know. After that, I read it again and highlight the main ideas. I also highlight other points in a different colour. These are important points, but less important than the main points.

S: I've got it.

A: The next thing I do … is make notes of the information I've highlighted. But I don't just copy out the information. When I make notes, I summarise the information, using a few key words or phrases. And I also make the notes using my own words – not the same words as in the text. Like this, I really understand the notes I'm making. If you just copy out sentences, it's possible you don't actually understand anything. And … er … well, that's about it, really. I don't think I can tell you anything else.

S: Well, you've given me some good ideas. Thanks, Anisha.

A: Anything else?

S: Er … well … there is something else … yeah …

Lesson 8.1 Track 2.9

Dr Wilson, Abolaji
W: Alright, Abolaji, you're next. Are you ready?
A: Yes.
W: OK then, start when you like.
A: Good morning everybody. Let me start with a question: Do you like sleeping? Today I'm going to talk to you about sleep. I hope to show you that sleep is a very important and interesting subject. But please stay awake – don't fall asleep during my presentation!

Scientists are starting to understand sleep much better than before, and I'll mention some new research in my talk. Because of the limited time, I'll cover three areas:
1 how much sleep we need
2 the types and stages of sleep, and
3 some problems with sleep in today's society.

So, let's look first at how much sleep people need. Most people spend around a third of their lives asleep, although the need for sleep decreases with age. A one-year-old baby needs about fourteen hours of sleep a day, a child of five needs about twelve hours, and an adult about seven to eight hours. However, different people need different amounts of sleep. Some adults need to sleep for ten hours or more a day, while others only need half that amount or less. Elderly people tend to sleep less than younger adults at night, but they doze more during the day.

Let's turn now to the different types of sleep, and I apologise for using some rather technical language here. There are two types of sleep, known as REM sleep and NREM sleep. REM means rapid eye movement. NREM means non-rapid eye movement. Most of our sleep – about 80 per cent of the sleeping pattern – is NREM sleep; during this time, brain activity falls to its lowest level. In REM sleep, the brain suddenly becomes more active – like the brain of a person who's awake. The eyes move rapidly and dreams occur. REM sleep is about one half of sleep time in babies, and about one fifth of sleep time in adults.

Track 2.10

OK. Turning to the stages of sleep, we can identify five stages in a night's sleep, as you can see on the slide. In different stages of sleep, our brains put together thoughts and experiences, then store them in an organised way, giving us clearer memories. According to Robert Stickgold, a sleep researcher at Harvard Medical School in Boston, it seems that different kinds of sleep improve different kinds of memories, and this might be why we have the five different stages of sleep. Recent experiments suggest that the final stage of sleep, REM sleep, is very important for organising our memories and helps to improve our learning. NREM sleep is important for making our memories stronger. Experiments have also shown that the brain works in a different way after we've had a good night's sleep.

The final area I want to talk about are things that can stop us sleeping well. One of them is too much light. Street lights and security lights mean that even when we're asleep, it's never completely dark. And the evidence suggests that the quantity and quality of darkness in our lives affects our health. Another problem is the 24/7 world, with the Internet, 24-hour shopping, global travel, etc. Because of this, our days are becoming longer and the nights shorter – and this could also damage our health, as we're not getting enough sleep.

To sum up, I hope I've succeeded in showing you that sleep is a very important and interesting subject. We sleep less as we get older, but everybody's different – some people need more sleep, others less. There are two types of sleep – NREM and REM; most sleep is NREM, but REM is when dreaming happens. During the five different stages of sleep, our brains organise our memories and make them stronger. But too much light and our modern way of life can have a negative impact on our sleeping patterns and, as a result, on our brains and our health. Thank you for listening. Are there any questions? Is anyone still awake?

Lesson 8.3 Track 2.11

Paul, Emma, Christine

P: OK then, so what shall we do after dinner? What's on at about eight o'clock, Emma?

E: Well, there's a classical music concert in the castle or else an open-air movie. What would you prefer to do, Christine?

C: I'm not sure, what kind of film is it?

E: It's an Indian film, a Bollywood film, you know, with loads of songs and dancing. This one's a romantic comedy.

C: Hmm, I don't fancy that. I'd prefer to go to the classical concert. What about you, Paul?

P: I think I'd rather see the film. I'm not that keen on the concert. I don't really like classical music. What about you Emma, what would you rather do?

E: Well, to be honest, I don't mind. I like all music. The movie sounds good because I've never seen a Bollywood film before, and they're good fun, the dancing's brilliant, so I've been told. But, the concert sounds good because it's in the castle, and I think that'll be lovely, a really good atmosphere for the music.

P: It's in the castle?

C: Yes, in the main hall. Are you more interested now?

P: Yes, I am. We haven't been to the castle yet, and I'd like to see it at night.

C: Great! Let's go to the concert then. What shall we do after that?

E: After that?

C: Oh yes, Emma, no one goes to bed before midnight during the festival. You have to see as much as you can.

E: OK, fair enough. Well, I'm more interested in the Japanese drummers than the one-man theatre show.

C: Yeah, the drummers do sound interesting, but perhaps we shouldn't go to a second music event.

E: Hmm, maybe Paul, which would you prefer to go to?

P: Oh, I'd love to see the drummers. They sound amazing. And it's a great chance to see something different and unusual. I'd rather see that than a play about Shakespeare.

C: But it says that the play's really funny. And how interesting is two hours of drumming going to be?

E: Oh Christine, I'm sure the Taiko drumming will be really interesting. I've seen some of it on TV, and I'd love to see it live.

C: OK then, let's go and see the drummers. But tomorrow, no music. OK?

P&E: OK.

Lesson 9.1 Track 2.14

Consultant, Shami

C: Come in. Hello. It's Shami, isn't it?

S: That's right.

C: OK, let me just have a look at the information here … you work in the Marketing Department?

S: Yeah.

C: And … you've been with the company for six years.

S: That's right.

C: Alright, first of all let's talk about your general feelings about your job. Do you feel the same way now as you did six years ago?

S: Well, no, not really. I mean, I think I used to be more enthusiastic. Maybe it's because I'm older now.

C: Well, you're still only 28. That's not exactly old!

S: No, I suppose not.

C: What else has changed?

S: I work longer hours now. When I started, I didn't use to finish work so late. Now, I go home after seven nearly every day, but I don't think I really achieve any more.

C: I see. What about the company? Is it helping you to develop new skills?

S: Yes, up to a point. I've done one or two management training courses in the last couple of years. I think I'm ready for promotion now.

C: What about other aspects of the job? Do you get the opportunity to travel much?

S: No, not much. But I don't really mind that. You see, I have to look after my mother and …

Track 2.15

Consultant, Rory

R: Good morning! I'm Rory Carroll.

C: Hello Rory. Have a seat. Well, you seem to have the longest service record – seventeen years!

R: That's right.

C: Well, you're obviously happy here!

R: I am, yes, although it used to be more fun.

C: Why's that?

R: Well, it was more sociable. I used to go out more with my colleagues, after work and for lunch. When I first started here, we had very long lunch breaks, sometimes for two hours. Now it's more like thirty minutes. And we all used the gym together. That doesn't happen much now.

C: Did you use to work more as a team?

R: Yes, I suppose we did. It's interesting you mention that. We're more on our own now. I also used to travel a lot more too. They've cut down on that.

C: Has anything changed for the better?

R: Yes, there are more opportunities to learn new skills and develop your career. It's more professional now. Also, they didn't use to pay you properly. The money's much better now! That's probably why I'm still here!

C: What about yourself? Have you changed at the same time as the company?

R: No, I don't think so. I think I'm pretty much the same person I was all those years ago.

Track 2.16

1 She used to work late.
2 Did you use to go out more with colleagues?
3 He didn't use to listen to me.
4 She didn't use the gym every day.
5 They used their opportunities well.
6 Did the company use the results of the survey?

AUDIOSCRIPTS

Lesson 9.3 Track 2.17

Lu Han, Richard

L: So, which of our products are you interested in?

R: OK, well, we're interested in buying some digital music players, the IP4 model. How much are they per item?

L: Let's see. … Yes, they're $100 each.

R: $100? That seems rather high.

L: Really? I see. How much would you like to pay?

R: About $85.

L: I see. Well, I'm not sure that we can go that low, but we can offer you a discount. It depends on the quantity. How many would you like to order?

R: We'd like 500. What discount can you offer?

L: Well, I'm afraid we can only offer a 5% discount on 500, but if you order 1,000, we can offer 15%.

R: I see. That might be difficult. I'm not sure that we can sell 1,000. What about if we order 750?

L: Well, then we can give you a 10% discount.

R: Hmm, that's still a bit low. How about 12.5%?

L: 12.5%? I'm not sure we can offer that. Although, if you order 800, we can offer 12.5%.

R: Hmm, 800, well …

L: It's not very many more, and the discount is good.

R: Well, yes, OK then. We'll order 800.

L: Fine, and we'll give a 12.5% discount. So, the final price is $87.50 per item.

R: Shall we call it $87? Keep it a round number? I mean, we hope to buy more in the future …

L: That sounds fine. $87 per item it is, then.

R: Great. Now, what's your normal delivery time?

L: It's usually thirty days after your order.

R: OK, the standard time. Actually, we need delivery in two weeks. Can you do that?

L: Two weeks? No, I'm afraid we can't do that.

R: Really?

L: Really. I'm afraid they won't be ready for delivery by then. Thirty days is the best we can do, I'm afraid.

R: OK, that'll be fine. Perhaps we can change things next time.

L: OK then. So, you order 800 IP4 music players at $87 dollars per item, and we deliver in thirty days. Is that a deal?

R: That's a deal.

L: Excellent. Is there anything else you're interested in? We're offering a great deal on digital cameras at the moment.

R: Really? Oh? What's the deal? If it's a good bargain, I might be interested. Which model …

Lesson 9.4 Track 2.19

Louise, Visitors

L: Good morning everyone. Welcome to Cadbury World. My name's Louise and I'm your guide this morning OK, let's see where everybody comes from today. Put your hands up if you're from the UK. Uh-huh. Anyone from Birmingham?

V1: Yes!

L: Good to see one or two locals. Alright, so the rest of you are visitors from abroad? And where are you from?

V2: From the US, Florida.

V3: I'm French.

V4: Spain.

V5: Japan.

V6: We're from Turkey.

L: Oh, I had a lovely holiday there last year. Anyway, it looks like we've got quite a lot of foreign visitors today. Now, has anyone been here before? No, OK, so it's everybody's first time. Alright, your tour this morning will last about one hour. First of all, I'm going to tell you a few key things about the history of chocolate, then I'll say a little bit about the company and after that I'll say a few words about how chocolate is made. All that will take about ten minutes. Then we'll go round the factory. How does that sound?

V7: Good. Will we taste any chocolate?

L: Oh, yes. Don't worry about that. There'll be a chance to taste some of our delicious products at the end!

Track 2.20

L: OK. So, let's look at the history of chocolate. To start with, does anybody know where chocolate first came from?

V8: From Latin America, I think.

L: Yes, that's right. It was the Mayans (who lived in what's now Central America and Mexico) who first discovered the delights of chocolate in about 600AD. They found that they could make a delicious drink from roasted cocoa beans. Do all our foreign visitors know the meaning of roasted?

V3: Cooked in an oven.

L: Exactly. The Mayans called their chocolate drink chocolatl. It was a real luxury because cocoa beans were very valuable. In fact, people sometimes used to give them as presents, or even used them as money. Soon, chocolatl spread to the Aztec civilisation around modern Mexico City. In 1517, the Spaniard, Hernán Cortés arrived in Mexico. He travelled to meet the Aztec emperor, Moctezuma, who introduced Cortés to his favourite drink – chocolatl. They served the drink to Cortés in a cup made of gold. If you look at the slide, you can see them drinking together.

When Cortés returned to Spain in 1528, he loaded his ships with cocoa beans and equipment for making the chocolate drink. Soon chocolate became a popular drink with rich people in Spain. But it took nearly 100 years for the news of cocoa and chocolate to spread across Europe, as the Spanish kept it a secret. In the 17th century, chocolate houses – like coffee shops today – became popular in London and other European cities. But it wasn't until the 19th century that chocolate became cheaper and available to a large percentage of the population. Also in the 19th century, they found a way to make chocolate hard, solid – to make the eating chocolate we love today! So, that was a very brief history of chocolate. To sum up, it started as a drink in Central America, it came to Europe with the Spanish, it spread slowly across the continent and finally became something a lot of people could afford to eat.

Now, I know you're all very keen to start the tour, but let's turn now to the company just for a minute …

Review Units 7–9 Track 2.21

Anna, Rob

A: I'm bored. Let's go out this evening.

R: OK. I'd love to go to the theatre. I haven't been for ages.

A: I'm not sure about that. I'm not that keen on the theatre. What's on?

R: There's a play by David Mamet. The tickets are £20, £25 or £30.

A: Oh, that seems a bit high to me, for a play in our local theatre.

R: Well, what would you prefer to do?

A: Mmm, I'm more interested in something active. I think I'd rather go dancing.

R: I don't fancy dancing! No, I'd prefer to go to a concert.

A: A concert? OK, let's see what's on. But what about if we go dancing at the weekend?

R: I don't know. Look, why don't you go dancing with your friends at the weekend?

A: But I'd rather go with you.

R: If you go with your friends, I'll cook a really nice dinner for us on Sunday.

A: OK, that sounds fine!

Lesson 10.1 Track 2.22

Fifty countries founded the United Nations after the Second World War, on the 24th of October 1945, to be exact. After such a terrible war, they founded the UN in order to maintain world peace and security, to develop friendly relations between countries and to improve living conditions and human rights across the world. There are now 191 countries in the UN, that's nearly every country in the world, and representatives from these countries meet at the UN headquarters in New York.

For most people, the Secretary General of the UN is the face of this massive organisation. The Secretary General is the person that we usually see on the television news when the UN does something important. Over the years, the Secretary General has come from many different countries, such as Egypt, Peru and Sweden. The current Secretary General is from South Korea.

The UN works in a wide range of areas, with a general aim to improve the lives of ordinary people and to keep peace in the world. For example, the UN helps refugees, helps the economic development of poorer countries and runs the court of International Justice. Two areas that the UN is not involved in are entertainment and religious education.

Track 2.23

Beth, Vihn

B: Hi there, Vihn. How are you?

V: Hi Beth. I'm fine, thanks. You alright?

B: Yeah, fine. Are you ready to update the website? I've got the Secretary General's schedule for next week here.

V: Sure. Fire away. What's he doing on Monday?

B: Well, actually, he isn't doing anything early in the morning, but at 11.15 a.m. he's meeting the Syrian Foreign Minister.

V: Sorry, which minister? My computer wasn't quite ready.

B: Or you weren't listening! The Foreign Minister. Of Syria.

V: Fine. Got that now. Anything after that?

B: Yep. At four o'clock he's meeting the Ambassador from The Congo. And that's it for Monday. Ready for Tuesday? Or are you still waiting for the computer to catch up?

V: Sure, I'm ready. You can go as fast as you want now.

B: OK, so, at ten he's giving a statement to the Development Committee, about the UN's plans for next year. Then, after lunch, he's seeing the President of the Security Council. The meeting is at three, and it'll probably be a long one, so he's not meeting anyone else that day.

V: Sure thing. Wednesday?

B: Yes, Wednesday, well, we've organised the morning, but we're not sure about the afternoon.

V: Fine, tell me about the morning now and we'll do the rest later.

B: Well, in the morning he's going to the Empire State Building where he's holding a press conference with the Messengers of Peace.

V: What time exactly? I can't really just say 'in the morning'!

B: Oh sorry, I thought I said. That's at 10.30.

V: Uh-huh. Fine. The press conference sounds a good idea. It'll get some publicity.

B: We hope so. Anyway, after that, at midday he's meeting the Brazilian President to discuss the rainforest protection plan.

V: Fine. Got that. What's next?

B: Well, that's what we're not sure about because on Thursday he's travelling to Europe. Before that, he might meet his assistants who are travelling with him, or he might phone the British Prime Minister. He's going to decide tomorrow. So, I'll update you then.

V: OK. Well, I'll put up the information that you've already given me, and then add that extra information tomorrow. How long is he staying in Europe?

B: Two weeks, and you won't need to put up the daily schedule while he's away.

V: Fine, I've got plenty of stuff to do anyway. Erm, may I ask, what are you doing tonight?

B: Oh, I'm going out for dinner with my husband, there's a new restaurant that's opened near us.

V: Oh, your husband …

B: Yes. Why did you ask?

V: Oh, no reason. Have a nice evening.

B: Thank you, you too. Are you doing anything?

V: No, no, a quiet night in for me.

B: OK then, well, talk to you again when the SG returns.

V: Sure, bye.

B: Bye.

Lesson 10.2 Track 2.25

Q: When was Fiat set up?

A: It was set up in 1899, in Turin, in Italy. The first factory was opened in 1900. 150 workers were employed there and they produced 24 cars. At the time, Italy had a population of 32 million people and most of them worked in farming. This was an exciting period in history: cinema and radio were invented around this time too.

Q: Where were cars tested in the early years?

A: On the roof of the factory! The Fiat factory at Lingotto was completed in 1922. It was the largest in Europe and had five floors. On the roof there was a track where cars were tested.

Q: When were car adverts aimed at women for the first time?

A: In the mid 1920s. Standards of living were rising and changes in society were occurring.

Q: Which newspaper was bought by Fiat in 1926, *Corriere della Sera* or *La Stampa*?

A: *La Stampa*. It means 'The Press' in Italian. It's a newspaper from Turin, but people read it in other parts of Italy too.

Q: What was set up in the late 1920s?

A: A lot of services for employees, for example, health care, schools, sports clubs and holiday camps for children. Other companies soon copied these ideas. Some of the services are still active today.

Q: Where were Fiat cars constructed in the early 1930s?

A: Fiat increased its activities abroad at this time and cars were constructed in France, Spain and Poland. The company also opened a bank in Berlin.

Lesson 10.3 Track 2.26

1

First, we want to deliver a magical experience, an electrifying atmosphere for competitors and spectators. Our aim is to inspire young people in Britain and across the world to play sport. We will do whatever we can to inspire children to choose sport, wherever they live, whatever they do, whatever they believe. These will be a memorable Games. A Games that will inspire young people to believe in the Olympic ideal.

2

And that magic begins with the venues. We'll use existing world-class venues, spectacular city centre locations, and most importantly, we'll

AUDIOSCRIPTS

create an Olympic park which is just seven minutes from the centre of London. In the Olympic park there'll be a magnificent 80,000 seat Olympic stadium and a fantastic aquatic centre for the swimming events. Half of the venues will be only five minutes from the athletes' accommodation and only ten per cent will be more than twenty minutes away.

3

The Olympic park will contain the Olympic village; we'll put athletes at the heart of the games. There'll be 8,000 double rooms and this accommodation will be modern, spacious and comfortable. Athletes will be just a short walk from the main stadium. They'll be at the centre of the Olympic experience.

4

The Olympic park will be only seven minutes from Central London by train via a new high-speed train service. Nine other railway and underground lines will form the basis of a comprehensive public transport system serving every venue. A special Olympic bus service will provide quick and easy journeys between venues. Finally, we'll give free public transport to all athletes, officials and spectators.

Lesson 10.4 Track 2.29

Speaker, Audience member

s: Good evening. Thank you for inviting me here this evening to talk about Interpol, the world's largest police organisation. Now, what do you think of when you think of Interpol? A lot of people get their image of Interpol from books or films. Perhaps they think of a French policeman from the 1960s, wearing a long pale coat. Or perhaps they think of something like a James Bond film, or *Mission Impossible*, with beautiful secret agents. Actually, Interpol is rather different to this and tonight I'm going to give you an idea about the real Interpol. First of all, I'll say a little about Interpol's history. Then I'll talk about Interpol today; I'll tell you how it's organised and, finally, what it does. There'll be some time at the end for questions.

Although the idea for Interpol was born in 1914 at a conference in Monaco, the First World War interrupted its development. It was eventually created in 1923, in Vienna, Austria, although it had a different name at that time. In the beginning, there were fourteen member countries. The work of the organisation was interrupted by the Second World War. In 1946, Interpol reappeared with a new headquarters in Paris, and it has remained in France since then. In 1989 the headquarters was moved to Lyon, where it is today.

Now let's look at the modern Interpol. First of all, how is it organised? Interpol now has 184 member countries. And let me point out that it's those countries that pay for it! 184 countries – that makes it the second biggest international organisation after the United Nations. The headquarters in Lyon operates 24 hours a day, 365 days a year. Staff from more than 80 countries work side-by-side, using the organisation's four official languages: Arabic, English, French and Spanish. There are also six regional offices around the world. In all, we have about 450 staff. Yes, that's right – perhaps 450 doesn't sound a lot to you. But that figure is just for the staff in Lyon and the regional offices. Each member country also has its own Interpol office. The staff there come from the national police force. Don't forget that most Interpol officers stay in their own country, and don't spend their time travelling the world fighting crime, as they do in the books and films!

In the final part of my talk, I'm going to say something about what Interpol does. Basically, we help police forces catch criminals. But, and I must draw your attention to this, we never break the law in any country.

One of our priorities is problems connected with drugs. Another important area is trafficking in human beings – people trafficking – especially women and children from developing countries. We also take a great interest in public safety and terrorism.

Another key priority is financial crime. Why? Because criminals are using new technology to get information such as passwords or credit card details through the Internet.

So, how can we catch these criminals? Well, the most important thing we do is to run a global police communication system, so police around the world can share information about crime and criminals. The system allows police in one country to check the databases of police in another country. Interpol itself manages several databases, including names and photos of criminals, fingerprints, etc. Another important thing we do is to provide training courses for national police forces, and organise international conferences on crime. In 2001, about 1,400 criminals were found thanks to the efforts of Interpol.

So there we are. To conclude, we can say that Interpol is over 80 years old, and has grown a lot from the organisation that was set up in Vienna in 1923. Today, our headquarters is in Lyon, France, and 184 countries are members. We fight international crime using modern technology. We do everything we can to make the world a safer place for you and your families. Thank you for listening. Are there any questions?

a: Yes, do you think organisations like Interpol have too much information about us – the public? For example, everywhere we go there are cameras taking photographs of us. There's no private space anymore. What's your opinion about this?

s: Hmm, now that's a very interesting and important question. Er, let me see if I can give you a short answer …

Lesson 11.1 Track 2.30

Presenter, John, Bruce

p: I've been a scientist for over 40 years and I've been making nature documentaries for the last twenty years and, to be honest, fifteen years ago I didn't believe that we were changing the world's climate. However, for the last ten years I've been travelling around the world to find out if, in fact, we *are* changing the world's climate. I've met many scientists and I've visited some of the world's most special environments. And now, I've definitely changed my mind.

We can see the early effects of global warming in the polar regions – the Arctic and the Antarctic. John Watts is a polar scientist in the Arctic.

j: I've been working here since 1980, and, recently, things have been changing very quickly. The sea ice is melting earlier every year and this means that life for the polar bears is getting harder and harder, because they can only find food when the ocean is covered with ice. There are now 25 per cent fewer polar bears compared to when I first came here.

p: Sea levels are rising because the polar ice and mountain glaciers are melting. This means that islands in the Pacific Ocean are disappearing under the sea. As well as this, the seas are also getting hotter. This is causing problems for both the rainforests and the coral reefs.

The warmer seas mean there's less rain in the rainforests. In the Amazon rainforest, the larger trees are dying and there are serious droughts. As well as this, the warmer sea water is killing coral reefs in many parts of the world. Coral reefs are very sensitive to temperature changes and we're now losing some of the richest environments in the world.

But, are we causing these changes or is it just a natural process? Bruce Sindall has a computer model that seems to answer this question.

B: With this programme, I can show how the temperature of the planet has been changing for the last 100 years and I can show what effect the burning of fossil fuels has on the temperature changes. The first line on the graph – the blue line – shows you the temperature changes because of natural processes, such as volcanoes and the energy from the sun. As you can see, the temperature goes up and down without a strong trend.

The second line shows you what happens when we include the CO_2 that is produced by the use of fossil fuels. As you can see, the average temperature has been increasing very quickly since 1950, and this will continue. The increase in CO_2 in the atmosphere has been increasing the planet's temperature.

P: So, is this the end of the world? Well, not yet. We have the power to slow, and possibly to stop, the rise in temperature. We have to produce less CO_2, and to do that we have to change the way we live our lives.

Lesson 11.3 Track 2.31

Poppy, Rick

P: Right then, so, the next project is *Wild City*. What do you think of this one?

R: Well, the best thing is that it's definitely a green project. I mean, you can't get much greener than a wildlife park, can you?

P: Indeed, you can't. And it certainly makes the local area a better place to live, doesn't it?

R: Mm-hm. Urban wasteland areas really ruin any local area – they make the whole place feel run-down and scruffy.

P: Exactly. So, what about the other points on the guidelines? The project solves a problem, doesn't it? Getting

rid of the wasteland. And of course, it involves local people working together.

R: Sure. But there are a couple of points that it doesn't meet, aren't there?

P: Well yes, but that's quite normal, isn't it?

R: Sure, but this project needs £5,000 a year. And we can't really give them that much money.

P: No, that's true. What do you think they need that money for?

R: Well, I reckon it's to pay for the local people who'll look after the park.

P: Hmm. I guess so. Well, they could do it unpaid, couldn't they?

R: Hmm, perhaps, but we've seen that fail before, haven't we? If no one gets any money at all, then things like parks soon get run-down. You know, there's more litter, you start getting graffiti, that kind of thing.

P: Mmm, yes, that's all true. Why don't we offer £2,000 a year?

R: Yes, that's fine. Right, well, there's one more point that the project doesn't meet.

P: Is there? Which one?

Lesson 12.1 Track 2.33

Darren, Nikki, Lesley, Peter, Keri

D: Welcome back. I'm Darren Bright and as usual at this time we're looking at today's papers. With me in the studio this morning are Lesley Diggot-Blake, the Minister for Sport, the journalist and commentator Peter Jones and the actress Keri Miller. Remember – this show is interactive, so if you want to comment on anything, or ask a question, just send your emails to *brightinthemorning* – that's all one word – *@sixtv.com*. The address is on your screen now, and Nikki over there will receive all your emails. Morning, Nikki.

N: Hi Darren.

D: Our first topic this morning is sport and in particular this letter in a newspaper from Michaela Scrivin about minority sports. Michaela wants more investment in minority sports and more stories about them in the media. Then, she says, we would be more successful in international competitions. Lesley Diggot-Blake, what do you think? Would we be better at minority sports if we spent more money on them?

L: To be honest, I was a little surprised when I saw this letter, because we've actually been investing a lot of money in minority sports over the last few years – last year, for example, £60 million was spent on new facilities around the country.

Also, we're building a lot of facilities for the 2012 London Olympics and people doing minority sports will use them. There was something else that surprised me. Michaela suggests that our sportsmen and women haven't been very successful in minority sports in recent years. Think about our gymnasts a few years ago. Beth Tweddle was a gold medal winner. Can I say, though, that success isn't just about money …

D: Alright, sorry to interrupt, we'll come back to you later, but we've got our first email. It's from Rod, in Brighton. Rod says: 'What can you read about judo in the newspapers? Almost nothing. Can you see badminton on TV? Fat chance! The media is only interested in football. If the media showed more interest in other sports, kids would want to try them.' Peter Jones, you're a journalist, what's your view?

P: Well, I couldn't agree more. I think it's a great pity some sports, like football, get so much media attention while others like badminton or table tennis are often ignored. And this problem isn't going away any time soon, either. The BBC has recently decided to stop *Grandstand* – its famous sports programme. I used to watch *Grandstand* on Saturday afternoons when I was a kid and it introduced me to all kinds of different sports. Without that kind of programme, kids won't have the chance to watch those minority sports. However, the 2012 Olympics offer some hope. Because the UK is the host nation, we can enter more teams than usual. Hopefully, people will see more different sports on their TVs.

D: Alright, we've got another email here. It's from Heather in Plymouth. Heather says: 'I think kids should do a lot more sport at school. I've heard that in Sweden kids have ten hours of sport a week. If I was the Minister for Sport, I'd give every schoolchild the opportunity to do a much wider range of sports. What about hockey or judo for all? If they had more opportunities, they wouldn't be so unhealthy.' Keri, hockey and judo at every school?

K: Absolutely. It's really important that kids get the chance to experience different sports from an early age. I was really lucky because I went to a school where we did hockey, and fencing and archery, but nowadays, most kids aren't so lucky. Most

AUDIOSCRIPTS

schools just concentrate on the same one or two, you know, football, basketball …

D: OK, here's another email from Gareth in Cardiff. He says: 'In Britain, we think …

Lesson 12.3 Track 2.34

Dr Mannit, Alex

M: Well, Alex, thanks again for agreeing to take part in this research. The interview starts with a short questionnaire, and then we'll talk more about your personal experience.

A: OK.

M: Right, well, here's the first question: If you had to do an exam next week, would you …
A) work with friends in a study group and prepare with them?
B) work with friends and study on your own?
C) only study on your own?

A: Well … that's a difficult one … I have studied on my own for exams before, but for my last ones I worked in a study group, you know, with my friends, and I liked that.

M: So, which would you do? A, B or C?

A: Right … erm, let me see … I think I'd do B, a bit of both.

M: OK, and the next question: If you had a tennis game with a friend, would you …
A) train hard before in order to win the match?
B) practise a little and do your best?
C) let your friend win?

A: Well, I don't play tennis.

M: I understand, but if you did, what would you do?

A: OK, then I'd do A – I hate losing.

M: Fine. And finally: If you could buy any car you wanted, would you buy …
A) a fast sports car, like a Ferrari?
B) a classic car, like a Rolls Royce?
C) a reliable car, like a Honda?

A: Hmm, let me think … well, to be honest, I'd buy a Ferrari. I'd love to have such a fast car.

M: OK, well, thank you for that, and for answering honestly. Would you like to know what your answers mean?

A: Yes, I would. Can you tell me now?

M: Sure, let's see. You chose B for the first question, so you're quite sociable. You chose A for the second one, so you're very competitive. Finally, you would buy the Ferrari. This shows you are happy to take risks. From these answers, I think you would like team sports, and, as competition and risk are very

important for you, I think you should try rugby or perhaps white-water rafting.

A: Really? Well, the only sport I play is football, and I love that.

M: Well, that's a competitive team sport, isn't it?

A: That's true.

M: And have you ever tried adventure sports?

A: No, I haven't, but I think I'd like to try white-water rafting. It looks fun.

M: Well, as I said, I think it would suit your personality.

Lesson 12.4 Track 2.37

Lecturer, Students

L: OK everyone. That's it for this year. I hope you've enjoyed the course and feel that you've learned a lot. Here's a little handout with some tips on how to prepare for the exam. Before we look at that, can I also mention a few general points about doing exams?

First of all, when you're revising, don't do lots and lots of practice tests. Of course, it's good to do *some* practice tests but, after a certain point, you don't learn anything new. It's better to spend the time improving your general level of English by reading books and newspapers, by watching a film in English, or by just doing some grammar self-study.

Secondly, make sure you're not tired on the day of the exam. Don't go to a party the night before, and don't stay up until three in the morning revising. You need to be fresh so that you can think quickly in the exam.

Thirdly, don't be late for the exam. It seems obvious, doesn't it? But last year one student was two minutes late and he wasn't allowed into the exam room. They sent him away … Right, now, once you're in the exam, what's the most important thing?

S1: Use correct English?

L: Well, clearly, that's important, but the most important thing is … do exactly what the exam asks you to do. Follow the instructions on the exam paper. Make sure you understand what the questions are asking you to do. Read the questions two or three times before you start.

Some of the questions are multiple-choice questions, and you have to choose one answer from a, b, c or d. First of all, decide which ones you think are definitely wrong, and cross them out. Then choose from the others. If you don't know which

answer is correct, make a guess. You might be right. Don't leave any gaps. Answer every question.

There are also questions that ask you to write something. Now, let me ask you a question. Let's imagine you're doing a piece of writing in an exam. Is it a good idea to do a draft, that's a first copy, and then make a final copy?

S1&S2: Yes, I think so.

L: Well, actually, no. I think this is a waste of time. In my experience, there's almost no difference between the draft and the final piece of writing. And it usually takes ten minutes or more to rewrite. It's much better to spend that time thinking of good ideas, or planning your work.

S2: But sometimes we make mistakes and we need to change something or cross something out.

L: Yes, that's OK. After all, it's an exam. You're not expected to write a beautiful-looking piece of writing. The important thing is that it's clear. One final thing concerns timing. Don't spend too long on one question. If you can't answer a question, go on to the next one, and come back to it later, if you have time. OK, would you like to ask anything?

S3: Yes, can we use dictionaries?

L: No, you can't. And, actually, that's good. Research shows that students who can use dictionaries in exams waste a lot of time looking up words that they don't really need to look up. If anytime you can use a dictionary in an exam, try not to use it too much. Just check one or two key words. Right, well, good luck. I hope to see some of you again next year …

Track 2.38

Interviewer, Jenny, Bethany, Alan, Nabil

I: Hi, I'm from the university radio. Can I ask you what you thought about that exam?

J: Oh, I thought it was pretty hard, actually, but I suppose I've only got myself to blame. I didn't do enough revision – I started it too late. I couldn't remember much, so I couldn't do many of the questions. Next time, I'm going to do more revision and make a revision timetable.

I: Hi, we're making a programme for the university radio. What did you think of that exam?

B: Well, it was OK, but I didn't have enough time to finish the last question – but at least I wrote down some notes about my ideas for that question. I might still get a few marks for that.

I: Excuse me, how do you think you did in that exam?

A: Oh, I think I'll pass it, but I really messed up one question. It was an essay about women and sport, and, well, I thought I had a lot of ideas so I just started writing – I didn't bother to make a plan. And that was a big mistake. Halfway through, I didn't know what to say. I got confused and, well, I tried to start again, but it was too late. Next time I'll make sure I make a plan, even if I think I've got lots of ideas.

I: Hello, can I just ask whether the exam was OK?

N: Yeah, sure. It was fine, really. One question was a bit difficult – it was about different personality types and I didn't have very many ideas. But, I remembered my lecturer's advice, and made sure that I gave a lot of examples for each idea. So, in the end, my answer wasn't too short. And the other questions were pretty easy, so yeah, I reckon I've done well.

Review Units 10–12 Track 2.39

Ben, Penny

B: Talking of holidays, are you going to the dragon boat festival again this year?

P: I don't know. It's too far for a weekend and James is really busy at work. How about you?

B: Yes, we booked last week. We enjoyed it so much last year. We're leaving early and stopping off to see my parents on the way.

P: Oh, that's a good idea. Where are you staying in Vancouver?

B: We've booked a hotel near the festival. It looks quite good.

P: Mmm, I don't think we can afford a hotel this year. We haven't got enough spare money at the moment. What's the entertainment going to be like? I mean, do you know anything about the bands?

B: Yeah, but only that several bands are coming from south-east Asia.

P: Oh, that sounds good. I love Asian music. I don't know ... if we went this year, we'd have to be very careful with money.

B: Have you thought about camping? Your kids would love it.

P: You know, that's a really good idea. Yes, if we camped, then we could take our own food too, so it would be a lot cheaper.

B: Look, why don't I find out about some campsites in the area?

P: That's really nice of you, but have you got enough time for that?

B: Yeah, no problem. I want to check out some other things on the Internet anyway ...

Track 2.40

Tutor, Student

T: You wanted a meeting next week about your project, didn't you?

S: That's right.

T: OK, let's try to arrange one. Let me see ... I can do Tuesday at 11.00.

S: Erm, I'm in lectures all day Tuesday, I'm afraid. What about Wednesday at 9.00?

T: No, I'm not planning to come in till 11.00 on Wednesday. You couldn't do straight after lunch, could you, say 2.00?

S: Well, I could, but for only half an hour. I'm going to the dentist at 2.30.

T: I think we'll need more than half an hour, about an hour, I'd say. I'm free all day Friday.

S: Mmm, I'm taking the 10.30 train home on Friday, for the weekend. Nine isn't too early, is it?

T: Well, to tell the truth, yes. It takes me over an hour to get here. You aren't busy on Thursday afternoon, are you?

S: No, well, not until 4.00.

T: Well, what about 3.00 on Thursday then?

S: Yes, that's fine, thanks.

IRREGULAR VERB LIST

Infinitive	2nd Form (Past Simple)	3rd Form (Past Participle)
be	was/were	been
become	became	become
begin	began	begun
break	broke	broken
bring	brought	brought
build	built	built
buy	bought	bought
can	could	been able
catch	caught	caught
choose	chose	chosen
come	came	come
cost	cost	cost
dig	dug	dug
do	did	done
draw	drew	drawn
drink	drank	drunk
drive	drove	driven
eat	ate	eaten
fall	fell	fallen
feed	fed	fed
feel	felt	felt
find	found	found
fly	flew	flown
forget	forgot	forgotten
get	got	got
give	gave	given
go	went	gone/been
grow	grew	grown
have	had	had
hear	heard	heard
hold	held	held
hurt	hurt	hurt
keep	kept	kept
know	knew	known
learn	learned/learnt	learned/learnt

Infinitive	2nd Form (Past Simple)	3rd Form (Past Participle)
leave	left	left
let	let	let
lose	lost	lost
make	made	made
mean	meant	meant
meet	met	met
pay	paid	paid
put	put	put
read /riːd/	read /red/	read /red/
ride	rode	ridden
ring	rang	rung
run	ran	run
say	said	said
see	saw	seen
sell	sold	sold
send	sent	sent
shine	shone	shone
show	showed	shown
sing	sang	sung
sit	sat	sat
sleep	slept	slept
speak	spoke	spoken
spend	spent	spent
stand	stood	stood
steal	stole	stolen
swim	swam	swum
take	took	taken
teach	taught	taught
tell	told	told
think	thought	thought
throw	threw	thrown
understand	understood	understood
wear	wore	worn
win	won	won
write	wrote	written

PHONETIC CHARTS

Sound-spelling correspondences

In English, we can spell the same sound in different ways, for example, the sound /i:/ can be 'ee', as in *green*, 'ea' as in *read* or 'ey' as in *key*. Students of English sometimes find English spelling difficult, but there are rules and knowing the rules can help you. The chart below gives you the more common spellings of the English sounds you have studied in this book.

English phonemes

Consonants

Symbol	Example	Symbol	Example
p	park	s	sell
b	bath	z	zoo
t	tie	ʃ	fresh
d	die	ʒ	measure
k	cat	h	hot
g	give	m	mine
tʃ	church	n	not
dʒ	judge	ŋ	sing
f	few	l	lot
v	view	r	road
θ	throw	j	yellow
ð	they	w	warm

Vowels

Symbol	Example	Symbol	Example
i:	feet	əʊ	gold
ɪ	fit	aɪ	by
e	bed	aʊ	brown
æ	bad	ɔɪ	boy
ɑ:	bath	ɪə	here
ɒ	bottle	eə	hair
ɔ:	bought	ʊə	sure
ʊ	book	eɪə	player
u:	boot	əʊə	lower
ʌ	but	aɪə	tired
ɜ:	bird	aʊə	flower
ə	brother	ɔɪə	employer
eɪ	grey	i	happy

Sound	Spelling	Examples
/ɪ/	i y ui e	this listen gym typical build guitar pretty
/i:/	ee ie ea e ey ei i	green sleep niece believe read teacher these complete key money receipt receive police
/æ/	a	can man pasta land
/ɑ:/	a ar al au ea	can't dance* scarf bargain half aunt laugh heart
/ʌ/	u o ou	fun sunny husband some mother month cousin double young
/ɒ/	o a	hot pocket top watch what want
/ɔ:/	or ou au al aw ar oo	short sport store your course bought daughter taught bald small always draw jigsaw warden warm floor indoor
/aɪ/	i y ie igh ei ey uy	like time island dry shy cycle fries die tie light high right height eyes buy
/eɪ/	a ai ay ey ei ea	lake hate shave wait train straight play say stay they grey obey eight weight break
/əʊ/	o ow oa	home cold open show throw own coat road coast

* In American English the sound in words like *can't* and *dance* is the /æ/ sound, like *can* and *man*.

AUTHORS

Elementary and Pre-intermediate levels

Ian Lebeau studied Modern Languages at the University of Cambridge and Applied Linguistics at the University of Reading. He has nearly 30 years' experience in ELT – mainly in higher education – and has taught in Spain, Italy and Japan. He is currently Senior Lecturer in English as a Foreign Language at London Metropolitan University.

Gareth Rees studied Natural Sciences at the University of Cambridge. Having taught in Spain and China, he currently teaches at London Metropolitan University and University of the Arts. He also develops English language materials for the BBC World Service Learning English section and he makes films which appear in festivals and on British television.

Intermediate and Upper Intermediate levels

David Falvey studied Politics, Philosophy and Economics at the University of Oxford and did his MA in TEFL at the University of Birmingham. He has lived in Africa and the Middle East and has teaching, training and managerial experience in the UK and Asia, including working as a teacher trainer at the British Council in Tokyo. He is now Head of the English Language Centre at London Metropolitan University. David is co-author of the successful business English course *Market Leader*.

Simon Kent studied History at the University of Sheffield. He has 20 years' teaching experience including three years in Berlin at the time of German reunification. Simon is co-author of the successful business English course *Market Leader*. He is currently Senior Lecturer in English as a Foreign Language at London Metropolitan University.

David Cotton studied Economics at the University of Reading and French Language and Literature at the University of Toronto. He has over 30 years teaching and training experience, and is co-author of the successful *Market Leader* and *Business Class* coursebooks. He has taught in Canada, France and England, and been visiting lecturer in many universities overseas. He is currently visiting lecturer at London Metropolitan University.

Far left: Simon Kent
Centre left: David Falvey
Centre: Gareth Rees
Centre right: Ian Lebeau
Far right: David Cotton